FLYING THE LINE
AN AIR FORCE PILOT'S JOURNEY

FLYING THE LINE
AN AIR FORCE PILOT'S JOURNEY

*PILOT TRAINING,
VIETNAM, SAC,
1970-1979*

LT COL JAY LACKLEN,
USAFR, RETIRED

Two Harbors Press
322 First Avenue N, 5th floor
Minneapolis, MN 55401
612.455.2293
www.TwoHarborsPress.com

ISBN-13: 978-1-62652-473-6
LCCN: 2013918862

Distributed by Itasca Books

Front Cover lithograph: "Mountain Fortress" by Dru Blair, with permission.
Typeset by Steve Porter

Printed in the United States of America

No time left for you,

On my way to better things,

I've found myself some wings,

Distant roads are calling me.

From the 1971 song "No Time" by The Guess Who

An epithet for my pilot training graduation and, perhaps,
for my funeral as well.

Dedicated to the soldiers of the Vietnam War
on both sides.

Where, as always, we all lost.

What were we thinking?

CONTENTS

PROLOGUE

As a college American history major, I have always been intrigued by life details from past eras. Often writers from a given time write of momentous contemporary events but fail to provide details of everyday life or standard problems and concerns of people in general or of specific social sectors. I suspect they reason that everyone of the time knows those details and would not be interested in reading about them. Once that era passes along with its inhabitants, however, no one knows the details that everyone knew at the time.

While flying cargo aircraft for the Air Force, I often wondered about the lives of our cargo-hauling predecessors in the sailing ships of the 1800s. Herman Melville's *Moby Dick* gives an excellent description of whaling ships but is not quite what I was looking for.

Then I read *Two Years Before the Mast* by Richard Dana, a Harvard graduate who diverted himself to sea for a health condition, something he would not otherwise have done. He spent two years on a merchantman hauling finished leather goods from Boston around the Horn of South America to the American West Coast. The ship would then haul raw cattle hides back to Boston for processing.

Dana provides a rich description of the sailor's cargo-hauling life in the early nineteenth century that, in some ways, has changed little since. We both had similar concerns about our cargo, our ship, the weather, and our "captains" who occasionally went off the tracks on us.

As with Dana, I got diverted into a profession I probably would not have pursued had it not been for an outside force—in my case, the military draft.

I had interned as a news reporter for a local paper one summer in college and anticipated working for a newspaper upon graduation, but the threat of being drafted into the army and sent to Vietnam as a rifleman demanded a different solution. Going to Vietnam was not the problem; humping a rifle through a rice paddy was.

I will chronicle my trek through the Air Force, two wars, and around the world from 1970 to my Air Force reserve retirement in 2004. This first effort will cover my active duty period from 1970 to 1979.

This story is not about airplanes so much as it is about the Air Force community and the people who comprise it. Aviation is the stage, and we are the actors on that stage. As I warn in the following story, that community is comprised of a complex set of human interactions that swirl around the mission and often affect it significantly.

An entire generation of Air Force crew members has experienced the same saga I have, but, as one author said of writers, I am the one with the words to explain it, so I will. I hope to have spoken for that generation.

TENDING TO AFFAIRS

After several years of preparing myself to command a B-52 bomber crew, I thought I had studied all the required aspects: the aircraft, the other aircraft commanders, the command, and the mission. And things had gone well. My novice crew had dropped the "best bombs" on our first Operational Readiness Inspection (ORI), trumping a dozen more experienced crews.

However, just when you think you are gaining mastery of your task, fate can put a MiG on your tail and threaten to blow you out of the sky.

Social relationships are a difficult aspect of military life on somewhat isolated bases. In far northern Maine, few twenty-something females were available for several dozen young, single pilots to chase. This meant the most compatible females they would meet would be the wives of their coworkers.

Concurrently, some of the married folk, two to three years beyond the marriage ceremony, had discovered they had made a mistake in love and were trying to assess their prospects. This could make for a toxic social brew.

One day, my copilot's wife called. This was not unusual; my subordinate crewmembers' wives often spoke with me to arrange social gatherings. Had I been married, they'd have spoken with my wife, but I wasn't, so they spoke with me—except the copilot's wife wasn't speaking about anything specific; she was chit-chatting. I sensed she was going to tell me something I wasn't going to like, and, as she continued, I began to worry about what that might be. Was her husband beating her? Did he leave her? Was he drunk in a ditch? Where was she going with this?

Finally, after a pause, she unloaded it on me. She said the navigator's wife was interested in having an affair with me.

I'd prepared for many things, but not for this. I had been clueless that "nav wife" had any such interest. Although she was attractive, the potential for such a tryst had never crossed my mind.

This threatened the worst kind of trouble, trouble that could destroy a crew, end a career, or get a person shot. Aside from displaying dubious morality if I agreed to this, I would be guilty not only of abetting adultery, but of fraternizing with the wife of a subordinate. If discovered, it could easily be construed that I had used my position as her husband's direct supervisor to force myself on her. Even that would not address the betrayal of a friend and fellow bonded member of my crew.

I swallowed hard and asked if the navigator's wife had lost her mind. I insisted this must be a poor joke and to please tell me it was not true. The copilot's wife insisted it was true, but demurred that she was merely the messenger (this, in itself, seemed bizarre).

The next call, a few days later, came from nav wife herself. She asked if she could come to my house to discuss something. My decision to manage this seemed sound—get her one-on-one, shame her, chastise her, berate her, and get her straight. However, the venue she had suggested, that I ill-advisedly agreed to, was my place.

When she arrived, I sat her at one end of my dining room table while I sat at the other end with a good six feet of table between us. Distressingly for my task, however, she wore a thin, form-fitting sweater that accentuated her figure.

She asked if I knew why she was there, and I said I most certainly did. And with that, I launched into my concise, cogent, logical treatise of why this could not—and would not—happen, that such a liaison would threaten the crew and my career and would be a brazen betrayal of her husband, my friend and crewmate. I expected her to hang her head, feel ashamed, and apologize profusely when I finished upbraiding her.

Midway through my diatribe, however, I saw things were not going well. Nav wife measured me with the eyes of a poker player who knew she had the winning hand. My blistering, telling arguments appeared to have no effect. She seemed to already know all I would say, and it seemed not to matter. I ended by righteously avowing I would not betray her husband, and I was aghast she would do so in such a manner.

She paused a moment, looking down at the table for dramatic effect, then raised her sparkling eyes to mine with the faint smile of the cat about to swallow the canary, which told me a coup de grace was coming.

"You don't have to worry about betraying my husband," she said. "He knows I'm here. He sent me."

NOTES

THE BOOK TITLE:

The word "line" in the title refers to the line derived from a seventeenth century naval maneuver of war ships sailing in a straight line to fire broadside at the enemy. For the army, this equates to the "front line" of a battle. This has morphed into airlines who assign pilots to fly a set schedule displayed as a line on the assignment sheet, or a "line" of flying.

For my purposes, the line refers to the pilots flying airplanes, as opposed to support troops or command and staff officers at headquarters. Line pilots fly the aircraft and take the risks to deliver the product, be it bombs or supplies, for the military mission.

MUSIC TO ACCOMPANY THE TEXT:

Songs available on YouTube are cited to accompany the text. In electronic versions, the reader can click on the tag line to listen to the song. In print versions the songs will be listed at the end of the book and may be selected from the book website to play at the appropriate time. The music provides an essential accompaniment to the text to put you in the aura of the era.

I have attempted to select YouTube versions of the songs that do not include advertisements. However, it seems the higher the visitation of various versions, the more likely it is to draw ads. I apologize for any ads that might interrupt. The reader may wish to download songs on some iTunes venue to create a clean playlist.

I have also listed extra credit tag lines to enhance the Vietnam section.

PERSONALITIES

I refer to most of the people in the book by first name, or by no name, to allow me license to give straightforward appraisals of their actions without embarrassing them. I try to explain what happened, good and bad, because this *is* how it happened. I attempt to give an honest appraisal of my actions as well, and relate many unwise and unsavory experiences on my ledger that I am not proud of, but, again, these things happened, so they are recounted. Readers can judge as they will, and I plead guilty to many of the charges I anticipate will be leveled at me.

A final admonition, treat everyone fairly and kindly during your career; you never know which son of a bitch might write a book.

CHAPTER ONE: THE DRAFT

1. DODGING THE DRAFT

With great indignation I viewed my 1965 army draft notice as I stood on campus at the University of North Carolina in Chapel Hill. I knew that as a student, I was exempt from the "1-A" status that non-college students of my high school graduating class from the previous spring would receive. These "greetings" would send many of them to lug a rifle through the rice paddies of South Vietnam, but I had a free pass. My draft board had made a mistake.

I strolled directly to the registrar's office in Old South for a copy of my enrollment forms and dispatched all this 1-A nonsense back to my draft board in Greensboro, NC.

Only much later did I contemplate the unfairness of this college exemption that allowed the privileged class to avoid the combat dictated to those less highly placed on the social ladder. This was, after all, a draft where it didn't matter what your politics or druthers might be; you were going to be shanghaied by the US government to fight their war in Southeast Asia.

The rationale at the time held that the educated cream of the rising generation should not be impaired from their preparation to lead society in the future. It was better for the country and American society to leave college students unencumbered by military service.

I view this differently now. If the war is important enough to fight, everyone's sons and daughters should be required to go. It seems, in retrospect, too easy for the social aristocracy, of sorts, to embrace a macho foreign policy on the backs of someone else's children. If the aristocracy's children were required to serve, America might be less enthused about decamping in, and running amok in, foreign countries to prove some think tank's foreign policy theories.

The follow-up policy that replaced the draft accomplishes the same task, also poorly. The all-volunteer army consists mostly of non-college-educated soldiers led by officers from the service academies, ROTC, or officer candidate schools, where again, everyone is a volunteer. This, too, allows the elite policymakers to ship off other people's sons and daughters to the mayhem they demand to validate their often imperialistic worldview.

The new century finds 1% of the American population fighting in Iraq and Afghanistan, often on numerous yearlong tours. There should not be any complaints, the generals must think, because these soldiers all asked for it by volunteering.

Back in 1965, I mused at my safety from this increasingly ugly war, estimating it would easily be over by the time I graduated in 1969. Even World War II lasted only four years. Why worry? Why, indeed. I had much to learn about the new realm of warfare. I had no inkling I would be in an Air Force flight suit seeing Southeast Asia for much of the first half of the 1970s. This would be my war, as would the subsequent two or three before I retired in 2004.

2. Avoiding the Green Machine

As graduation approached in 1969, the green (army) heat was on. I got my 1-A draft notice and this time there would be no escape. If I did not find an option, I would soon be wearing army green.

I had not protested the war with many of my college classmates, but I was ambivalent about it. I had listened to the antiwar rhetoric from the peace cabal in my fraternity but never joined or contested them. It had not mattered to me...until now.

2

I clearly remember a confrontation in the living room of my frat house, the "Lodge," between a professor invited as a guest speaker and our frat house Big Man On Campus who led the campus antiwar movement. After a long-winded diatribe against the war, the BMOC asked if the professor did not agree that this endeavor was unjustified.

The professor began by saying, "Well, of course the war is justified," and proceeded to shred the just-proffered antiwar rationale so thoroughly that the peaceniks sat in stunned, stupefied silence when he finished. They had been guilty of reinforcing each other's views without testing them against the competition and their position collapsed under the assault. I realized I agreed with the professor at the time, although I tend to agree with the BMOC and peaceniks now, in retrospect. This gradual yet catastrophic reversal makes me wonder if we ever know anything assuredly, or if truth flits around like a butterfly in a flower garden as life unfolds.

This solidifying of my position at that lecture, along with the perhaps naïve view that one must experience war as a universal human endeavor, led me to embrace service with at least tepid enthusiasm. As a boy I had toyed with the idea of being a pilot and this seemed an excellent method to avoid the dreaded rice paddies where punji sticks and leg-removing land mines lurked.

Aside from the political argument over the war, the fraternity provided another harbinger for me I should have heeded more than I did. A frat brother one year ahead of me enthusiastically bought into the Marine Corps ethos and could barely constrain his desire to get into the war as a platoon leader who would live in the rice paddies I was ducking. He graduated in 1968, one year ahead of me, and fairly sprinted out the Lodge door for Southeast Asia. Less than a year later, just prior to my graduation, he returned crippled, bitter, and vehemently antiwar. His wound, apparently a rifle shot to the leg, left him hobbling around the house on a cane, a shadow of his former self as a strutting, strapping member of the university wrestling team. He would proselytize up and down the hallways about his revised, dark view of the war. I should have gotten into a deep discussion with him, but I did not. He was preaching against my action plan and I didn't want to hear it. Later, much later, his view would resonate with me.

Meanwhile, my Air Force application got hung up somewhere in the system and imperiled my non-army future. In desperation, I petitioned the Marines for a pilot position and they eagerly swept me under their wing, an officer/pilot recruit from the "People's Republic of Chapel Hill" who had seen the light. In reading their literature, however, I found I had a 90% chance of getting helicopters, and those landed in the rice paddies with lots of bad guys shooting at them, so the Marines would be a last resort. It almost came to that, however.

I received my orders to report to Raleigh for my army induction physical along with what turned out to be several dozen other soon-to-be inductees. As I stood in line in my underwear in a large assembly area, I tried to explain to the sergeant that I was actually going to be an Air Force pilot, yes I was, and was this army physical really necessary? He scowled at me and barked for me to get back in line. I was not enjoying this army stuff.

Political strings soon saved me, however. My mother, as a Democratic activist, knew one of the North Carolina senators. Her appeal to him broke free my Air Force application from whatever desk it had been buried in and I was saved. It proved to be a delayed enlistment so I would not report to Officer Training School (OTS) until January 2, 1970. When I got the notification it said my anticipated length of duty would end in 1990. Ha! I thought at the time. 1990! You must be kidding. I'll be long gone from the military by 1990! I still had so much to learn.

Ironically, three months after I signed myself away to the Air Force, the military instituted a lottery to select inductees. This more fair system replaced the draft and took people based on their birth date. A random selection of dates put birthdays in rank order from 1 to 365. Mine, December 2, was #328; the highest number called turned out to be #195, which meant they would never have called me into the service. However, as a consequence of the lottery, support for the war started to plummet now that everyone's kids were vulnerable to the draft.

The high draft number didn't bother me because I now looked forward to starting pilot training which provided me with needed direction. Without the military, I was unsure what type of job I might have sought. I applied to the *Raleigh News and Observer* to be a reporter until my delayed induction. They seemed enthusiastic to have me until they discovered I'd leave in six months for a six-year military commitment. Instead, I moved to Hartford, CT, to room with a frat brother, where I sold cameras at the now-defunct G. Fox department store until the week after Christmas, 1969.

Many years later, after the military career and after 9/11, I shared a cautionary parable with the Air Force pilot training students I instructed in the classroom and pilot training simulator in Mississippi.

I'd ask all history majors to raise their hands. I'd usually find one hand in the air out of a class of twenty or so, most of whom were engineers of some stripe, often from the Air Force Academy.

Every class needs a history major, I explained, because some time in your career the Air Force will order you to line up four abreast and march off some sort of theoretical cliff. Once so ordered, I would continue, the engineers among you will quickly calculate how long it will take the first rank to reach the cliff, how many ranks will go over per minute, what the acceleration rate of the falling bodies will be, and with how many g's the bodies will hit the rocks below.

The history major's imperative task, I conclude, is to broach the question unasked by the engineers: "Why are we marching off this cliff?" The engineers would not ask, they would just do it, but someone had to question the apparent insanity of the task.

Chapter Two: Training

Officer Training School (OTS)

USAF photo

"Eeeeeeeys right!"

OTS broke me down and rebuilt a military personality within me just as it was meant to do. I could play the military guy thereafter, but I don't think it altered my core personality as a reflective history major. I never was a perfect fit with my military world, a truth that displayed itself repeatedly over the years.

I departed Greensboro on New Year's Day 1970 to drive to San Antonio to begin a thirty-four-year military journey. I drove the "(red)neckmobile," the 1963 Ford Galaxy convertible I had bought in college that was named by my snooty New England prep-boy frat brothers at Carolina. I was one of the few non-prep, regular high school members of my twenty-man pledge class and occasionally suffered for my lack of "proper" education at Deerfield or Exeter. During rush week, I had been asked where I had prepped. Well, heck,

7

in high school, I answered, naïvely.

As I drove, I recalled a statement a fellow short-term worker at the G. Fox department store in Hartford, CT, had said to me that fall: "You are about to start a great adventure." As an ex–Air Force pilot, he knew what I would discover, that this journey would be a marvel few get to experience.

That experience started when I checked into the billeting office at Ellington AFB, TX, for the night. My travel orders listed me as a staff sergeant even though I insisted to the clerk I was headed for officer school. But I got the very low-priced room, so I didn't really care what they called me.

By the afternoon of the 2nd, I had found my barracks at the Medina Annex of Lackland AFB. I parked the neckmobile in the parking lot behind the building, got my suitcase out, and locked the car, little realizing I would touch it only once in the next three months so thoroughly would I be incarcerated within the system.

The clarifying moment that my world had changed occurred when I reached my assigned room to find "OT (Officer Trainee) Scott," one of my roommates, turning to greet me with a smile.

I saw a single bed by the right wall and a bunk bed against the left wall. I swung my suitcase up and dropped it heavily on the single bed. OT Scott's face suddenly snapped to attention with stern authority.

"I just made up that bed to specs, mister, and you just wrecked it!" he growled.

I would soon find out about beds made up to spec and would expend much effort pulling the "Chinese laundry" (bed sheet seams) tight through the loose metal mesh my mattress laid upon while lying on my back under the bed.

Thankfully, OT Scott proved an excellent instructor since he had been prior enlisted and knew the ropes, and Chinese laundry, very well. He played mother hen to me and OT Furlong, our third roommate.

The OTS program provided one of the imperative military education lessons as my classmates came from every geographic corner of the country. This geographic diversity matched the personality diversity that instilled a worldly view few of us had prior to OTS.

The OTS day began at 0500 each morning with the "OT of the Day" bellowing from the end of the hallway that "The time is 0500! By order of Col D.A. Curto . . . !" and the uniform of the day would be such and such and other daily announcements.

All feet would hit the floor about ten seconds after the bellowing began because we had to pull ourselves from the bed as you would a foot from a sock. We did this to preserve the remnants of our bed make-up specs. By slipping in and out at the head of the bed, we retained about 80% of the bed-making basics so we could yank it into quarter-bouncing-off-the-blanket tightness in minimum time. This also meant you slept on your back like a corpse in a coffin and never moved during the night.

Then the mayhem began in the latrine. Even though urinals lined one wall, no one ever... ever . . . used them. Anyone who did would be assigned the duty to clean them. Since they were never used, they only had to be hand-dusted prior to inspection.

This resulted in lines at each stall initially, with every OT trying to shave and dress in the minimum time allotted. If the first formation was PT (physical training), we rejoiced because preparation required only shorts, T-shirt, and running shoes (actually, sneakers; running shoes were just showing up in the stores). However, if we had classroom activity first, we had to dress in the full Class A uniform with blouse (suit coat) and tie. Later I would refer to this as the Halloween costume designed either to scare little children or to impress a girlfriend's parents.

The day would be scheduled for both class and PT with the six OT squadrons on Medina alternating which schedule they would follow. There were three other squadrons on Lackland, but they might as well have been in a different universe as we never saw them except toward the end of the three-month course at the OT Club on Lackland.

I gamely tried to keep up in squadron 3, nicknamed "Rodney's Rangers," with our gold jerseys. I don't know who Rodney might have been, but I think he had departed long before.

The one officer I remember was a diligent also-ran for promotion, Capt. Barber. He seemed old for a captain and was probably an enlisted retread who would never go anywhere in rank. He did, however, run the one-mile course with us and challenged anyone to beat him, the only officer to do so. Since we had several nationally ranked cross-country runners in the class, he didn't always win, but he could whip my butt with ease.

My first attempt at the mile put stitches in my side and left me hobbled and walking by the end. Eventually I turned in a 6:30 after three months of effort, the fastest I ever ran a mile. I imagine Capt. Barber drew great solace in whipping up on young twerps such as me. He knew he'd probably never rise to higher rank as most of us would, but he could take his revenge on the track. He was also the tight military disciplinarian with a drill-sergeant demeanor who knew he could perform our duties better than any of us could and seemed to take great pride in his excellence at the chore. Capt. Barber, wherever you are, I salute you for the pride and enthusiasm you took in your task.

At the switch between class and PT, we harched (marched)—apparently the "h" sound is easier to shout than the "m"—as a flight, in formation, to the chow hall for the noon meal. The food was above average in quality and plentiful, for what good that did us with upperclassmen hovering around incessantly and hounding us ("Are you eyeballing me, mister?). They also allowed us, at times, only thirty seconds to eat what we could. You'd be amazed at how much you can shovel down in thirty seconds. This rapid ingestion imperative has stayed with some of us for life. A meal is something to be quickly dispatched because . . . well, because those damn upperclassmen might show up!

The large drill pad adjoining the barracks often displayed the hilarity of novice flight leaders trying to put their flights through their parade maneuvers. "Forrrrward, harch! To the rip [rear], harch!" the rookie commanders would bark. In several instances, flights would be marched off the pad because the leader could not remember the command to reverse course. My flight was once marched off the pad into the mud, where the flight leader got us stuck marching in place, splashing mud all over our laboriously polished shoes and crisply pressed trouser legs as he fumbled for the correct directions to get us back onto the pad. The pad also found many an OT marching off demerits on the weekend, alone. I got to do so when a flight commander found a *Playboy* magazine above my locker. I got a demerit for each page and marched endlessly that weekend.

I should pause now to explain the point of OTS. The regimen is designed to destroy whatever persona you had in civilian life and to rebuild you as a military person. You might return to some aspect of your previous personality, but you would always be able to call upon your military persona when required.

Sleep deprivation peeled back any personality veneer that had protected you in the past. The five hours of sleep allowed each weeknight soon laid bare your core personality for all to observe and that is what the Air Force wanted to see and evaluate. Sometimes the results were not pretty. One of my lower classmen cracked fairly quickly and sat in a chair in the middle of his room, singing to himself and refusing to move until they led him away. Others just threw up their hands and SIE-ed (self-initiated elimination from the program). One day they were there, the next they were not.

The kinder, gentler military now allows seven hours for sleep; for the better, I judge.

Another imperative demanded there could be no excuses. The system assigned far more tasks than anyone could possibly accomplish in the time allotted. This ensured every OT would fail, by design. When they did, there could be no excuse and they must respond with: "No excuse, sir!" Of course, this laid them open to unending remonstrations and ridicule for their "poor" performance; heck, they just freely admitted to being incompetent!

This had a salutary effect of instilling future suspicion in the OT that alibis for failure should always be suspect, that any individual can rationalize poor performance as due to outside influences when it is actually laziness or inattention to detail that caused the failure. As the program progressed, even the average OT, such as I, found that he could find effective efficiencies to accomplish far more than he imagined and in a superior manner. Military mission, and the objective of OTS, accomplished.

Given the pressure applied to the OTs, it is imperative I explain what future OTs must know. The initial screaming, shouting, and over-the-top criticism, coupled with initial incompetence at the demanded tasks, puts significant mental pressure on the new cadet. Add in loss of sleep and a lack of any escape from the harassment, and each cadet will soon confront the question: Do I *really* want to do this? Is being an officer and a pilot worth this stress? Of course, this is exactly the question the military wants to force the cadet to confront. Some find it is not really what they want and act accordingly, although in 1970, this meant an immediate transfer into the army enlisted ranks and a free ticket to Vietnam.

The crunch time arrived for me on day three. My roommates and I had set an alarm to awaken thirty minutes early, at 0430, to get ahead of our chores—specifically, tightening up our beds so they would make a quarter bounce. In retrospect, this seems insane, since the five hours allotted for sleep fell ludicrously short of that needed, and we were cutting thirty minutes off that. But we deemed it necessary to get our beds up to spec so we could last a little longer before being upbraided for our incompetence, which as I have explained, we had to freely admit.

So on that day, at 0430, under my bed with a small flashlight in my mouth (lights could not be turned on until 0500) pulling the Chinese laundry tight, I confronted the imperative question. I decided I would use the Alcoholics Anonymous method: one more day. If I can't take it after one more day, I'll quit.

But then something marvelous happened; after day three, things stopped getting worse and started getting better. I began acclimating, as much as I could, to the lack of sleep; I started getting my act together with the guidance from OT Scott and began to think I could survive in this ridiculous alternate universe.

Had things continued going downhill for weeks, I'd have been toast, but I needed some indication that things would turn soon, and I got it. For anyone starting this process, take comfort that things will not continue to get worse indefinitely; the tide will turn. Accept that you are meant to get yelled at and to fail, and the course will become somewhat acceptable and allow you to endure.

Much of the pressure on the new OT is delivered by upperclassmen that are a mere six weeks ahead of the lower class. The sadistic among them take out their pent-up frustration and rage on the newbies, much as frat boys do on pledges. I have no problem with stern authority to adjust behavior, but gratuitous mental savagery is destructive and despicable.

On day two as upperclassmen, a group of us decided to haze the newbies. After three of them had spent a good hour trying to get their beds up to specs, I strode into their room. As they were required to do, they snapped to attention and shouted, "Room, ten-hut!"

I scowled at them sternly. "Gentlemen," I said, "we have a report of contraband in this room." (This could be something as innocuous as, um, a *Playboy* magazine). "Is this true?" I demanded.

All three responded with the standard shout of, "Sir, no, sir!"

"I see; you deny it? Well, I feel an inspection is warranted," I said.

With that, my two cohorts entered the room and flipped all three mattresses onto the floor, making a shambles of their previous hour's work.

As all three of their faces turned purple with rage, a rage they were forbidden to express, another of my cohorts then raced into the room, as planned, to exclaim breathlessly that we had the wrong room!

"Oh," I said. "Sorry, gentlemen, there has been a mistake; carry on."

With that my cohorts and I left. Once around the corner, we began dancing in silent laughter, almost unable to control our glee with our prank. Much of this was driven, I am sure, with desired revenge against our upperclassmen that had tormented us, but these were not those upperclassmen, a crucial distinction. After about thirty seconds, we reentered the room with the three purple faces while laughing from our depths.

"At ease, you guys!" I guffawed. "You should see your faces! Bwah-ha-ha, you could probably rip my head off right now, right?"

The three glanced at each other, not knowing how to react.

"Relax, men, we're going to remake your beds for you. Take a break. Besides, you have no idea how to make the bed yet, but we do. You'll get it soon enough. No hard feelings?"

The purple faded from their faces, and soon they thought the entire episode hilarious themselves. We played the required game for the next six weeks, but they knew where we were coming from and where we wanted to guide them. That is how it should be done but seldom is, I fear.

The standard weekly routine demanded a Saturday morning inspection by the upper-class brass whose shoulders were adorned with navy-style striped epaulets. The four-stripe insignia threw almost as much terror into us as an actual 2nd lieutenant!

Inspectors would arrive at the room wearing their pristine white gloves and begin swiping for dirt or "dust bunnies" under the beds and on top of the closets. After room inspection, we had to stand personal inspection on the drill pad.

Once, being behind in my preparations for some reason, I barely made it into the ranks on time for the call to attention. The cadet commander stood before the six squadrons, facing them from a platform, and bellowed, "Group!" followed by each of the squadron cadet commanders turning their heads sideways and bellowing, "Squadron!" whereupon the commander shouted, "Ten-hut!" and all of us snapped to attention from "parade hest" (rest).

Then the inspectors—the officer flight commanders—began reviewing someone else's squadron, walking down the ranks viewing the uniforms. Our inspector paced down the rank, stopping momentarily at each OT. He arrived before me, glanced me over, started to move on, and then stopped. He frowned. Something was wrong, but he couldn't immediately discern what it was. Finally, he puffed up triumphantly and growled, "No US lapel insignia!" This proved a marvelous coup for him and a demerit-producing disaster for me. I might as well have left my nametag in the room. I spent the rest of my Saturday harching forlornly on the pad to pay for my oversight.

Several detailed memories remain from those three months at Medina Annex. One night early in the process, I sat alone in the room laboriously polishing my boots to a mirror shine when I paused and stared wistfully out the window at a driving rain. From my compact desk radio came the perfect complementary song, "A Rainy Night in Georgia" by Brook Benton. For some reason I found this wistfully embracing, a fellow sufferer singing an enabling tune. Yes, a rainy night, but one that would pass and that we would survive.

A second vivid sensation surrounded me near the end of the January-to-March tenure. Spring had begun to sprout in southern Texas and, as I stood in the two-abreast, six-rank flight formation preparing to harch to breakfast in the dark and rain, it hit me—the fragrance of new grass, something the winter had denied me for three long months. Yes, a hopeful season and a hopeful graduation arriving together. I wanted to crow like a rooster in triumph.

The final incident proved less enthralling. On my final weekend, I got a pass off base and drove the neckmobile, for the first time since arrival, to the San Antonio Riverwalk. With a marvelous sense of emancipation, I sat at an outdoor table next to the walk dressed in my OT uniform and ordered a beer.

Before the beer arrived, I notice some commotion flaring up across the river channel. Over the hill, a small young man ran unevenly toward the one-hundred-foot-wide, concrete-channeled river that flowed through the storefronts, a policeman in pursuit.

I watched with interest as the man jumped into the river and began walking strenuously through the chest-deep water. He clambered from the water as the policeman turned and ran for the nearest bridge to continue his pursuit. In an apparent incoherent rush, the dripping fugitive ran directly at me and bowled me over in my chair, apparently not even seeing me until we tumbled to the turf. I seemed to have accidentally apprehended the fugitive as we lay struggling in the grass. Another onlooker joined me in attempting to subdue the wild-eyed youngster. I lay on one arm, the other fellow lay on the other. Somehow, this slight young man lifted me off the ground with one arm, apparently enabled by some sort of drug enhancement.

Moments later, the policeman arrived to cuff the kid and carry him away. I took this as an unfortunate omen—my first taste of freedom and I get run over by a fleeing criminal.

CHAPTER 2: TRAINING

Our final military function finished off our indoctrination with a "Dining In," a military pomp and circumstance at a formal banquet celebrating our graduation as newly minted 2nd lieutenants. This included what turned out to be a ridiculous exercise in buying our mess dresses, or formal military attire (and, no, it did not include a dress; bear with me). At the time, this included tuxedo-level black pants with a short, black formal jacket for winter and a white one for summer. The ridiculousness centered on the cut of the garments, measured to tight specifications by several local San Antonio firms that specialized in this. We attended the Dining In in mess dresses we would, and could, never wear again since they were tightly tailored to our never-to-be-seen again svelte OTS bodies. By the time of our next Dining Out/In ("In" means military only; "Out" means spouses may attend), we would have put on a few pounds that these closely tailored uniforms would not allow. My white jacket eventually turned a light tint of yellow in my closet, and I never wore it again. Within a decade or so, the military demanded a new, different mess dress, so my OTS ensemble seldom, if ever, saw use.

I've found the military seems very concerned with three things: changing the uniform needlessly and repeatedly, changing the titles and numbering of regulations as soon as everyone has learned the previous edition, and renaming the commands, such as altering the Air Training Command (ATC) to Air Education and Training Command (AETC). My final command, airlift, has shifted from MATS to MAC to AMC. This seems to come under the topic of rearranging deck chairs on the *Titanic*. Are these the issues that should constantly perplex our generals?

At the end of our final formation on the drill pad, we all threw our wheel hats in the air and sprinted for our cars to put Medina Annex in our rearview mirrors, something we had dreamed of doing since the second day in the program. A gaggle of enlisted men stood between us and our cars, hoping to garner our first salute as officers, and therefore, to score a dollar off us for

17

the privilege the custom dictated. I dodged them and ended up awarding my dollar to a pleasantly surprised master sergeant in Washington, DC, at the Andrews AFB pay counter the next time I had the uniform on.

I spent the next thirty days on leave, on my mother's couch in Greensboro, sleeping as long as I damn well pleased and trying to decompress from the OTS ordeal. I later regretted blowing that much leave and spent several years trying to recover the loss.

By then it was time to drive the neckmobile from the San Antonio airport, where I had left it to fly home, to the forlorn sagebrush wilderness of Big Spring, TX, for Undergraduate Pilot Training (UPT).

PILOT TRAINING

USAF photo

As I approached the main gate at Webb AFB, TX, I appreciated how a cavalryman must have felt approaching Fort Apache a century earlier. For many miles in any direction, the view seemed to offer nothing but rocky landscape and sagebrush, except for the base.

The town of Big Spring served as a halfway point between the cities of Abilene to the east and Midland to the west and would have been a town George Strait would have transited on his way from "San Antone" to "Amarillo by Morning" as he sang in his song of that name. If the cowboy saloons and used car lots had been removed, the town would hardly have existed.

This proved a favorable factor, since Undergraduate Pilot Training

19

(UPT) would allow scant time for going out on the town. This was a second demanding mental crucible following the OTS crucible that left me frantically running just to break even with the pace.

A few years later, the Air Force decommissioned Webb as the Vietnam pipeline dried up, but in 1971, the pace was torrid as hundreds of pilot candidates entered this system designed to fill wartime cockpits around the world.

I checked into my billeting room, a two-bedroom suite with a shared living room probably built just after the Second World War. My roommate, Terry, was a Marine pilot candidate training with the Air Force, since his preassigned aircraft was the C-130 cargo aircraft instead of the usual Marine fighter or helicopter.

At the in-processing physical, I confronted another aviation reality. The flight nurse put down eighteen-inch paper squares, inked the bottoms of my feet, and had me provide a footprint. I laughed at this initially but looked around at my very somber compatriots. "What the hell is this for?" I asked. One of them told me: after a plane crash at three hundred mph riding a hundred thousand pounds of jet fuel, the only remaining morsel of me might be the soles of my feet inside my boots. They would need these footprints to identify me. I became somber too. Today this task requires only a saliva swab from the mouth for a DNA sample, yet they still take the footprints since there might not be anything left to swab.

At the first group meeting of eighty in my pilot training class 71-07—the seventh class of fiscal year 1971—processing details had to be completed, like dividing us into two sections and parceling out our basic flying gear, including flight suits, helmets, and gloves.

As the Officer in Charge (OIC) read down the list of names to divide into sections, he frowned, then chuckled.

"I see we have Lieutenants Hollopeter and Spermo. You two are going into different sections," he announced to great levity among the group. Hollopeter and I would spend many a hungover Saturday morning in a small, nondescript Mexican restaurant on the outskirts of town enjoying the best Mexican food I will ever eat.

Flight suits were handed out and, for some reason, I got suits with the name "Ketchum" sewn on the chest (Velcro had not yet been invented). Apparently Lt. Ketchum had flunked out of a previous class and I got his flight suits.

The officer dividing up the class wore his hair in a short crew cut and fairly growled his instructions. I suspect he, like Capt. Barber, was an enlisted retread since he seemed the oldest major I had ever seen. He also administered my T-41 check ride, where he held his face in his hands in frustration during the ground evaluation when I could not fully explain a carburetor's function on the plane's engine. I wanted to volunteer that I could explain the importance of the Magna Carta for him instead but decided that probably would not extricate me from my dilemma.

STARSHIP TROOPERS

After this first meeting of the class, I returned to my barracks with my issued equipment. I took my helmet into the bathroom and locked the door.

Standing before the mirror, I put on my gleaming white helmet with the oxygen mask dangling to the side. Surveying this improbable view for a moment, I slowly hooked the oxygen mask across my face. After a frantic moment trying to find the flange on the end of the hose to allow air into the mask (momentary breathless panic), I stood before the mirror again. Here I was, former college party boy, appearing as a dog-fighting aerial ace sneering at danger, an envied hero among men and desirable hunk among women.

Photo by Jay Lacklen

Starship Trooper lost over Texas on a cross-country.

Then, the final affectation, I twisted open the visor lock on the top of the helmet and lowered the dark filter snugly against the oxygen mask. Behold, Starship Trooper, 1970 version! I asked myself if I could really be transformed so easily into a mythical hero among men, an American avenging angel bound for the war zone in Vietnam. Could the Viet Cong possibly resist the overpowering coolness of Starship Trooper?

As I discovered, to my dismay, the Starship Trooper self-image had no effect, by itself, in the real world. It did give me a potent dose of self-importance but one that my first flight instructor had quickly deflated by revealing my inept mechanical knowledge.

The allure of this inflated self-image persisted, however. Even as a senior C-5 cargo pilot years later, I would catch my reflection in one of the cockpit side windows—sun shining directly on my face, svelte boom mic to my mouth, and sunglasses—again displaying me as an ultra-cool man-among-men doing daring, heroic things.

I am reminded of such foolishness as I ponder the image of current American soldiers in Iraq and Afghanistan. They shame the relatively sloppy image of Vietnam-era soldiers who had sleeves rolled up on baggy jungle fatigues.

Today's war heroes have trim helmets topping closely tailored, computer-designed camouflage uniforms. They have myriad pouches and pockets on their trousers in the best outdoorsman fashion; their torsos are covered in form-fitting armor plate with all sorts of grenades and implements tightly attached; and, of course, they hold the M-16 rifle at the ready to mete out Starship Trooper justice to anyone the Trooper deems worthy. Add dark, alien-looking goggles or protruding night vision gear, cameras, and helmet lights, and you have a space creature of formidable proportions.

This visage appeals to outdoor camping/hunting enthusiasts and is captured in a form reminiscent of football uniforms. How could any young, red-blooded American male resist the offer to become a Starship Trooper, an instant hero among his peers with his pick of women? I couldn't, and I don't expect the current crop can resist it, either.

Unfortunately, Troopers have bought an image that has little to do with an unspoken reality: they must be prepared to kill other human beings and to have other human beings try to kill them, the ultimate human contest. As they will soon discover, Starship Trooper outfits provide no protection against copper-plasma-tipped roadside explosive devices or the ground when your plane crashes into it at five hundred mph.

Starship Trooper regalia also does not make you right, or righteous. You might be righteous, but that has nothing to do with the Trooper image, although the two are often confused. How could someone who looks so absolutely, terrifyingly cool be wrong?

I think the military will always be able to meet their recruiting goals—their advertising agencies will see to that. With terms such as "Army strong," "The few, the proud . . ." and spiffy uniforms to convey gravitas, they will always have young men searching to validate their manhood by dressing up as a Trooper.

Recruitment posters showing the new Starship Troopers standing astride the adventurous sands of Arabia and proclaiming that they are fighting heroically for freedom should bring forth another American generation of volunteers to fight their war as my generation fought ours. Alas, the Starship image will have nothing to do with the advisability of the cause, nor the eventual results of the conflict.

But I did not understand any of this standing before the mirror in 1970. I was going to war, and we were going to win.

FLYING: T-41

We soon hit the flight line for our initial demonstration—"dollar rides"—but not at the base. T-41 (Cessna 172) training took place at the Howard County Airport northeast of town. Also, instead of Air Force instructors, we were taught by civilian contract pilots. These guys had come up the hard way,

USAF photo

Cessna 172, dubbed Air Force T-41.

paying for their own training because they loved flying. My instructor, who if he'd been a cowboy might have been named Slim, seemed about forty years old and had long, wavy, greased-down hair that he must have thought made him look like Elvis, but to me made him resemble a motorcycle gang member. Regardless, to me he became "Elvis."

Most of us put on flight suits for the first time in the facility's men's room, for me the first of ten thousand times, and took our seats, four to a large square table, in a long room containing eight such tables. When my section flew, our sister section received academic instruction on the base in the large squadron building next to the barracks, and vice versa.

Terrible things began happening almost immediately. For the first two weeks, fellow students would disappear from one day to the next, eliminated from the program. At the end of the first week, I was the sole survivor at my table. By the third week, I was the sole survivor of my second table. There were fewer dropouts after the T-41 phase, but only forty-seven of us got our wings out of eighty who sat together that first day in the auditorium. Most of the officer eliminations from the program resulted from MOA (manifestations of apprehension), or fear of flying itself, or due to the inability to fly without getting airsick.

The high attrition rate resulted from the Air Force taking almost anyone who wanted to fly and could pass a physical in order to feed the voracious Vietnam pipeline. In the next generation, most applicants would have to have a private pilot's license to be selected to ensure MOA and airsickness would not be a factor. Attrition rates dropped dramatically.

While I had flown commercially as a passenger, I had never set foot in a small airplane or flown anything. It turned out I would be pretty good at such things, but I started far behind many of my more experienced classmates. For all I knew, I would panic or puke on the first flight, but I didn't.

Airsickness can be devastating. I found if I tried to read in the windowless courier compartment of the C-5 in turbulence, I would feel the wave of nausea rising within me. Even if I put down the book and ran forward to look out a window, the nauseating momentum would continue unabated for half an hour. Looking out a window prevented this, but I'd have been a goner from the program, too, if that had not been the case. As it was, I did not enjoy getting bounced all over the sky in a little airplane. Elvis would chuckle at my complaints and explain, why, shucks, these are just thermals—hot air columns—rising rapidly off the hot Texas plain.

Elvis would demonstrate various maneuvers, steep turns, vertical S climbs and descents, and landings. Those all went well enough, but soon we got to stalls and slow flight.

Stall recovery requires stalling the airplane, where the wing no longer has enough lift to fly. When you stall, you fall. I was not enjoying this. It would get worse in the T-37 jet I flew next, where we would stall and spin the plane and recover as it dropped thousands of feet. In the T-41, the stall gave the same sensation as falling off the crest of a roller-coaster track; suddenly, you are falling steeply. The solution is fairly simple—as the plane falls, it regains airspeed and begins flying again. That is, it begins flying again as long as you have enough altitude, especially if you add full power as you begin falling.

Slow flight remained a mystery to me throughout the T-41 phase. In this maneuver, you slow until you barely have enough speed to fly and the controls become sloppy and largely ineffective. Then you must make coordinated turns left and right. I had absolutely zero feel for this coordination with the rudders, so I faked it and somehow got by on the check ride.

Landings proved dicey since the runway had thermal updrafts all afternoon; the winds swirled from one angle or another and the plane would float and hang in the air, leaving it, and me, dancing at the mercy of those thermals and winds. Watching students land on hot afternoons provided more thrills than anyone wanted. Planes would wobble and yaw ten feet off the runway, then fall heavily onto the concrete, flexing the wings at the impact. Or the plane would be driven into the runway without flaring, which would result in a harrowing twenty-foot bounce into the air.

A crosswind required that the plane be "cross-controlled." Elvis tried to explain this to me, initially without success. In exasperation, he finally found a model airplane and walked me through it.

"OK, the wind is coming from the right, what would you have to do to hold centerline?" he asked.

"Tilt the right wing down," I said.

"Good, but while that wing is down and the wind is blowing against the tail, what will the airplane do?"

"Ah, um, swing clockwise around the vertical axis?" I guessed.

"Yes," Elvis exclaimed with a smile, "so where will the nose go?"

"To the right of centerline," I said.

"Correct," he said. "So what must you do to straighten it out?"

"Push in the left rudder?"

"Yes," Elvis exclaimed with a smile. "You have right wing low and left rudder. Crossed controls. Got it?"

Finally, I got it. Elvis was exultant. He, a high school graduate, had schooled a fumbling college boy who would fly the airplanes Elvis would kill to have flown but knew he never would. I'm sure he felt the sting of injustice in this. He, who loved flying as much as life, would be denied high flight, while this upper-class, draft-evading student fleeing the army would soar across the world in giant airplanes. I'm sorry, Elvis.

After about ten flight hours, the time came for Elvis to turn me loose for my solo. I thought I was nowhere near ready, but Elvis insisted; it was time for me to spread my wings and fly, so to speak. On final approach, Elvis requested a stop-and-go landing, which meant we'd stop, he'd get out, and I'd go. I tightened my grip on the yoke, again with the feeling you have just before you drop over the crest on the roller coaster. (Have I mentioned I am terrified of roller coasters, Ferris wheels, and looking out windows of tall buildings? Go figure.)

We stopped on the runway. Elvis gathered up his checklist and books, reached over and shook my hand, wished me luck, and got out. The tower was on me quickly to get off the runway because another T-41 was on final approach. They cleared me for an immediate takeoff with official urgency in the controller's voice. Moving mechanically, I advanced the throttle, accelerated, and stabbed at the rudders to maintain centerline. Then I pulled on the yoke and was airborne.

I got the flaps up, gained airspeed, and then looked in horror at the starkly empty right seat. *Holy shit!* I thought. *I have to land this thing all by myself!* No Elvis to come on the controls at the last second to save me, as he had several times. Now the OTS admonition returned: "No excuse, sir!" Yes, no excuse could rescue me now. I managed to land with only a small skip and a modest thud.

There are two seminal moments in my flying career I will always remember: rolling down the runway after that first solo T-41 landing and, years later, turning around before I got on the crew bus and gazing at the B-52 bomber I had just flown for the first time as an aircraft commander. The rooster arose in me each time, threatening to crow to the gods that I had done it and needed no excuses. No matter what other failures or fiascos I have in life, no one can take those two moments from me.

As I walked back to the flight room, the boys awaited me outside the building. They lifted me high as I put up faux resistance, carried me to the water trough, and tossed me in to applause at this ritual dunking for a successful solo. Cock-a-doodle-doo!

The mellowest memory I have of T-41 training happened on the way to the Howard County airport. One bright morning, the blue Air Force bus rattled and jostled down the final roadway into the airport with most of us lost in thought about our upcoming flights. One of the guys had strapped a small transistor radio to the overhead handrail, leaving it dangling by its strap. As the airport came into view, the Beatles started singing "Here Comes the Sun" on the radio, the song encouraging us with its positive, hopeful message on this first step in our flying career.

FLYING: T-37

During Air Force training, it seemed as soon as you became minimally proficient in one aircraft, they moved you on to a more

Sunrise at Howard County Airport.

demanding one, ensuring there would be no time to relax. The next one for us would be the "Tweet," or T-37, a small twin-jet trainer that was antiquated even then. Though relatively slow and unglamorous, the Tweet proved sturdy and resilient; it needed to be. A thousand or so Air Force pilot training classes beat the living hell out of this poor airplane, spinning it, crunching it on the runway, and generally abusing it with our rookie ineptitude.

Pilots prefer to fly a hot airplane as an instructor, but the true measure of an instructor is his instruction, not the airplane he instructs in. T-37 instructor pilots (IPs) did far more to shape future pilots than those in the T-38 and should have out-swaggered the T-38 guys in the bar. The Tweet IPs' hands rocked the cradle of the Air Force pilot corps.

The Tweet represented a drastic change from the T-41, as it went from prop to jet engines and from single engine to twin, centerline (equal on both sides) thrust. The single-prop T-41 demanded constant right rudder to

29

counteract the torque of the prop; the T-37 did not require rudder in regular flight since the power was balanced on each side of the centerline.

I saluted the T-37 in our yearbook:

USAF photo

Recent Air Force T-37 Demo Team.

Hail to thee blighted bird.

Sorely did we curse thee and many of our class did ye claim.

*With clouted snout and bubbled head, your speed lacketh
and your noise exceedeth.*

*In summer's heat did we spin you, stall you, roll you, crump you, and
overstress you, yea, but we could not finish you.*

*Our parting words for thee, flung over fleeing shoulders,
were vile indeed,*

*But none so vile as you might have shouted to us if you
could but speak.*

CHAPTER 2: TRAINING

We left Howard County Airport to make way for the next T-41 class and moved back onto the base flight line with military instructors.

I met my T-37 instructor, 1st Lt. John Booker, on the first day on the base flight line. He had played football at Texas A&M and had remained at Webb after his own pilot training as a FAIP (First Assignment—Initial Pilot training, or, as often referred to, a "FAIP" worse than death). He had become a fairly seasoned instructor, however, and had a string of successful students to his credit by the time I arrived.

Booker spoke softly and earnestly during initial briefings, explaining maneuvers and airspace rules for the base. We learned the airplane systems in academics and had to have a fairly extensive knowledge of the nuts and bolts of the machine before we hit the flight line. Booker's favorite answer to my aircraft and procedure questions was: "What does the book say?" In other words, I should have already known the answer and shouldn't be asking him.

Booker's calm and earnest demeanor in the flight room, I soon discovered, did not extend to the cockpit. He proved to be a dreaded "screamer" IP, who would pound the instrument panel shroud with his ham-sized hands while loudly berating me for my inadequate performance. I recall being under the instrument hood, a fabric visor fitted over the helmet to block any view outside the aircraft, and watching dust jets shoot down from the panel shroud as Booker pounded it in disbelieving disgust at my flying.

Finally, after suffering a Booker diatribe about my weak and tepid aircraft handling ("The aircraft is flying you; you aren't flying the aircraft!"), the area controller cleared us to descend from 24,000 feet to 18,000 feet. Having had just about enough of Booker by this point, I decided to show him non-tepid flying. I descended toward 18,000 at a high rate of descent and then snatched the control stick back abruptly to level off, pulling four g's in the effort, meaning I briefly weighed seven hundred pounds and Booker one thousand pounds. *Take that, screamer boy!* I thought. Booker groaned at

31

the g's and let loose a string of expletives but, tellingly, kept his mouth shut all the way back to base, perhaps smiling to himself at the response he had elicited from me.

Booker apparently carried the military hazing ritual, probably learned at A&M, over to the cockpit as a strict disciplinary method to drive his students to excel. Maybe that worked with some students, but I chafed under it and dreaded the condescending, belittling attitude from him from the moment we took our seats beside each other in the cockpit. In full autocratic mode, he would occasionally reach over, grab my oxygen mask hose, and shake it, thrashing my head back and forth to emphasize some error I had committed.

My classmates refused to believe Booker could do such things in the cockpit since he played the gentle giant in the flight room before and after the flight. With my ears still smarting from his airborne lectures on my inadequacy, he would debrief me calmly, quietly, and respectfully in a total reversal of his cockpit demeanor. I decided the gentle giant was his normal personality and the airborne screamer an affectation he felt would be effective.

Lt. John Booker

In one sense, he may have been right. If I couldn't stand the pressure of him screaming at me, how would I react in a dicey aircraft emergency? If I ever make a movie on piloting, I'd use poetic license for cinematically describing a severe emergency. I'd have the pilot recognizing the impending disaster and alerting the crew. Then, to illustrate the situation, I'd have the pilot look to his right to find the Grim Reaper seated in his jump seat staring straight ahead impassively, a vulture circling above an animal in distress, watching and waiting. The pilot would recognize that his skill and knowledge must be sound or the Grim Reaper would reap the pilot and everyone else on board.

The Reaper image serves another purpose. An aggravating pilot training feature requires students to stand up at their seat, with the entire student and instructor force watching, and answer emergency procedure questions. Students often consider this unnecessary harassment, and the embarrassment of a floundering answer before your peer group can prove acute. It is supposed to be, because some day the Reaper will ask the questions of you, and you'd better know the answers when he asks.

Years later when I flew the C-5, every so often I would walk back to observe passengers ascending the stairs to the upper-level troop compartment. As I watched families with children embark, it would remind me they had entrusted their lives to me. They depended upon me to know what I was doing. While I might have been tempted to take risks on my own behalf, I could not take any risks on their behalf.

For all training rides up to my first major check ride (T-37 transition check), Booker had awarded me "G," for good, ratings. Many of my classmates suffered strings of "F" (fair) or "U" (unqualified) grades, but I was smoking the course, up to that point anyway.

On the check ride, I was doing very well until I did a split S (rolling the plane upside down and pulling down and through to level flight) in the upper altitude area, above 18,000 feet. I don't know what happened, but I didn't pull hard enough and blew through the bottom of the area, a major violation. My grade for the check was a "U," which knocked me out of any possibility of getting my choice of aircraft at graduation, since they are awarded by class rank, and a "U" check ride dropped me way down the list.

As I returned to the flight room, word had already spread of my check ride bust. As I had seen with many others who had left the program, a pall of disaster now surrounded me, an aura of defeat and impending course failure I had seen envelop many others. I was crestfallen. I'd come so far, and now classmates spoke to me with a tinge of pity in their voice, suggesting perhaps I, too, would be gone soon.

Booker, the screamer, debriefed me on the check ride from the check pilot's comments. I expected him to upbraid me for choking under pressure and making him look bad as an instructor, that I was a damn history major who had no business in a cockpit. I wasn't sure I could survive such an assault and continue in the program. I clenched my jaw, awaiting the tirade I feared was coming.

Instead, incredibly, Booker told me calmly this would be but a minor bump in the road, that I was easily capable of flying airplanes and was excelling in this course. He insisted I should not worry about it. If I had judged his instruction method harshly, his assured confidence in me right when I needed it erased all negative feelings toward him. He gave it to me straight and true without emotion. I took the recheck, did well, and never failed another pilot training check ride. Thus Booker's skillful hands saved, and shaped, this future 12,000-hour Air Force pilot.

On a somber note, Booker, then a captain, died in a training accident in his F-15 fighter while refueling over the Gulf of Mexico a few years after I graduated. I never heard any of the particulars, although given the circumstances, I presume he had some sort of midair collision with the tanker or another F-15. They never found Booker or his aircraft. His death chilled me, since I found him an excellent pilot well trained to his task. If he could die so quickly, so could I. If someone who taught me much of what I knew about flying had died in a crash, why was I still alive? If the "devil takes the hindmost," I was certainly well behind Booker. As the years unfolded, there were several instances where the Reaper visited my cockpit, but I survived. Luck of the draw, I suppose. Anyone who climbs into a cockpit must accept that death can claim them regardless of how well they fly or how thoroughly prepared they are. Not being good and prepared could kill them more quickly, but in some cases, nothing the pilot might do can save him.

My first emergency arrived during one of my T-37 solo flights. I had an airplane equipment malfunction while taxiing out for takeoff, so I taxied to the run-up pad where a maintenance tech met me and fixed the problem. However, during the repair, the tech accidentally turned on the oxygen system on the right seat environmental panel. As I taxied out and took off, the 100% oxygen reserve was streaming out of the right seat oxygen hose.

I was headed for the high area, above 20,000 feet, so oxygen would be a necessity lest I black out from hypoxia, or oxygen deprivation. As I climbed through 18,000 feet, I ran a routine checklist and noticed my oxygen tank reading zero. I did a double-take, not believing it could be true. I leveled off and called the supervisor of flying in the Runway Supervisory Unit (RSU).

I told him, stammering, that something seemed to be wrong with my oxygen. He asked what the gauge read. "Zero," I responded. He asked my altitude; I said 22,000. He calmly but clearly told me to declare an emergency, descend immediately to 10,000 feet (the level at which supplemental oxygen is no longer required), and return to base.

An emergency! *Oh, my God*, I thought, *I'm having an emergency!* "Ah, Center, I'm declaring an emergency and descending to 10,000," I said on the radio. Center didn't seem to find this as extraordinary as I did and cleared me to descend. I pulled the throttles to idle, extended the speed brake, and came screaming out the sky as if on fire. I would later mock and tease new copilots who suffered low-level panic over their first emergency. Shame on me for that. I had my hair on fire unnecessarily for this routine emergency and had no room to ridicule anyone later.

The full spin has always been the signature training event in the T-37 and has claimed many lives over the years. The pilot slows until almost in a stall, then slams in full rudder that sends the plane into a flat, sickening, panic-inducing, 360-degree rotational spin, doing a full turn in about a second, as the aircraft plummets from the sky. If the pilot does not enter the spin correctly, the plane will flip upside down and spin; as if watching the earth spin in a blur is not enough, now you are watching it upside down. Correct recovery procedures must be used or the plane will continue to spin into the ground. The pilot must step on the rudder opposite the spin direction for a few seconds, then slam the control stick forward, breaking the stall and entering a dive that will increase forward airspeed and allow recovery. The rule book says the student gets one try at it. If it doesn't work, the IP takes over. Occasionally, even that does not work and the plane will continue to spin and, sometimes, flip upside down. At eight thousand feet, the rule book says both pilots should eject. Usually they did. Those who tried one more recovery sometimes hit the ground without recovering.

Given my fear of roller coasters and Ferris wheels, the spin should have terrified me, but it did not beyond the normal apprehension level all pilots feel. I treated the view outside the cockpit glass as a movie to watch and fortunately never experienced any of my fear of heights.

I reached an epiphany on a night navigation ride in the Tweet. I flew with a different IP for some reason, headed west toward El Paso in the dark. As we returned to Webb, things had quieted down at cruise. I stepped back mentally and reflected upon my pilot's world and whether I would fit into it.

The instrument lights bathed the small cockpit in a soft, red glow as I scanned the instruments. The vertical velocity indicator, which showed the rate of climb or descent, bobbed around zero, as it should have at cruise. On the radio, I had the navigation aid monitor switch pulled up so I could ensure its reliability. At regular intervals it announced its moniker, "Hobbs . . . VOR," from its location in Hobbs, NM, located off our left wing. Gazing out the canopy, I saw a full moon that illuminated the desert landscape in a ghostly light. This allowed an unusually vivid visual perspective of the mountains at night with nearly unlimited visibility. I relaxed and, for the first time, felt comfortable in a cockpit. *I can do this*, I thought, *and now I want to do this. I'll embrace this world of red instrument lights, bright blue airport taxi lights, stunning panoramas out the windows, and an entire world to explore in a series of marvelous machines that transport me into this special realm.*

As the small clump of lights that was Big Spring came into view, I shook the stick lightly, signaling I was taking control of the plane, and instructed the IP, "I'll take it from here on in, sir. Tell Center I'm ready for descent." I was in my new home.

Flying: T-38

USAF photo

Student two-ship training mission.

Leaving the Tweet behind, we moved down the flight line to our T-38 flight rooms to meet our instructors. Mine was 1st Lt. Tom Jones, and I would be his first student after FAIP training. The squadron commander, also named Jones (his first name was "Sir" to me, and he was not related to

Lt. Jones), pulled me aside and told me Lt. Jones was one of the best students to go through FAIP training recently; I soon found this to be true.

Lt. Jones graduated from the Air Force Academy, something I tried not to hold against him (just kidding!), and he proved the antithesis of Lt. Booker in flight. Jones treated me as a fellow pilot and comrade, similar to my treatment of the lowerclassmen at OTS. He never played "gotcha" on me to make himself look good by making me look bad. At any rate, as a strict Mormon, his strongest epithet was, "You tuna!"

(As an aside, Academy "ring knockers" often seemed to presume the same preparation advantage over me that my prep school frat brothers had in college, similar to how a medical doctor might view a med student who studied in the Caribbean after failing to gain entry to an American medical school. I found many "Zoomies," but not Jones, to be company automatons incapable of independent thought and, as I have said, to require civilian history majors to ask them why they were streaming over a cliff in brain-locked obedience.)

The T-38 got a pilot's blood pumping just approaching it. Its sculpted, streamlined fuselage and shiny, white skin seemed made for speed. As I pressed the throttles into afterburner for takeoff, I found myself riding an earthquake down the runway that snapped my head back against the headrest.

Lt. Tom Jones

This thrust and speed required the student pilot to

adjust his aircraft expectations. The T-37 had thick wings and small engines and needed a relatively large movement of the control stick to maneuver. But the T-38, flying at much higher speeds, needed only the lightest stick correction to attain the same result. This took getting used to and, on my first takeoff, I got the plane into pilot-induced oscillation, where the aircraft started "porpoise-ing" up and down erratically. I wasn't helping the situation; I was making it worse by the second. So Jones took the plane away from me to let it settle down.

On our first "dollar" ride, Jones put the T-38 into a steep dive and took us through Mach-1. I can't say I felt anything as we passed the threshold, but at least I could say I had done it. The T-38 had two-thousand-pound-thrust engines at the time that needed the help of flying downhill to break the sound barrier.

Aside from the lighter stick forces required, the student must also focus much farther in front of the aircraft because it is so fast. Instrument approaches flown at a leisurely pace in the T-37 whizzed by far more quickly in the T-38, forcing the pilot to project his awareness farther down the road.

The T-38 also required the use of a G suit to resist the sometimes high g loads from pushing the pilot's blood into his legs. This temporary blood deficit in the brain resulted in the pilot's vision going from gray and grainy to a total blackout if the g-forces continued. I found this unnerving. Fully conscious and with my eyes open, I could see nothing.

The suit was nothing more than a thin air bladder that encased a pilot's stomach, thighs, and calves. As the g level increased, a ball-and-valve contraption on the left horizontal ledge by the left elbow would inflate the G suit—the higher the g's, the greater the inflation. This proved very uncomfortable with g-forces crushing you from above, and the G suit crushing you from below.

The G suit also provided T-38 guys with an ostentatious symbol of their perceived higher-level status in the pilot pecking order, and they often wore them long after they had landed. The suit reminded everyone the T-38 pilots flew the more prestigious aircraft, since they required the suits in their higher-powered environment. I think some of them would have worn them downtown to the bars if allowed.

Several instances of flying the T-38 stand out in my memory. First, on an instrument ride, when I had to fly in the back seat instead of the front and with a curtain pulled the entire length of my canopy to block any outside view, I almost did the unthinkable. Since it was a smooth day, I felt no sensation of speed as the IP flew on the initial climb out. I then noticed that part of the instrument curtain was caught under the canopy. Reflexively, I started to reach for the canopy handle to raise the canopy and free the curtain. My hand got nearly to the handle before I froze. Had I lifted that handle, my canopy would have opened into the 250-knot wind stream and instantaneously departed the aircraft, leaving me directly exposed to that air stream. I almost threw up right there in terror of what I'd been about to do. I'd never have lived that down.

Second, on my first T-38 solo, I got into multiple troubles. In one of the maneuvering areas, I decided to do repeated loops, merrily climbing and losing ten thousand feet in each loop. As you pull through the top of the loop, you must look up to see the earth coming back into view. As you finish the loop, there is nothing but earth before you as you streak straight down. I was having a fine time until Center called me and asked which area I was supposed to be in. I gave him the area name, and he informed me I had strayed into the adjacent area in my frolic, and why didn't I get my butt back into my own area.

That, however, was mild compared to what was coming. I returned to the Webb pattern, shot an instrument approach, and requested the closed (close in) visual pattern to get another quick landing. As I rolled out on final, I noticed the controls were behaving very strangely. I had to use huge control stick movements to get my desired response from the plane. As I pondered this, the RSU officer came up on tower frequency and asked, "T-38 on final, confirm no-flap?"

AAAAAAH! I had forgotten to put the flaps down to improve lift for the slow final approach and now, belatedly, realized I was about to stall the plane a few hundred feet above the ground, something that could have fatal consequences. I slammed the throttles forward into full afterburner, orange flames shot out the back of the plane's engines, and I felt a blessed power surge that pressed me back into my seat. Stunned at my lapse and whispering, "Oh, fuck! Oh, fuck!" to myself, I heard the RSU controller on the radio again a moment later.

"On the go, [meaning me], gear?"

AAAAAAH again! I had forgotten, in my panic, to raise the gear and had now exceeded its maximum extended speed limit. However, it did come up and eventually go down one more time as I full stopped.

photo by Jay Lacklen

Classmate Roy Shields prepares for a mission.

I wobbled away from the plane after landing and skulked back into the flight room. I didn't know if I could possibly get away with this. As it turned out, I could not.

One of the loudest, most obnoxious of our section's IPs had been the RSU officer asking me the questions from the tower, and he soon arrived to skewer me in front of the entire flight. "Lieutenant Lacklen, were you Rod 22?" he asked loudly, knowing full well I had been.

"Er, yes, sir, I was," I said.

"Did you write up a gear overspeed when you landed?" he pressed, glaring at me angrily as if he had just caught me in bed with his wife.

"Er, no, sir."

As he looked around the room to ensure everyone was listening, he continued, his voice rising, "Well, let me count up the busts for you on this flight—one for flying an illegal [for a student] no-flap, one for over-speeding the gear, and one for not writing it up in the maintenance forms. That is three U's on one solo ride, mister. Where the hell is your IP? Now, get your ass back out to that airplane and write up that gear!"

Captain Obnoxious had known he had a student by the balls when, after asking for no-flap confirmation of me on final, he had seen the orange flames explode from the back of my engines, a sure sign I had hit afterburners; I didn't even need to answer him. Had he not seen that, and had I not answered, his next, panicked command would have been "T-38 on final, burners now!" because, as my nose-high, wallowing aircraft movement warned, I'd have soon started stalling and falling. But I beat him to the punch. Then, as I streaked past the RSU with my gear still down, he knew he had me again, and he did.

Earlier in the T-38 program, he had grilled three of us by asking a question concerning some button you had to push at a given groundspeed to activate nose wheel steering when taxiing the aircraft. When none of us knew the answer, he stood up and erupted with a shout of, "You guys don't ... know... *shit!*" that startled everyone else in the flight room. Now, alas, I had run afoul of him again.

Argh—the only U's I received in UPT aside from the initial T-37 bust, and they all came on one solo flight.

We did our solo out-and-back to Amarillo, and I managed to embarrass myself yet again. Fort Worth Center cleared me for a visual approach to the airport that I claimed I could see but had misidentified. Now clueless what to do, I called the IP on the ground with the other cross-country solos and told him I didn't know where the airport was.

I was close enough he could see me, so he said, "Look at your three o'clock, Tort 08."

"Oh, now I see you," I said. I wished that conversation had not transpired where my peer group could listen to it. I became one of Little Bo Peep's lost sheep in the retelling of the story at the bar.

A final treat before graduation came on my T-38 cross-country to Hamilton AFB, CA, just north of San Francisco. This flight would transverse half the continent and provide a visual approximation of a space trip as we flew westward at 42,000 feet on a clear winter night with another T-38. The sky turned a deeper and darker blue as the sun moved farther below the horizon, and soon it seemed we might be in orbit, far above the earth in our small craft, dwarfed by the immensity of the sky and dark earth below. *Can it get any better than this*, I wondered, *flying a sleek aircraft eight miles above the earth en route to San Francisco?*

Assignments came down a few weeks before graduation and I had to take the dregs, which turned out to be a blessing in disguise. My busted T-37 check ride and two academic test failures put me three from the bottom of the section. I had asked for something to Vietnam, so I guess I actually got my first choice, of sorts, in the C-7 Caribou, a small cargo aircraft. If I recollect correctly, only four of us would be stationed in Vietnam—Ed Moreland and Phil Greenawalt with me in Caribous, and Bob Gymryk in C-123s just down the coast in Phan Rang. Many others would transit Vietnam in C-130s and C-141s. Since only a handful of fighters were in our selection, I don't know if any were stationed in-country.

I have been surprised by how few of my classmates I have run into during my career; I would estimate no more than a half dozen of the forty-seven who graduated with me. As far as I know, none have died in aircraft accidents, a marvelous accomplishment.

In a disturbing pattern, Lt. Jones died in a T-38 training accident about the time Booker died in his F-15. On a two-ship formation flight to San Angelo, TX, the two aircraft had just begun a go-around when the number-two ship reported Jones's lead plane did a snap roll at low altitude into the San Angelo dam. The accident investigation board found the tail section "slab" had malfunctioned and split, meaning half of the horizontal surface went full-up and the other half full-down, inducing a corkscrew snap roll. The number-two ship said it happened in a split second. Jones and his student never started the ejection sequence. As with Booker, the good can die young even in airplanes.

GRADUATION

This final day presented a personal travail. I invited both my mother and father to the ceremony. Although they had been divorced for a few years, I didn't think there would be a problem with this. However, to my deep chagrin, there was.

My mother showed up; my father did not. I could not fathom why he would pass up this event, no matter how great his problems with my mother. If I had a child graduating from pilot training and headed to a war zone, nothing, and I mean *nothing*, would keep me away. I have never figured out what kept my father from attending. I had been on good terms with each parent, despite their animosity with each other, and expected both to join me in celebration of a major accomplishment. Put another way, there are certain things you show up for in life regardless of your animosities; they are required formations, to put it in military parlance. This was one of these—

and Dad didn't show. While I remained cordial with him until his death twenty years later, his failure in this duty put permanent distance between us and hurt me deeply.

Training for Vietnam

C-7 Caribou School

I had several schools to complete after pilot training before I reported to my squadron in Vietnam. First stop, C-7 Caribou training at Dyess AFB in Abilene, TX.

Dyess was just a hundred miles or so east of Big Spring and sat on what I considered the "Texas green line," where enough Gulf of Mexico moisture fell to keep the landscape green. Big Spring lay beyond the green line and served as a warning for the sagebrush and semi-desert that held sway all across west Texas, New Mexico, and Arizona.

The training squadron introduced me to the "real Air Force," where instructors were not worried about my piloting ability but only with how

USAF photo

C-7 Caribou.

well I could adapt to their particular aircraft. Getting me on the line as a competent copilot was their only goal, and each of them knew exactly what would be required since they had all spent at least one tour in Vietnam.

The Caribou caused me a significant shock, however. It could not have been more different from my pilot training jet aircraft.

As a small STOL (short takeoff/landing) cargo plane, its emphasis provided a radical departure, especially from the supersonic T-38. The "Bou" had a wingspan of ninety-five feet and a tail height of eighteen feet. Most would find it had a somewhat ungainly, unattractive compromise of features to allow it to land on short, unprepared strips in all corners of Vietnam. It cruised slowly enough (120 knots) that we could fly with our side windows open and our elbows protruding into the slipstream. That open window, incidentally, served as the only available air conditioning, a definite incentive to get airborne as soon as possible. The three-man crew included two pilots and a flight mechanic/loadmaster.

The biggest adjustment for me was switching back to a piston-engine prop aircraft after jet trainers. The engines were "radial," with the pistons in a circle, something I can describe but not explain—the history major strikes again. The props were three-bladed Hamilton models that provided enough power to lift our paltry eight-thousand-pound or so cargo limit off a 1,500-foot runway.

The throttles proved the most startling idiosyncrasy, as they were on the cockpit ceiling, of all places. The pilot moved them with his arm bent at a right angle, straight up from the elbow, to grasp the levers. I found this bizarre but acclimated to it quickly and felt very comfortable with it. On a maximum performance runway stop, I could almost imagine myself as a cavalry officer halting his troop with an upraised arm and hand as I moved the throttles backward into reverse.

CHAPTER 2: TRAINING

The aircraft was fairly basic and uncomplicated, especially compared to my upcoming planes, the B-52 and C-5. Academics took about two weeks and flying about three weeks, with half a dozen or so flights.

I was paired with a fellow pilot, "Milo," whose career would closely parallel mine over the next thirty years. We would share the same airplane— the B-52—after Vietnam, and the same hooker in U-Tapao, Thailand, a few years hence.

While training in Abilene, I had promised to look up an older couple who had been friends of the parents of a high school buddy. When I called, they invited me to spend the weekend at their house to escape the Air Force for a few days. They were of my parents' generation, at this time in their late forties or early fifties.

I mention them because something bizarre happened during the visit. On Sunday morning, I was awakened in the guest bedroom by the wife who had pulled a chair next to my bed and held a glass of orange juice in her outstretched hand. She thought I might want some, she said.

The "some" of what I might want suddenly seemed capable of more than one interpretation, since she wore a nightgown that had an outer veil of a very thin and wispy material that did not do its job of obscuring very well (or, from another viewpoint, very minimally well indeed). My mind began calculating the situation, but it was not computing.

Had she been my age, I'd have known exactly what she was proposing, but our age difference made me incredulous. I had previously, briefly, imagined she must have been quite an attractive young woman who had aged well enough, but, come on, she was twice my age!

The crucial interaction was at hand. I could reach for the glass or for her wrist beyond the glass while looking into her eyes. I took the glass and thanked her. She paused, smiled thinly, and left.

I've often pondered what would have transpired had I gone for the wrist. Who would lead in such a mismatch—wisdom and experience, or youth? Or would the contest to wrest control provide much of the zest for the tryst? I suspect wisdom would control but allow youth to think it did.

I still wonder where her husband fit into this scenario. She could not have pulled this off with him in the house unless he knew. And if he knew? Oh, dear, that leads to interesting possibilities. (This proved a harbinger of a somewhat similar, upcoming, proposal described in the book prologue.)

Perhaps she was testing to see if she still possessed allure. She did, but the questions surrounding the offer made it hard to risk accepting. What if I had misinterpreted her intentions and she had run shrieking to her husband, who would throw me out of the house and report my perverted behavior to my buddy's parents? If she wanted to seal the deal, she should have been explicit in her offer to include an explanation of where hubby fit into this. I suppose I made an acceptable target for such attention—young, single, and never-to-be-seen-again. Maybe hubby had been caught cheating and owed her one; I don't know.

I did not return the next weekend, the last before I left for Survival School. In retrospect, I should have returned, taken the wife aside, challenged her on her behavior, and explained why I went for the glass instead of the wrist in case my interpretation of her actions had been correct. Who knows what that might have wrought? ("Oh, Fred! I need you to go shopping for me at the grocery on the other side of town!") This is regret for an action not taken rather than remorse for one I did. I seem to have plenty of both.

SURVIVAL SCHOOL

When I reported to Survival School at Fairchild AFB, WA, some American pilot POWs had already been incarcerated in North Vietnamese prisons for six years and would not be released for two more years in 1973.

This school attempted to prepare us for being shot down, to avoid capture, and to provide the means to survive prison camp if captured. Some of our instructors had indeed escaped from either North Vietnamese or Viet Cong prisons and knew the subject well. Since I would be flying cargo in South Vietnam, I didn't really think this would apply to me. I didn't realize I would return in 1973 as a B-52 bomber pilot, which might put me in real jeopardy of a vacation in the Hanoi Hilton, the North Vietnamese prison that housed most of our captured pilots.

First came escape and evasion (E&E) training, showing us how to travel cross-country without getting caught. After some Boy Scout–style instruction on making a camp and navigating cross-country, teams of ten or so students launched on a trek across the Washington Cascade Range. Using topographical charts and compasses, the teams attempted to find a rendezvous point several miles distant. Since this was summer, we battled with foliage that ensnared us and obscured distant topography. In the winter, there was little to snag your clothing, and the view was virtually unlimited in all directions. Of course, it could be exceptionally cold and the snow could prove precarious, especially around lakes and ponds. The only near-disaster my team encountered was unknowingly approaching a steep drop-off into a ravine that we did not discover until the last moment as we moved through the thick foliage.

Arriving at our rendezvous point, we met our instructors, set up camp, and, over the next few days, attempted to put our training to use setting snares for squirrels and chipmunks, with zero success. We set up to cook our evening meal with some transported food, but the main course would eventually be the team's pet rabbit. During our several days in the camp, one of the students had been assigned to care for the rabbit. In a cruel twist, the caretaker belatedly discovered he would be the one to dispatch the rabbit with a karate chop to the neck. Our rabbit keeper tried halfheartedly to accomplish the task but succeeded only in greatly distressing the rabbit, which jerked and flailed while being held by its hind feet. The instructor for our team grabbed the rabbit and *whack*, it was done. After cleaning the carcass, we dined on pet rabbit that night.

The course syllabus saved the most onerous task for last—capture by the enemy and prison camp. We started by crawling across a simulated battlefield at night in our green fatigues. We had to slide under wire barriers and crawl on our bellies while trying to avoid trip wires that would set off flares or alarms and result in our capture. Of course, we all had to be captured, which we were, and delivered into the interrogation camp.

This being summertime, the battlefield excursion dehydrated me badly. After my capture, I sat with a group of fellow detainees dying for something to drink. Finally it was provided, some tepid tea sweetened with sugar. While rudimentary in composition, I have never in my life tasted anything as good as that tea.

Once in the camp, the loud exhortations began. The camp "guards" did their best to replicate a North Vietnamese prison camp environment. We had loose-fitting bags placed on our heads and had to walk around blindly with our hands on the shoulder of the "war criminal" in front of us.

Aside from this group harassment, the individual torment proved the most taxing segment. The three major features of this included the cage, isolation, and interrogation.

I knew the cage was coming and knew I would be deeply stressed by it. I have a problem with claustrophobia that I discovered while crawling through suburban sewer tunnels as a child. If I happened to be in the middle of the line, I would feel panic rising if everyone stopped and I was blocked from going forward or backward. (I'd never have made it in the submarine corps.) I had also read, as a teenager, accounts of prisoners being buried alive, unable to escape their coffin. Pondering such thoughts would bring on visions of the

Edvard Munch painting "The Scream," which is what I wanted to do in such situations.

But I knew I could not scream, or even complain, as they boxed me. But, then, what would they do to me if I failed this test—ship me to Vietnam? As I was led into the box room, I saw slat-sided crates of various sizes for various-sized "criminals." I hoped for a large one but, of course, they put us into one that barely fit us. My method to resist consisted of not touching the open-slatted sides of the box. I scrunched up tightly on my knees and elbows so that I felt none of the box's constraints on me. I then closed my eyes and imagined I was not in the box. This seemed to work until my muscles started aching, and I feared trouble if I moved and touched the wood. Fortunately, they let me out before panic hit. I don't know how long I was in the box— probably five minutes—although it felt like fifteen.

Next came the one-on-one interrogation in a small room with a simulated North Vietnamese Army (NVA) interrogator. It fit the stereotype well—one bare light bulb swinging over a Spartan wooden table and chair.

The interrogator began with taunts and insults aimed at eliciting a forbidden response from the prisoner. First came disparagement of the prisoner's mother, her lascivious predilections and shady reputation. Next came disparagement of any prisoner whose physique differed in any way from perfection. Woe unto those with big ears, a big nose, who were over- or underweight or balding. The interrogator would zoom into any physical feature about which the prisoner might be sensitive. He sneered at me that my head was too big for my body, but I already knew that. I briefly wondered how *his* face would look after I smashed his nose flat, but that was the reaction he was fishing for. Point taken. All this continued as the interrogator's thug partners arrived to shove the prisoner around the room and against the walls. This physical roughness was meant to goad the short-fused barroom brawler types who otherwise would not tolerate such treatment. Interestingly, none of the camp personnel ever used profanity. We were war criminals, capitalist pigs, or, for the poor overweight, bedraggled, full colonel prisoner in our group, a syphilitic old goat.

The final hurdle put us in the compound jail cells, rows of six-by-four-foot-square rooms for the night. Each had bare walls and a door with a sliding viewing hatch so guards could check on us. We were forbidden to lie down and ordered to stand throughout the night, despite our utter exhaustion by this point. About every thirty minutes, the guards would make the rounds, sliding the hatch open to see if we were lying down sleeping. Also, every so often they would shout down the hallway as if they had caught someone on the floor, which meant everyone leapt up to stand for a short while. Mercifully, after a few hours of this, they relented and let us sleep.

The most contentious subject surrounded the Soldier's Code of Conduct, especially Statement Five:

> 5. When questioned, should I become a prisoner of war, I am bound to give only name, rank, service number, and date of birth. I will evade answering further questions to the utmost of my ability. I will make no oral or written statements disloyal to my country and its allies or harmful to their cause.

How much must a prisoner endure? The line for each man depends upon his condition and the methods of torture used. In the early days, the North Vietnamese didn't have to worry about leaving bruises on the body or blood on the floor because no one would know. Later, when outside observers were allowed to see the POWs, the prison personnel had to abide somewhat by the Geneva Conventions, something they definitely did not do in the early days.

While the North Vietnamese undoubtedly used measures forbidden by international law, and should be damned for doing so, I'm not so sure our skirts were clean on this. As described later, the South Vietnamese tiger cages on An Thoi and Con Son Islands easily constituted torture and, while we did not run those camps, we knew damn well what was going on and did nothing. A Pulitzer Prize–winning photo showed a South Vietnamese commander performing a summary execution of a Viet Cong prisoner with a .45 bullet to the head, something threatened by the NVA on our prisoners but, as far as we know, never used.

If I attempt to view the North Vietnamese from a neutral viewpoint, they might have had mitigating factors in their prisoner treatment, as those being held had, in many cases, unleashed aerial mayhem on them for years, especially us B-52 pilots in our three-ship cells carrying 108 five-hundred-pound bombs each. The B-52 presence over the battlefield was not evident until the hundreds of bombs falling from seven miles high exploded and unleashed their shock wave, which would kill even those outside the area of the explosions by rupturing internal organs. America used the B-52 indiscriminately for years as a terror weapon and dropped four times the tonnage in this war as we dropped during WWII.[1] At the time, I would have said, well, too bad, the NVA still must abide by the Geneva Conventions.

But then came 9/11/2001 and our own suffering under a "terror bombing" using commercial aircraft. Although 9/11 was aimed mainly at civilians and the B-52 raids at military targets, we often inadvertently hit civilian targets. Even attacking military sites, the shock waves emanating from these explosions must have killed many civilians in Hanoi and Haiphong. Estimates of North Vietnamese civilian casualties from American bombing range from 50,000 to 182,000.[2] We inflicted this terrible toll in a country with only one-tenth the population of the US.

When compared to North Vietnamese barbarity, we do not come out well in comparison. We invaded Iraq in 2003, seemingly as a jilted lover might pick a bar fight to assuage his pain and humiliation from 9/11. In so doing, we started a conflict that resulted in the deaths of perhaps hundreds of thousands of Iraqi civilians[3], in addition to about five thousand of our own soldiers. Saddam Hussein, while a murderous cad on his own account, was, for 9/11, an innocent bystander who had nothing to do with this abominable attack and had none of the weapons of mass destruction we accused him of having.

Further, under both Presidents G. W. Bush and Obama, we indulged in rendition, or farming out our torture to third-world nations to do our dirty work.[4] At Guantanamo and elsewhere, we waterboarded at least several prime terror suspects and claimed this was not torture, even though we had prosecuted Japanese and Americans for using this method in World War II, and had signed international treaties swearing we would not waterboard.

Conservative sophists attempt to escape this dilemma by avowing we do a mild form of waterboarding for training on some of our own elite soldiers and it doesn't harm them. Nonsense. What our soldiers get is a tepid appetizer of the full-course torture meal, far less than that used on our prime suspects.

The essence of torture lies in the unknown for the victim. How long will a procedure last? Not knowing what the torturer has in mind exponentially increases the pressure on the detainee.

For instance, I often go into a sauna. I can stand the terrific heat because I know I can get up and leave when I wish. But suppose I could not leave when I wished. If someone else had the power to keep me in the sauna as long as he wanted, especially if that person wished to torture me, what effect would this have on my ability to resist? Yes, I can take the sauna heat on my terms, but this says nothing of my ability to survive the same on someone else's terms.

This is why military waterboard training is not torture and does not compare to actual waterboarding. The trainees know they will not be placed under heavy duress, and the trainer will stop the process before damage can occur. The trainee knows the process will be abbreviated and relatively mild.

54

The torture victim, however, does not know and must assume this process will continue until he breaks; the "sauna door" will remain locked until he capitulates. Further, what part of "we prosecuted Japanese and Americans for waterboarding" do the sophist apologists not understand?

The decision by the Bush administration to "do what was necessary" to gain intel on future attacks and to find nonexistent weapons of mass destruction filtered down through the ranks and led to the ludicrous abomination of torture at the Abu Ghraib prison in Iraq (a country where, again, we should not have been in the first place). Once you turn the torture dogs loose, they may eventually devour you.

If Americans can do what we did to prevent future terror attacks, what can we say of the North Vietnamese for doing relatively less in retaliation for our terror bombing that unleashed more firepower on that small third-world country than the entire bomb tonnage unleashed by the US in World War II? The eleven day, Christmas 1972, B-52 bombing campaign alone dropped twenty-thousand tons of bombs on the cities of Hanoi and Haiphong that approximate Minneapolis/St. Paul in size.

I know this view will enrage the "America, right or wrong" crowd, but this same crowd represents the "jilted lover picking a bar fight" that facilitated our tragic foray into Iraq, a blunder that cost us and the Iraqis terrible blood and treasure for insufficient reason. We largely abandoned the good fight in Afghanistan against al-Qaeda terrorists to indulge our wounded ego by pummeling Iraq with "shock and awe" that sank us into a quagmire. While the relatively recent sting of 9/11 makes our Iraq mission feel vaguely justifiable, future generations will ask why we panicked, lost our minds, and invaded Iraq.

But such questions would not resonate with me for several decades. So, having completed Survival School, I headed to the Philippines for jungle survival training, or Snake School, en route to Vietnam.

55

Several times, the method of transport to and from Southeast Asia would be on KC-135 tankers. We became cattle in this cattle car, a dozen B-52 crews, or Survival School classes bound for Vietnam, sitting on web seating down the sides of the cargo compartment. In a seemingly sinister conspiracy, the plane would often take forever to taxi and take off, leaving us sweltering in the back, since the air conditioning could not properly do its job on the ground. The worst episode had the plane about to take off from Travis AFB, CA, but then find its takeoff clearance canceled for an emergency aircraft on a long final approach. Once the emergency aircraft landed, tower changed the active runway to the opposite direction, which demanded we taxi the entire two-mile length of the runway to take off. We had all sweated through our flight suits, and I began to imagine we were illegal immigrants trapped in the back of an eighteen-wheeler being smuggled into the States and about to die of dehydration and heat prostration locked in the trailer. Then, however, the plane would get airborne and climb to 35,000 feet, and suddenly we were freezing in our saturated flight suits, one extreme to the other. Thanks, tanker toads.

Experienced crews knew the ropes on these flights. As soon as the gear and flaps came up, they would dive for a section of the metal cargo floor to claim for sleeping upon. Once the floor space was taken, those left out were screwed and had to sleep in the web seats for the long overwater flights. Newbies watched curiously as the diving for the floor began, only to realize they should have done likewise.

A bit of lore transpired on one of these trips on the Hawaii-Guam segment for my first tour as a B-52 copilot in 1973. In these days before inertial navigation systems, the tanker navigator had to guide the plane to the island of Guam and get to within TACAN radio beacon range—two hundred nautical miles—or disaster could ensue. If the pilots did not obtain a TACAN lock-on on the way by the island, it would be easy to run out of gas trying to return to Andersen AFB on the north end of the island.

About an hour out of Guam, the young tanker navigator came back and asked our B-52 navigators to give him a hand. When they reached his station behind the pilots, he explained that he was unsure he would get close enough to pick up a TACAN lock on the field and feared we might miss Guam and experience disaster. They laughed and thought this was a joke until they saw a tear run down the tanker navigator's cheek. Our navs' jaws dropped and they frantically began reviewing his computations and celestial readings. Among them, they directed a new heading that, thank the gods, just managed a two-hundred-mile lock-on to Guam that we would have missed to the south had they not intervened.

SNAKE SCHOOL

Prior to leaving home for Vietnam, I had read Barbara Tuchman's biography of US Army General "Vinegar Joe" Stilwell and his exploits in Southeast Asia during World War II. Having already been mentally steeped in the jungle environment from the book, I felt as if I had stepped back to the Second World War in the Pacific as I arrived at Clark AFB on the island of Luzon in the Philippines, northwest of the capital of Manila. I would spend two weeks completing jungle survival training, which proved far more fun than regular Survival School.

The Clark O'Club offered a sprawling cabana-style building that Vinegar Joe might have frequented, all teak wood and tiki torches as splendor for the American military maharajahs that had arrived in the early 1900s to subdue the dreaded Moro insurgents.

The club interior featured large dining rooms and several large, lavish bars suitable for cocktails or gambling on rows of slot machines. It lay nestled within, and surrounded by, banyan trees that provided shade as well as a tropical atmosphere to go with the high humidity and frequent rain squalls during the rainy season. I've found few better venues for contemplation than an expensively decorated teak wood bar with a tropical view on a rainy afternoon. As with most dreamy philosophers, my insights seemed to become more profound as I knocked down another Mai Tai cocktail delivered by white-coated Philippine waiters. Occasionally I'd wonder how I managed to qualify for this marvelous maharaja status.

As I ruminated in the several club bars, I half expected to see Vinegar Joe step to the bar to join John Wayne, Kirk Douglas, and Patricia Neal from the World War II–era movie *In Harm's Way*, or to see Henry Fonda and Glenn Ford from the movie *Tora, Tora, Tora* at a nearby table discussing where the Japanese fleet might be. Actually, the second movie was made two years after this visit to the Philippines, but who's counting?

On my first foray to this marvelous realm, I met a perplexing creature, a fellow 2nd Lt. who bore a striking resemblance to Errol Flynn, with a pencil moustache and jet-black hair. He cut a dashing figure, and somehow we wound up drinking a few on the outside lanai bar on a sunny jungle afternoon.

"Errol" seemed to want to discuss himself at length and explained he had personal connections to the Air Force chief of staff and had been marked for high rank. In order to punch the tickets for this high rank, he, too, was headed to Vietnam. Very early in the discussion, I noticed he began slurring his words and had obviously started drinking well before I arrived. As his self-described magnificence continued to expand, I began to wonder, if this were true, why was he not holding forth in the bar with base commanders instead of some fellow Second Louie he'd never met? I decided Errol was a fake and a drunk who would probably be shipped home early as a head case.

He did look like someone out of a Flying Tigers group picture, however. I'll give him that.

I ate every available meal and spent every free moment in the O'Club and remembered it fondly over the years, including right up to after it had been extensively renovated in the late 1980s when I visited as a C-5 pilot. Alas, they had just finished the renovation when nearby Mt. Pinatubo volcano blew itself up and covered the base in six inches of volcanic ash in 1991, followed four days later by a typhoon that scored a direct hit on the base. The locals must have thought God had it in for them and an earthquake must be on the way to finish them off. I'll discuss this catastrophe in a later book, since the calamity was twenty years in the future when I visited in 1971.

I must mention the nearby town of Angeles City. If the locals wanted to seek salvation by throwing virgins into Mt. Pinatubo, they would find none in this town. When the devil comes up to the earth's surface, he resides in Angeles City, home to every perversion known to man and maybe some not yet discovered. Sending a crew there to crew rest is to risk having mangled and wasted, yet smiling, dregs return. On this score, Angeles City made Saigon and Bangkok look like nunneries and choir cloisters.

Snake School would be my first jungle experience, and it left me needing my "jungle fix" for the rest of my life. While Melville longed for the sea in *Moby Dick*, I long for the lush green of the jungle when I have been away too long. My jungle haunts would include Vietnam, Thailand, Guam, Panama, Costa Rica, Nicaragua, Puerto Rico, and Hawaii. I've decided if you put me in a jungle, I wouldn't know which country it might be in if I didn't already know. It seems any jungle will do to slake my fix as long as it displays the deep green punctuated with vivid floral colors of red, yellow, orange, and purple and with the fragrance of orchids wafting on the air.

The first week of the school taught us jungle survival—to include things we could eat, things we should not, and how to cut a vine to make it trickle fresh water from its core. First aid in this environment seemed pertinent since nefarious things can happen to injuries in the jungle environment. All in all, I decided I would not like to crash-land in the jungle and suffer these consequences even without little brown men in black pajamas chasing me.

Photo by Peter Bird

Drinking from a sliced vine on jungle mountain.

The two highlights the school provided were the E&E laboratory and a night on jungle mountain. For the E&E exercise, we loaded into large convoy trucks for transport to the field. On the way there, on a dusty road through the jungle, local Negrito children ran behind us, shouting, "Hey, Joe!" The Negritos are an indigenous people who live a Spartan existence in the jungle throughout Luzon. When we reached the exercise area, we would be "hunted" by Negrito men familiar with the jungle. *This will be rich,* I thought, *a Chapel Hill frat boy trying to escape from indigenous jungle hunters in their own backyard. Fat chance I'll have.*

One of my pilot training buddies on the trek with me said, only half-joking and after the Negrito kids had run behind us shouting, that the

Philippines wouldn't be so bad a place if there weren't so many foreigners here, an inadvertent insight to a common American predilection.

At the E&E exercise area, we dismounted from the trucks and gathered for instruction. An area of jungle a few acres across had been outlined with colored markers for us to hide within. It had a few trails but consisted mostly of thick jungle foliage and underbrush. About fifty of us would hide in this area to be hunted by three Negrito trackers who would be awarded a fifty-pound bag of rice for every ten he "captured."

We had thirty minutes to hide before the instructor announced that the hunt would begin. I walked briskly toward the middle of the area and slid into the foliage between two trails about twenty feet apart. I wriggled in about twelve feet off the trail I had used and eight feet from the second trail. That seemed brilliant on my part, because I had left no trace of entry from the nearest trail. The jungle proved so thick I could not perceive either trail from my hiding place and felt sure no one could detect me.

As it turned out, I was one of the last captured, and the Negrito tracker had cheated, in my estimation. He tagged me from the trail I had not used and had apparently just been fishing in the area, since he had covered most of his designated patch of the exercise area and either felt one of the missing escapees must be in this area, or else he smelled me, which is how some thought they found us.

After the E&E exercise, our instructors demonstrated various signaling techniques to alert rescue helicopters to our position. The first, a small handheld pyrotechnic rocket, could punch through a triple jungle canopy to allow the rescue chopper to identify our location. We held this in our hand pointed skyward, an inch-long miniature shotgun shell with a firing pin that mimicked a butane lighter mechanism, which we would flick downward and release so that a spring-loaded pin would jab into the bottom of the rocket and send it on its way. It took me a few tries to get comfortable with this hand rocket, since flicking the firing pin downward tended to cause my hand to jerk and ruin my aim. As instructed, we always held this high above our head before activating.

Next came the multipurpose flare that resembled a stick of dynamite in size and shape. One end had small protruding nipples around the rim for identification in the dark. (I chuckled, thinking I had some experience finding nipples in the dark, har, har, har.) This end, when the tab on it was pulled, resulted in a standard effervescent torch-like flame effective after dark. The other end tab, when pulled, would begin pulsing out a vibrant orange smoke column for daytime identification.

The final method for identification used a flashlight contraption slightly larger than a pack of cigarettes but shaped about the same. Turning on the unit produced an intense light pulse about twice a second. In actual use, this had presented problems because this light flash closely mimicked a rifle's muzzle flash, sometimes making it difficult to distinguish the good guy trying to signal you from the bad guys shooting at the rescue chopper. For this reason, the apparatus had been equipped with an optional blue filter to distinguish the good guy so the chopper wouldn't mistakenly fire on him.

The last field exercise instructed us on vectoring a chopper to our location with a compass. Even though this simple system worked well, there was one wrinkle in the process that had to be recognized. When sighting the helo across the compass, you must remember to read the heading off the bottom of the compass pointing at you, not the heading on the far side pointing at the chopper. Of course, when it came my turn, I bungled it and read the useless heading from me to the chopper, to the great consternation of the instructor who had taken great pains to explain this potential error to us. Frat boy strikes yet again.

The Snake School finale lay a short helicopter ride from Clark to a nearby jungle mountainside where we would spend the night. I'll say right here I do not like helicopters. If the engine quits, you are going to land almost immediately below, regardless of how catastrophic that might be, as free-wheeling autorotation of the blades means you can at least cushion the impact. If the engine seizes, however, it is game over. The aircraft becomes a falling rock, leaving those on board no option but to kiss their ass goodbye on the way down. Most fixed-wing aircraft have more than one engine and, even in the case of total power loss, can glide to earth and have some selection of crash location, unlike a chopper.

The ride to jungle mountain went well, however, and the chopper dropped us on a clearing near the top of the mountain ridge. We ducked to avoid any chance of decapitation by the helo blades and walked into the jungle to our camp on a gradually sloping grade that eventually dropped steeply down the heavily forested mountainside.

Once there, our instructors demonstrated fire-starting with sticks, something we couldn't seem to get the knack of doing. They also demonstrated the cutting of "water vines" for water and pointed out edible vegetation and, conversely, tubers and leaves to avoid.

After a campfire meal, we prepared our sleeping positions for the night. Rule One said we had to be suspended off the jungle floor, since any number of crawling things, especially ants, would want to join us should we lie on the ground. This meant stringing up a hammock between two trees. This took planning, since we all had to find two suitable trees the right distance apart to string our hammocks. After I had mine rigged up, I found myself suspended about two feet above the ground once the hammock sagged with my weight—not perfect, but sufficient to avoid the crawling things.

Since there was precious little to do in the inky blackness after sunset, even with the campfire, we all climbed into our hammocks for the night. Sleep did not come easily. You cannot gracefully roll over in a hammock and, in trying, may roll yourself onto the ground with the creepy crawlers.

Other disturbing events also occurred. After about an hour, I looked up the hammock line above my head that ran to the tree a few feet away. There, disconcertingly, I saw two bright, small eyes looking at me in the dim light from the campfire embers. Whatever it might have been seemed smaller than a cat but larger than an insect. I presumed whatever it was, it would not come walking down the hammock line to visit. I pulled my covers over my head, bravely, and wished it away.

The second macabre event came in the early morning mist. Something awakened me, I'm not sure what exactly, but I peered outside my blanket and looked down the hillside toward the now-dormant campfire. A line of men walked silently up the hill toward me through the mist, clothed only in loincloths and carrying basic bows and arrows. If this were a planned demonstration, the instructors had really pulled off a good one. Soon, however, it became apparent this was not a planned event. For all I knew, these were head-hunting cannibals who had found a camp full of juicy meals. To my relief, instead of drawing their bows to skewer sleeping victims in their hammocks, they continued to walk through the encampment and to form a small camp just above us on the hillside. These were the country cousins of the suburban Negritos that had hunted us the day before near the base.

The hunting party joined us for breakfast and some spoke pidgin English. Though we had rudimentary communication, we mostly sat and contemplated each other. I'm not sure which group viewed the other with more wonder. In addition to their bows and arrows, they had blow-dart tubes for picking birds or monkeys out of trees. They wanted to show off their bow and arrow prowess, much to our delight. They could nail a coconut off a stump at one hundred feet with aplomb and to cheers from us, the awkward, over-encumbered-with-equipment jungle neophytes who were about to depart on the big metal bird. They waved to us as we lifted into the sky, and they strode back into the jungle, each group on its separate missions. The Negritos would hunt monkeys with bows and arrows; I would eventually hunt other humans with strings of five-hundred-pound bombs as a B-52 pilot. I had to reexamine which group put the better face on humanity.

The next day we caught the flight to Cam Ranh Bay, Republic of Vietnam, to begin our tours.

CHAPTER THREE: VIETNAM

SEPTEMBER 1971–MARCH 1972

Photo by Peter Bird

C-7 Caribous on the ramp at Bam Me Thuot in the Central Highlands.

So, finally, I had arrived in the war zone. Soldiers in past wars had found themselves on the fields of Marathon, Antietam, Flanders, or Iwo Jima, while I had decamped into a relatively squalid little conflict in a jungle-covered third-world country halfway around the earth. It wasn't much of a war, but it proved the only one available to me for a few decades. My motivations were divided about evenly between observer and participant status. As a young child races to the street to see a circus parade pass by, I had gone in search of war to observe human nature turning on humans.

Unlike the war of our fathers, World War II, the very concept of democracy was not in question. If we lost, there was no danger of invading soldiers raping our women, as happened when the Russian army swept through eastern Germany in 1944. America had not mobilized for this war as the previous generation had for theirs. We projected ourselves into this conflict as part of a larger superpower struggle with Communism and the Soviet Union because, as one philosopher observed, we thought we could win easily and cheaply, and were wrong on both counts. How risky could it be, we thought, for a superpower to beat up on a third-world country that used water buffaloes to plow their rice paddies?

Of course, it was not that simple. The threat of other superpower intervention, be it the Soviets, who armed the opponent extensively with modern weapons, or the Chinese, who might join the conflict if taunted, constrained us and evened out the odds. The Chinese threat, specifically, dictated we could not invade North Vietnam (NVA) as we had North Korea a generation before, an option that might have assured a quick and decisive victory. The same threat allowed the NVA sanctuaries in Laos and Cambodia, meaning they could employ the classic guerilla strategy of fighting only when they had an advantage and retreating to the sanctuary zone when they did not. The NVA had become highly practiced in this type of warfare, having conducted it for over thirty years and having bested the French at the decisive battle of Dien Bien Phu in 1954. They had long known the guerilla warfare we were just learning.

A more insidious problem with our South Vietnamese allies also crippled our effort. Billions of dollars flowing into the country created fertile ground for corruption and income disparity. As this became apparent, our efforts to "win the hearts and minds" of the South Vietnamese population shattered and created a fertile fifth column among the population that actively abetted the enemy beneath our noses.

On a lower level, I'm sure the importation of several hundred thousand white and black boys with money, which bought favor with Vietnamese women, turned more than one young Vietnamese man into Viet Cong. I have no objective proof of that except that were positions reversed, I'd have taken a very dim view of "me." Recall the retaliation wreaked on French women who consorted with Nazis; they had their hair chopped off, and worse. Male umbrage at interloping foreign males with a monetary or military power advantage can be considered a universal male predilection. We exclusively enriched the South Vietnamese military elite and beguiled Vietnamese women with our dollars, two of the worst things we could have done.

Our final disadvantage would be the timeline. The Vietnamese had all the time in the world; we did not. We could get away with an ineffective war strategy for a few years, but eventually the country would ask why we were not winning against a bunch of water buffalo farmers. General Westmoreland, the commander of the war, could rationalize our supposed success until the Tet Offensive in 1968 that saw Viet Cong penetrate the American Saigon command compound. Even though the Viet Cong lost decisively militarily during Tet and never recovered from the carnage, they obliterated the falsely positive progress reports from General Westmoreland and set in motion antiwar sentiment in America that effectively won the war for the North Vietnamese.

To digress for a moment, General Westmoreland seems a caricature of our problem in Vietnam. He presented himself as the command general from central casting—tall, trim, immaculately groomed with a very short tapered haircut, impossibly starched and pressed khaki uniforms, and an impressive command presence. Observing his public briefing demeanor, one might wonder how he could possibly lose to the buffalo farmers. We should have suspected Westmoreland's seeming invincibility.

US Army photo

General William Westmoreland

I had seen this phenomenon before, as I thought back to my high school wrestling days. Before the contest began, we would line up across the mat from the other team progressively by weight class. This meant you would be staring directly at your upcoming opponent. Distressingly, it seemed I always drew the captain of the other squad at my midlevel weight. But I noticed something else about my opponents. Those who were physically sculpted and over-muscled turned out not to be a significant worry. They often could not wrestle very well and had no choice but to pump iron to become selectively strong, in a narrow weight room sense. What struck terror in me was an opponent with a physique that did not inspire confidence, being very thin and rangy, or even slightly pudgy. This meant he had succeeded because he probably possessed cat-like quickness and a high level of skill in wrestling moves and did not need to overcompensate with muscles.

From this perspective, Westmoreland proved a muscle-bound klutz. He could lift heavy weights, that is, military maneuvers, but could not seem to blend them with any appreciation of the necessary societal and political moves to succeed. The false confidence he inspired turned out to be disastrous for our country. He presented another example of the Starship Trooper conundrum; how could someone who appeared so terrifyingly competent and invulnerable ever be wrong? The history majors in President Johnson's administration failed to successfully question why we were going to march off the cliff that was Vietnam.

CAM RANH BAY

Cam Ranh, a major shipping port facility, lay midway up the east coast of South Vietnam on the South China Sea, with the Central Highland mountains to the west. Nearby coastal towns included Na Trang to the north and Phan Rang to the south. Directly west in the mountains lay the hub airports of the Central Highlands, Ban Me Thuot and Da Lat.

The base belonged to II-Corp, one of four military sections of South Vietnam that included the large middle swath of the country.

Most of my flying out of Cam Ranh would be in II-Corp and in IV-Corp in the southern delta, when I flew one-week rotations out of Tan Son Nhut Air Base in Saigon.

On arrival, my unit, the 458th Airlift Squadron, picked us up and delivered us to our hooches close to the flight line. The 458th had recently moved to Cam Ranh from Phu Cat in the Central Highlands in a consolidation effort that seems to have marked the beginning of the American drawdown of forces.

HOOCH LIFE

The hooches were Quonset-style two-bedroom dwellings, little more than a curved metal roof that would approximate a tunnel if the ends were removed. Four men lived in each hooch, which was divided down the middle, lengthwise—bedrooms on one side, living area on the other. Eight hooches formed a unit, four on each side facing each other, with latrine and shower facilities on the cross-bar of the "H" shape. Generally, each flying squadron had one twenty-four-man hooch unit for its pilots.

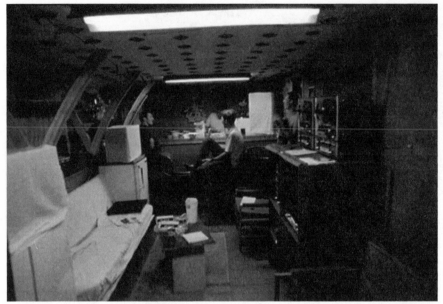

Photo by Peter Bird

Standard four-man hooch with requisite tape deck stereo systems.

Our hooch had two permanent fixtures: our maid, Baby San, and our dog, Douche Bag. They remained constant as the transitory residents of the hooch came and went from the States. I don't think Baby San ever said a word to Douche, but they recognized each other as permanent residents and coexisted peacefully.

Baby San must have been in her thirties, but it was hard to tell. She was fairly attractive and about five feet tall. However, I never knew of her cavorting with any of the clientele. She was all business. She would wash our clothes, shine our shoes, and clean our hooch in exchange for the meager salary the military paid her and for the presents we brought her from Saigon, usually nuoc mam fish sauce. She walked with that sashaying, turkey-toed sway of peasant women and usually wore black pajamas and the ubiquitous conical straw hat, our own Viet Cong look-alike.

I got along with her well, except the time I thought she had lost my socks. I looked everywhere for them and decided she had taken them to the washing machines and lost them or sold them downtown. I told her my socks were missing, with the clear implication she was responsible. Bad move, Lacklen! She ripped open the bottom drawer of my dresser, pulled back a shirt, and there they were, all the allegedly missing socks. I then endured a severe, finger-wagging tongue lashing in Vietnamese that I'm not

Photo by Stan Owens

Hooch maids doing our laundry the old-fashioned way before the washing machines arrived.

sure I'd want to have translated, a real school-boy lecture—richly deserved—about bad manners and the improper slander of hooch maids. It took two bottles of nuoc mam to calm her down.

I have no idea who procured or named Douche Bag—someone long departed from the theater. She was a docile and amiable dog who loved to have her belly rubbed, as long as you belonged to our hooch. She turned junkyard dog when a stranger tried to enter, however. My buddy Milo came looking for me one afternoon and entered the totally blacked-out hooch. He said he got one foot in the door when he heard an ominous growl from the interior. He departed, thinking he had encountered at least a pit bull. Douche was overweight and fairly waddled as she walked. She stood maybe a foot tall at the shoulders and weighed about twenty pounds. I'd guess at the breed mix, but I'd have no idea of the dominant lineage, although her head resembled a miniature black Labrador. With Douche on guard, we never locked anything, knowing she would protect our elaborate stereo systems and everything else we left lying around.

Milo's hooch dog in the 457th was named Reno, a much larger and friendlier hooch pooch that seemed a collie-setter mix, with a long russet coat. Reno ranged far afield from his hooch, while Douche did not. Reno also seemed to know everyone on base, and everyone knew him.

When Cam Ranh closed down in 1973, I heard they unceremoniously drove around and shot all the hooch dogs after the troops had left. That bothered me, although there probably were not many alternatives. At least they didn't end up downtown fried on a stick.

When I heard of the hooch dog massacre, I recalled Douche trotting to the south end of the hooch complex with me, but not a foot farther, as I left with my duffel bag and suitcase for the States in March 1972. Apparently the duffel bag signaled her of arrival or departure of her temporary masters. I dropped my bags in the back of the squadron pickup and turned for a last look at my abode. Douche cocked her head toward me, as if asking for confirmation I was leaving. I gave her a last rough rub on the head and told her good-bye. I should have told her I was sorry I was moving on while she had to stay behind. She paused a moment, then turned and trotted back to "her" hooch to await her next temporary master. Since we had just given all the C-7s to the Vietnamese, I'm not sure a new master ever showed up.

Cam Ranh Bay was actually a pretty good base, with good facilities and a marvelous beach. The major drawback was we couldn't leave the base, for security reasons. The small villages across the inlet that separated the base from the mainland were apparently not always secure and there was not much reason to visit.

The Viet Cong occasionally lobbed mortars into the base. The one time I remember a mortar landing on the base, we had gotten a siren and a Code

Red (I can't remember exactly what they called it) over the PA system (Giant Voice). Everyone was supposed to hide inside their hooch behind their sandbags, but I climbed on top of the hooch to see where the action was. I noticed a dozen other heads popping up on surrounding hooches for the same reason. We all wanted to see the war parade passing by.

The O'Club was about a quarter of a mile south of our hooch. It was smallish but cozy and comfortable. Heavy drinking was always in order, and everyone would repeatedly sing along with the song "We've Gotta Get Out of This Place" by The Animals while banging their drink glasses on the bar with the beat.

One night I drank too much at the club but wasn't worried because I was not scheduled to fly the next day. Someone called in sick, however, and suddenly I *was* scheduled to fly. I'm sure our passengers got concerned as their copilot occasionally threw up in a barf bag. I'd have had to ground myself in the States during peacetime, but for the war, I had to perform. I let the pilot do all the flying while I did enough puking for both of us. That was a long, painful day, and it took me a week to recover. I estimate the guy I replaced had called in "sick" for a similar self-inflicted malady that exacerbated my pain.

In many ways, we seemed to be on a normal Air Force base. We'd eat regular meals at the chow hall, do routine runs to the base exchange (BX), and play racquetball games almost daily when not flying. I'd only be reminded of being in a war zone when I looked across the rice paddies to the one mountain to the west with a large downward-pointing triangle of white that I presume resulted from some sort of artillery targeting over the years.

We only made it to the beach once, and I didn't even go in the water. One of our foursome did, however. Ox-cart swam out about one hundred yards with a snorkel and flippers. As we watched him, he suddenly turned and stroked for his life toward shore. I told him it seemed he only touched the

75

water about every fifty feet in his panic. He had spotted a large hammerhead shark maneuvering beneath him and spared no effort to get back on shore. We thought he was just showing off his swimming prowess until he came gasping up onto the beach with his explanation.

On my non-flying days, I would often be required to report to the squadron for desk duty. I got the standard comeuppance on day one. In life, we often move from the top of one ladder to the bottom of the next, and the captains in the squadron quickly put me in my place on the bottom rung. I had become accustomed to strutting around, letting everyone know I was an Air Force pilot with wings, by golly! Well, everyone in the squadron had wings, too, and combat experience to boot, so that gained me no advantage. The duty officer snapped at me to make coffee for the commander as if ordering a plebian to sweep the floor, failing to realize he was speaking to "Ace" Lacklen, pilot extraordinaire. I know, on a much higher level, one-star generals are told to do the same by three-stars at the Pentagon and suffer similar chagrin. So I learned that I had once again become a fraternity pledge that could be ordered around with impunity by the brothers despite my self-image as Starship Trooper.

I also got a bitter taste of the Air Force Officer Effectiveness Report (OER) system. One day at the hooch, a squadron 1st Lt. knocked and wanted to talk to me. He didn't come in and remained in the doorway, perhaps fearing I'd clock him when he explained why he had come. He initially failed to realize I didn't know shit-from-Shinola (Shinola was a shoe polish from the brown-shoe days of the 1950s) about OERs but soon saw he could easily sell me the snake oil. He held out my first OER and explained that I had gotten an "8/3" rating out of a possible "9/4," the first number being a performance rating from one to nine, and the second a future potential, or promotability, rating from one to four. *Wow*, I thought, *I'm only one notch below the top that only future four-stars probably get. I guess they know what a fine job I've been doing.*

After comparing notes and asking around, alas, I found that an 8/3 was lower than whale shit in the scheme of things, because the system had suffered rampant inflation and 90% of officers got a "firewalled" 9/4. This meant most of my pilot training buddies with cushy flying billets in the States or Europe were scoring 9/4s while I, war zone hero, was getting knifed in the back with an 8/3! I should have poured my beer on this guy's head.

The OER system proved an excellent method for a commander to look good to his troops while delivering his real opinion to senior officers behind closed doors. More on this later.

My time in Vietnam came fairly late in the national endeavor. The intense years of 1968 to 1969 had passed, and within eighteen months the withdrawal would be complete. I can only imagine the systemic economic shock when America turned off the giant economic fire hose. One day soon after I departed, Baby San, Douche, Reno, and the area surrounding Cam Rahn woke up and found the GIs were gone, along with their dollars. The artificial socioeconomic edifice built on the dollar must have collapsed quickly, leaving many abandoned and scrambling. When the hooches emptied, Baby San and Douche found themselves on their own in a desperate situation. As bad as we made things by being there, we created another disaster when we left and took our sustenance with us.

FLYING THE LINE

Photo by Peter Bird

C-7s in the foreground at Cam Ranh and a C-5 shown on takeoff roll.
My first and last assigned aircraft, smallest to largest.

As the smallest cargo aircraft in the inventory, the C-7 was capable of landing on the shortest runways. We would deliver supplies in the C-7 to small army units in the field that had sometimes rudimentary landing strips. In some cases, we could get into fields no one else could, generally those with 1,500 feet of concrete or metal PSP (pierced steel plating) surfacing, as shown in the photo above. We would haul the cargo from large bases, such as Cam Ranh Bay, that had a large shipping port, or Tan Son Nhut in Saigon, where the larger cargo aircraft brought in supplies from the States, to the small runways around the country. Ironically, I went from the smallest Air Force cargo plane to the largest, the C-5, later in my career.

Our regular Cam Ranh missions covered II-Corp up and down the coast and throughout the Central Highlands. The usual stops included Ban Me Thuot and Dalat Cam Ly in the highlands and Nha Trang on the coast. A standard day would include about eight stops, usually under VFR (visual) conditions and rarely at night. No one really followed our progress, and "Hilda," the controller in Saigon, only wanted to hear from us if we had problems. We were responsible for showing up at the assigned bases, but arrival and departure times were flexible, unlike C-5 times would be in later years. If we wanted to take a detour and buzz the giant Buddha lying on its side, or take a sightseeing trip around Con Son Island, no one cared.

On my first C-7 mission, an eight-field schedule in the Central Highlands, I committed a horrendous yet hilarious (to everyone but me) mistake. The crew, usually the copilot, refueled the Caribou by pumping the gas from a nozzle with a long hose into a wing tank that could only be reached by walking across the top of the wing to the vent, halfway to the wingtip. The nozzle looked like the standard kind you'd use to fill your car but had one important difference that I discovered the hard way. A brass cap fit over the end of the nozzle and hung from a bungee cord when removed. I didn't know this.

I dropped a cargo strap with a big metal hook/clasp on the end to the fuel truck guy and pulled the nozzle and hose up to me on the top of the wing. I placed the nozzle into the tank opening but suspected something wasn't quite right, so I peered into the tank to make sure the fuel would be flowing and pulled the fueling trigger.

Since I had not removed the cap, the fuel slammed into the cap, pushed it a few inches outward, and reversed course directly into my face. I shouted in disbelief and wobbled to both knees, fifteen feet above the tarmac on the wing, blinded with aviation gas in both eyes. I wanted to race for the water jug to flush my eyes but realized I wasn't going to race anywhere since I couldn't see. I now stunk of gas, was blind, and was stranded on the wing, unsure of how to get back to the fuselage for the water jug.

Photo by Peter Bird

Pete Bird refueling on the wing.

My aircraft commander (A/C) and the ground crew found this hilarious; I did not. I felt for the rough, no-slip walking strip on the wing with my hands and crawled back to the fuselage, miserable and humiliated. This gave new meaning to "wet behind the ears," since I was wet there and several other places. When I had climbed back into the plane, the other pilot brought me water for my eyes while trying to suppress his mirth at my ineptitude. I stunk of avgas the rest of the day, a source of renewed levity when people at each station would sniff and say they smelled gas. "Go ahead, Lieutenant, tell them why they smell gas!"

A further rookie error also embarrassed me. The aircraft commander directed me to "call the army on their frequency to ask if they had Artie." I didn't know who Artie might be or why the army would have him and asked for clarification. The pilot chuckled at me, yet again, and explained I was asking if the army had any artillery (arty) firing going on near us. "Oh," I stammered.

On one score, I did mask my ineptitude. I reported to the aircraft for this first mission wearing my flak vest. As I neared the plane, I noticed no one else was wearing their heavy, bulky vest, so I took mine off to see what they would do with theirs. As we climbed into our cockpit seats, the aircraft commander shoved his vest under his seat, so I did likewise. As I finally figured out, if we were going to get shot, it would come from beneath us and that is where the flak vest would do the most good.

A few weeks later, I got a quick reality check when I had to fly my initial in-country line check ride on a mission to Nha Trang, a short hop up the coast. I somehow had imagined that the system would take it easy on me for my first check ride, but nooo. Arguably the most difficult check ride of my career hit me right off the bat in a war zone and in a horrendous monsoon squall.

Matched with a crusty old major as a check pilot, I rued my luck when the morning dawned cloudy, rainy, and gusty. The check pilot told me the first leg would constitute the check ride, a short leg to Nha Trang with an instrument landing system (ILS) approach. I had come to pride myself on my ILS approaches, but most of those were flown under pristine conditions, and this one promised to be anything but pristine.

Things went well until I started the ILS. The C-7, due to its large tail required to provide aerodynamic leverage at slow speed, is horribly susceptible to crosswinds. The gusty monsoon rainstorm thrashed the plane to and fro on the approach, causing it to bounce and shudder. This made staying on the localizer and glide slope exponentially more difficult than the standard approach. The windshield wipers slapped back and forth noisily and represented one of the few times I ever used them.

I fought to keep the plane within its parameters and grew desperate to break out of the rain clouds to ease my task. The cloud ceiling (beneath which I could see) varied somewhat depending upon the local storm cells, and we were still on instruments as we neared Decision Height at two hundred feet above the ground. *Just how bad is fate going to stick it to me today?* I wondered, as I realized I might have to go around and try it again if we failed to break out of the clouds. Finally, right at minimums, we broke out, and I saw the field beneath me through the driving rain. I landed hard and in a crab (turned into the wind and not aligned with the runway) that caused the plane to lurch awkwardly as the wheels, now on the runway, yanked the plane back to runway alignment.

"Well," the check pilot growled, "you got it on the runway, so I guess you pass."

Gee, thanks, and fuck you! I thought. *I just flew a courageous (for a rookie) approach under terrible conditions and you guess I passed? Ha!* I thought a medal would be appropriate, but I took the small victory and kept my mouth shut.

Ironically, that specific C-7 aircraft ended up at the air museum at Dover AFB, DE, where I flew C-5s for many years.

The Central Highlands could present challenges. The often austere fields lay between ridge lines or, in one case, sat on a planed-off hilltop that sloped away in all directions. I once watched my aircraft commander make three attempts to land on one. The steeply sloping terrain made judging the landing difficult. All normal visual cues told the brain you were still far above the field, and yet, suddenly there it was, immediately below you, leaving the plane too high to land.

Finally, on the third frustrating try, the pilot, although still too high, decided to put it down anyway. I couldn't believe he would try it, but I had no control over the situation except, perhaps, to scream.

Photo by John Stymerski

Caribou diving for a runway.

The pilot dove the aircraft at the 1,500-foot runway, then yanked back hard on the yoke just above it. Unfortunately, the dive had increased our airspeed, so the plane floated, possibly catastrophically, down the short runway. We touched down with about seven hundred feet remaining on the slippery PSP metal runway before the terrain dropped steeply into the jungle. The pilot slammed on the brakes and yanked the engines into reverse. The plane skidded and rotated slowly sideways as the reversed props threw up a huge dust cloud that enveloped us. Even though I couldn't see the precipice through the dust, I knew it was approaching and we'd be lucky not to roll off the end and down the steep slope.

We stopped, blessedly, on level ground. The pilot took the throttles out of reverse, and the dust cloud slowly dissipated as we both sat gasping and speechless. Looking forward, I could not see level ground, only the jungle a hundred feet below. We had stopped with just enough runway overrun remaining to turn sharply to taxi back to the cargo ramp area. Another five feet and we'd have been bouncing down the slope into the jungle, and infamy.

Several runways in the area were renowned battlefield locations from before my arrival, though I never landed at them. Two of these were An Khe and Doc To, two army outposts almost overrun by NVA troops in the late 1960s. Caribous had performed dicey cargo airdrops to the troops surrounded by the enemy. The most famous almost-overrun post lay farther south at Khe Sanh, a hugely contested piece of real estate where our army weathered constant artillery bombardment while the VC and NVA suffered relentless pounding from the air as the price for pressuring the army outpost.

I seldom went north of II-Corp into I-Corp ("Eye" Corp) except on one mission to Da Nang. This put me much closer to the border with North Vietnam. Except for Quang Tri, Da Nang represented the northernmost major American outpost. I don't know if the monsoon weather colored my view, but Da Nang seemed to have an ominous pall of danger over it. This was the front line where hot warfare could break out at any time.

Other fields down the coast, Qui Nhon for instance, already showed the effects of the war's initial drawdown. For years the home of F-100 fighters (Huns), the base and its large runways were now nearly empty and irrelevant to the task, with no fighters still present. We sat alone, a sole aircraft on several square miles of abandoned concrete.

While II-Corp was my home, my favorite flying took place in IV-Corp in the Mekong Delta.

FLYING THE DELTA

My most vivid memory flying the Mekong Delta in South Vietnam is flying over the flat, green plain covered in rice paddies on a brilliantly sunny day listening to Cher sing "Gypsies, Tramps and Thieves" on Radio Australia on the High Frequency (HF) radio. Bright blue above, bright green below.

Photo by Mike Loughran

Unknown Caribou driver. Note the throttles on the ceiling.

I couldn't believe the turn my life had taken. Just two years before, I was starting my senior year in college, and now I was flying an Air Force transport in a war zone halfway around the world and loving it. I enjoyed the panache of being in a war, yet with very little real danger to me. I would often later feel guilty saying I "fought" the war because for all practical purposes, I was above the war. I had never killed anyone (yet), never had anyone shoot at me, and only heard one rocket land at any base I was on. Mine was the softest, most comfortable perch for the war and I tried not to claim any heroic status for having gone. Others suffered horribly or died to provide my panache and subtle war veteran sheen, so I tried never to volunteer that I had served there.

I was proud of the service but, over the years, many of my generation began fabricating war exploits for political purposes, or used their Vietnam service for perceived advantage. I find this particularly galling when my relatively affluent peers, who took alternate methods of avoiding Vietnam, decided having gone might provide an advantage for them, so they created a phantom service record. I have no mercy for those publicly outed.

PAPPA TANGO

Pappa Tango was the navigation beacon identifier for Phan Thiet, South Vietnam, a small fishing village on the coast east of Saigon and south of Cam Ranh Bay. I remember it fondly for its small rock lobsters that cost 10 cents apiece. I'll use this memory to recount flying in the Mekong Delta, the lower quarter of South Vietnam centered around the capital, Saigon.

Thirty-three years later, I flew through Vietnamese airspace in an Air Force C-5 enroute to U-Tapao, Thailand. I had to pause before transmitting to the Vietnamese controller to keep from calling her "Saigon Center," using instead the now-proper "Ho Chi Minh Center." That rankled. I dearly wanted to send a message by using Saigon, but I didn't. The name Ho Chi Minh connotes a gray old man with a scraggly beard; Saigon connotes a vibrant, voluptuous, dynamic, naughty city of lights and noise. The comparison seems appropriate, and the Vietnamese suffer still with the lesser symbol.

Although stationed at Cam Ranh Bay on the central coast, we rotated Caribou crews to Tan Son Nhut Air Base outside Saigon to cover the Delta on a weekly basis. Included on these missions were, by far, the most interesting locations in Vietnam.

I'll start with the last day of the rotation. We'd fly north to Song Be, back to Saigon, west to Tay Ninh, back to Saigon, then return to Cam Ranh with an intermediate stop at Phan Thiet on the way.

Song Be sat next to a lone mountain on the delta plain that guided us visually to the field straight north of Saigon about sixty miles. We brought supplies for the surrounding army posts but rarely stayed long. The most notable Song Be memory was of the Vietnamese kids who lived around the field. I had brought candy on a previous rotation, and they would send scouts to the plane to see if I was on board. When the alert was given, a gaggle of twenty or thirty kids would race to the plane and mob me, beseeching the candy they knew I would have. They would tug and pull at my arms and flight suit as I held the candy canister over my head. After teasing them briefly, I would surrender the canister and watch the scramble as the wrapped candy poured onto the tarmac.

Photo by Jay Lacklen

Children beseeching candy at Song Be.

Tay Ninh was a grocery run, and among those groceries for the army were multilayered cartons of steaks. I spoke with the port representative, a gruff black army master sergeant and asked if all these steaks were eaten or if they threw some away. He caught my drift and said, charitably, that they often threw some away. So, yes, we could pinch a twenty-steak box and no one would notice. So we did.

We had to put it in a small floor compartment just behind the pilot seats on the center aisle that was the coolest section of the plane, but only at altitude. Our air conditioning system consisted of opening the pilot windows, so the only cooling came with altitude and (very slow) speed. With the party steaks acquired for the evening meal at Cam Rahn stowed in the "cooler," we taxied for takeoff. Tay Ninh's control tower consisted of a large, empty oil drum with a portable VHF radio sitting on it. When traffic arrived or departed, a controller would pick up the phone receiver/transmitter and manage the flow. Tay Ninh represented the last somewhat secure outpost on the western frontier that included the Parrot's Beak region on the Cambodian border. No one ever relaxed out here, and the facilities had a hunkered-down appearance, as if the next mortar would arrive at any time. I was glad to leave.

On one earlier Tay Ninh mission with 1st Lt. aircraft commander Norv Selvidge, a highly distraught Air Force major began gesturing wildly in front of the airplane as we parked and shut down the engines. He clambered on board and stalked to the cockpit. He then began blistering Selvidge with an incomprehensible diatribe about some complaint with air support that Selvidge and I had nothing to do with. It became obvious the poor guy had lost it and broken down mentally. Selvidge humored him, feigned concern for his complaint, and promised to relay the complaint, whatever it was, to the commanders back at Tan Son Nuht. Somewhat mollified, the major left, and left us bewildered. We sat silently for a few moments pondering the crushing pressure we knew existed out here in the field.

After a quick turn at Tan Son Nuht, we flew to Pappa Tango in the late afternoon. The field ran along a high bluff above the city and South China Sea, a very picturesque sight. The lobster vendor squatted next to the runway, friendly and gregarious with his broken pidgin English. "I get lobsta for you, GI?" he'd say. Yes, I told him, beaucoup lobsters. We got a hundred silver-dollar-sized rock lobsters for ten bucks.

The GI/Vietnamese lexicon proved humorous at times, a curious mix of pidgin English and French. At the Saigon Airman's Club I heard a Vietnamese band playing a current hit called "Yellow River" by Christie. Alas, when the Vietnamese singer sang it, it came out as "Jellow Liver." I'm sure we butchered Vietnamese just as badly.

Everything was valued as either "numba one!" (best) or "numba ten!" (worst), with no value in between. I'm not sure where this value scale came from, but it was well-established by the time I got in-country in 1971. The next-favorite epithet was "Cheap Charlie," spoken without the "r" in Charlie. The Vietnamese used this on us when they didn't think they had been properly compensated for whatever service they had provided. Yes, this usually meant the Saigon hookers who never thought their price, or your tip, was enough. (Before I get myself in trouble here, I never partook of Vietnamese hookers. For other parts of Southeast Asia I visited, I plead the fifth.)

We were back at Cam Ranh in thirty minutes, where our hooch compatriots had prepared the battlefield by starting the charcoal grills and icing down the beer. We then would make a grand gesture of presenting the army steaks and Vietnamese seafood for the feast, along with exclamations that war is hell. Even Douche Bag would become uncharacteristically sociable with the prospect of steak scraps.

The Saigon rotation became my favorite mission, and I volunteered for it continuously. The extra trappings of time off in the big city, interesting air fields to visit, and availability of army rations to be pilfered, provided a respite from the cloistered base at Cam Ranh, where we were never allowed out the front gate.

The air fields in the delta proved fascinating and diverse, and I'll cover them in turn:

<u>Tonle Cham</u>: a small outpost on a jungle hill near the Cambodian border. The hill was defended by three separate lines. At the bottom were

89

the Montagnards, local tribesmen who had allied with us for the war (and who suffered significantly for doing so after we left). Next up the hill came the South Vietnamese behind seemingly impenetrable hedgerows laced with concertina wire. Finally, at the top, was a small American Army contingent who ran the show and had communication with MAC-V in Saigon for any support that might be required, from artillery to air strikes.

This was one of the first frontier outposts overrun by the North Vietnamese in 1975, and I can't imagine how they did it on this series of dense hedgerows that lined the hill with well-fortified trenches and firing positions. I couldn't climb that two-hundred-foot hill in a day, even with no one shooting at me, but the NVA overran it in a few hours, although I don't know if it was fully manned at the time or if the defending force surrendered prior to being overrun.

As we touched down on the short, austere PSP runway, I thought I had landed in Xanadu. Alongside the runway, loin-clothed local villagers were leading elephants dragging teak logs from the heavily forested jungle hillside across the runway from the fortified camp. Later, the American commander, an army captain, said a tiger had been killed by an American Claymore mine just outside the base perimeter the week before. *Good God, where have I landed?* I thought. *I'm in the same neighborhood as elephants and wild tigers!*

Things became more bizarre when, after visiting the top of the hill fortress for lunch, we picked up our passengers. I'm not sure if they were Vietnamese or Montagnards or Martians. They wore bandanas of several subdued colors on their foreheads; were ferociously armed with assault rifles, hand grenades, and knives; and looked as if they'd probably enjoy killing humans before, during, and after a meal, and think little of it. If there were an American among them, he had gone totally native and I couldn't recognize him. While flying to their destination in our cargo compartment, they lit a fire in a small stove to cook a meal. This was highly illegal, but I certainly wasn't going to tell them to stop, or even critique them. We dropped this probable hunter-killer team at our next stop, and they walked into the jungle silently. They were fighting the real war I was flying above. I felt grateful they were on my side, but I'm sure the other side had counterparts just as ferocious and fearsome. In all probability, these two opposing groups must have made each other what they were, and what I saw.

An Thoi: an island off the southwest coast that served as a US Navy station that had a three-thousand-foot PSP runway. We always tried to arrange to arrive during lunch because the navy had, easily, the best food of any of the services, especially the coffee. We also made our necessary purchase of nuoc mam, a pungent Vietnamese fish sauce created by stacking layers of fish on wooden racks in the hot sun and letting them ooze into a container at the bottom of the racks. I never tried to eat any, especially after smelling it, but it made the perfect present for our hooch maids back at Cam Rahn, who would thank us profusely for bringing them a bottle. A C-7 flight mechanic once broke a bottle of nuoc mam on the aft ramp and it took the plane out of service for a week as they tried to rid it of the stench.

An Thoi was close to the infamous tiger cages used to house South Vietnam's political prisoners, and you could see the cages from the air as you departed. These were little more than holes in the ground with grates over them that allowed the prisoners to bake in the stifling heat. While tacitly an ARVN (Army of Vietnam) operation, we knew exactly what they were doing and made no attempt to remedy these inhumane conditions that violated every treaty we had ever signed. I imagine the tiger cages did more to alienate Vietnamese, north or south, than almost anything else we did during the war. In retrospect, I wonder why the American adult supervision at the prison didn't do anything about this. This was far more barbaric than the treatment our POWs received in the Hanoi Hilton, and it begged to have quid pro quo inflicted on us up north. This bothered me even more when I returned in

B-52s just before the hot war ended in 1973, when it became possible I'd wind up at the "Hilton" at the end of a bad mission.

Can Tho: the most centrally located field south of Saigon. It billed itself the home of "Pleasure City ALCE" (Air Lift Control Element). Fortunately, or unfortunately, I never had the pleasure of finding out why this compound was so named, but I can imagine. I thought Saigon had about the most potential "pleasure," but Can Tho must have had some claim, be it Thai basket jobs or other exotic erotic potentialities. I'll refrain from describing the basket job, except to say that it went around and around.

Vung Tau: the coastal resort city east of Saigon that could have provided the model for the 1980s TV series *China Beach* (which was based on a beach near Danang). Somehow, the Aussie C-7s claimed this garden spot as their province during my tour. Such a deal. I'd like to know who negotiated *that* agreement. We were trapped at Cam Ranh Bay and couldn't even get off base, but the Aussies got China Beach? Besides, they got to wear bush hats while flying and could grow their moustaches to huge handlebar proportions. Americans did get a sort of revenge. When arriving for R&R in Sydney, the Aussie women would capture the American soldiers as they entered the terminal and would hold them as sex slaves for their entire seven days before returning them, tired but smiling, to their return flight. You can have your moustaches, mates, and g'day!

Saigon: the phantasmagoria of Southeast Asia rivaled only by Bangkok. Thriving, boisterous, dirty, elegant, wicked, decadent, vibrant, and in a hurry, this city displayed everything that was right or wrong with South Vietnam. Capitalism flourished alongside rampant corruption. French elegance in language, architecture, and cuisine stood alongside abject shanties, dirty klongs (sewer ditches), and fried dog or cat sold by street vendors. The traffic was mayhem, only loosely affected by traffic lights. Rampaging rivers of diverse vehicles would collide at large traffic circles that seemed always on the verge of suffering fifty-car pileups that never quite seemed to happen. Car horns blared—offensive weapons as vehicles veered within inches of each other while paying absolutely no attention to traffic lanes. Traffic moved very swiftly considering the overwhelming congestion, and a thick fog of exhaust hung over the streets and stung the eyes. I suppose it could be argued which city has the worst traffic congestion and mayhem, and Saigon would have been in the top three I saw, along with Cairo, Egypt, and Bangkok.

In retrospect, a Saigon restaurant named Le Cave served me the best meal I have ever had. I've had excellent meals in many countries, but this meal was artistry, a lobster thermidor that made me gasp in astonishment when I tasted it. The French waiter performed perfectly, showing up exactly when needed and not bothering us otherwise. (American waiters tend to ask how the meal is while walking by briskly and exactly when I have a mouth full of food, and then refusing to look toward me when I need something.) This meal gave a glimpse of the departed French presence, and it was an excellent one.

Driving through the city, the huge, blocky MAC-V compound stood out garishly, the white palace of the American maharajahs. I worked for them, and even I didn't like the look of the place—corporate headquarters for the, at times, half-million-man army camped in this poor, little third-world country. When I think of this compound, all the cute quips come to mind. We should have just bought North Vietnam because, in their terms, they'd have all been rich had we rained down the billions of dollars squandered on this project on them instead, turning them into the capitalists we wanted them to become. No punji sticks, no napalm, no B-52 strikes, no Tet Offensive, no vast wards of permanently crippled soldiers on both sides, no dead 55,000 Americans and hundreds of thousands of Vietnamese. Such a better capitalist outcome.

The sad fact that Saigon fell and was submerged into a Communist economic hell is one of the region's great tragedies. Saigon did capitalism as well as any place I have ever seen. They sucked money off GIs with an aplomb that would have astounded any nineteenth-century American moguls. But they did it by providing exactly what we wanted, with a smile and quickly. And if they didn't know exactly what we wanted, they found out in a hurry. Ironically, they were better capitalists than we soldiers were. They knew the system better, did it better, and appreciated it far more than we did. They lived the naked capitalism we only vaguely thought about, and then not very well or precisely. And we thought we could teach them? They would have been teaching us, had we the sense to listen to them.

Some soldiers stationed in Saigon got lost in the marvelous mayhem of the city. This was termed T-locking, which I think approximated the Vietnamese term for living downtown on the economy and freely as a bird. This always involved a Vietnamese woman who acted as something between a wife and a maid while performing the duties of each. (I can hear the smart remarks from American wives who feel they are T-locking.) Many soldiers "went native" and disappeared into the city when not on the job. Even an American Army private could live lavishly on the economy where the dollar held mystical power, and many did.

There were sad sights, too—beggars, orphans, and war cripples. One night as we scrambled to get inside the Tan Son Nhut Air Base gate before the 2300 curfew, a withered, disheveled, gray Vietnamese grandmother wandered among us saying, in a trancelike state: "Suck, fuck, one dolla, numba one Amelican girl!" Yeah, right. I asked her if she really had a "round-eyed" woman. She nodded her head fiercely and said yes, right down that alley over there. Oh, yeah, I'm going to walk down that alley all right, Mama San.

While we found it humorous at the time, it displayed an abject desperation for a dollar. I should have given her ten. Besides, most of us would live our whole lives with "round eyes" and we were looking for something different here, a very different look, a very different outlook, a very different attitude. Right or wrong, many a variety of exotic life spices were available outside the gate, and many GIs were looking for exactly that because they knew they'd never be readily and anonymously available again once they got back to "the world."

I also discovered one place where rank did not have its privilege: the Tan Son Nhut Air Base Airman's Club. This facility dwarfed the O'Club and, due to a far larger clientele, had better entertainment and go-go girls, although this is where I heard the Vietnamese band singing "Jellow Liver." We stopped outside and huddled to discuss crashing the enlisted club. We didn't think we'd get caught in civilian clothes; how could they tell we were officers? Well, they could, maybe because we were six or so years older than most of the patrons. I felt a tap on my shoulder. An MP asked to see my ID card. Busted, ejected, banished for rank too high!

Saigon Tea: the lubricant of a billion-dollar industry, the sex trade in Saigon. Bar girls would make a deal—you buy them glasses of Saigon tea and they would sit and talk with you for a while. Stop buying them tea, no more bar girl to talk to. At $5 a pop in the sixties and seventies, this could get expensive pretty quickly for the green liquid that might have been tea but might have been colored water for all anyone knew. The phrase "you buy me Saigon tea?" was one almost every GI heard at some time or another, even if trying to steer clear of such temptation. I decided if I ever had a boat, from a dingy to a yacht, it would be named "Saigon tea." I still don't have a boat and don't really want one, but I need to name *something* Saigon tea.

PHU CAT TDY

After about three months in-country, the squadron sent me to Phu Cat in the Highlands to evaluate what had been my squadron's home before they moved to Cam Ranh. They wanted an evaluation for suitability to establish Vietnamese Caribou training once we left, and I spent about a week there.

Photo by John Stymerski

Phu Cat from the runway.

This put the war on a new level for me. I lived alone in a bunkered hut with a metal helmet, a flak jacket, a .38 revolver, and an M-16 rifle. These were necessary because the base perimeter was defended by South Vietnamese, with few Americans in the neighborhood. In retrospect, my best defense if overrun would have been the NVA soldiers laughing themselves to death at the sight of me dressed up as a soldier as if for a school play or a costume party.

My instructions said if the siren went off indicating a perimeter breach, I was to head a quarter of a mile across a gully to the ROK (Republic of

Korea) compound. Given such a situation, I was warned not to approach the compound except at the main entrance; otherwise I'd be considered a hostile by the ROK guards.

I didn't get nervous until nightfall as I sat outside my bunker looking across the runway at the hills beyond the far side of the base about a mile away. Occasionally the perimeter guards would fire phosphorus flares into the night above the wire barriers to light them up, checking for sappers or infiltrators. The flares would pop to life a few hundred feet in the air and float down slowly on tiny parachutes providing a harsh white light that shifted as if a giant lantern were being slowly swung back and forth above the jungle. I thought of these flares as the torches carried by demons lighting the stairway to hell.

As I lay in the dark trying to sleep, I again wondered how frat boy had wound up in such conditions. What the hell was I doing here? I attempted to tamp down my dread of the enemy forces roaming the countryside. Forty years later, I still wonder about the men on the other side of the perimeter wire at Phu Cat.

CONTEMPLATING THE NORTH VIETNAMESE ARMY

When I think of the NVA, I recall a famous line from the movie *Butch Cassidy and the Sundance Kid* where the two protagonists are being methodically pursued by a highly paid professional band of outlaw hunters. Both Butch and Sundance look back at their pursuers and ask: "Who *are* those guys?"

I view the NVA similarly. Who are these guys who dared to contest the mightiest military on earth, who suffered a million deaths from a country with only twenty-five million people[5], who stood and fought as hell rained down on them from the skies? They could not call in air strikes to save themselves as

97

we could, there were no "dust off" choppers to race their wounded to a first-rate hospital, there were no transport planes to move them into the theater; they had to walk or ride in trucks with B-52s lurking in the skies above them. Their "bedroom" was a hammock in the jungle for years at a time.

My only direct information comes from a novel by a former NVA soldier, Bao Ninh, who wrote *The Sorrow of War* in 1991.[6] Ninh is about my age and fought the entire length of American involvement in the conflict and, further, to the fall of Saigon, or the ten years from 1965 to 1975. I presume his characters are largely autobiographical.

Ninh has to be the luckiest NVA soldier who ever lived. Only he and nine others from his five-hundred-man battalion managed to survive a battle near the Sa Thay River near the Cambodian border in 1969. As he wrote:

> *That was the dry season when the sun burned harshly, the wind blew fiercely, and the enemy sent napalm spraying through the jungle and a sea of fire enveloped (the battalion), spreading like the fires of hell. Troops in the fragmented companies tried to regroup, only to be blown out of their shelters again as they went mad, became disoriented, and threw themselves into nets of bullets, dying in the flaming inferno. Above them the helicopters flew at treetop height and shot them almost one by one, the blood spreading out, spraying from their backs, flowing like red mud.*
>
> *The diamond-shaped grass clearing was piled high with bodies killed by the helicopter gunships. Broken bodies, bodies blown apart, bodies vaporized (pp. 4–5).*

Who were these guys who repeatedly walked into the terrible teeth of the world's preeminent war machine?

Just before the final push for Saigon, Ninh and his four-man scout platoon fought at police headquarters in Bam Me Thuot in the Central Highlands. Two of his comrades were incinerated into ash as the tanks they were riding exploded and burned.

The other remaining member of the group died at Ninh's side in the police headquarters building. A South Vietnamese police female Ninh had already shot, and who he had told to go outside with her hands up and she would not be harmed, instead pulled out a pistol and pumped four bullets into Ninh's comrade's back. She would have killed Ninh, too, and had leveled the pistol at him at short range, but she had expended all her ammo and the pistol clicked as she repeatedly pulled the trigger. Ninh emptied his entire AK-47 clip into the woman and then fell to the floor retching, saying this was the most distraught he had felt in ten years of war—quite a statement. A female of the "puppet" South Vietnamese forces had shown discipline and dedication equal to his, and this must have greatly disillusioned him.

Ninh quotes North Vietnamese officials as claiming the NVA was the best land army in the world. That might be true for this specific niche of warfare where they could employ their finely honed guerilla tactics from nearby sanctuaries against a militarily superior foe constrained by superpower geopolitics. Freed from geopolitical constraints, however, the US could have invaded North Vietnam and made short work of the NVA, but given those constraints, I would not dispute the accolade.

Yet, the NVA's extraordinary capability turned out to be a curse. They were so good they persevered and "won" but sacrificed perhaps two generations of young men to hitch their society to a collapsing political system that would mire them in poverty for decades. Destitution became the spoils of their dearly paid-for victory.

Ninh provides hints that the soldiers knew their political system might be suspect. They mocked the simplistic Communist slogans forced on them and ridiculed the political class for their rigid orthodoxy. Perhaps Ninh should have considered what this would mean should victory arrive, a tacit validation of the inept, foundering Communist system. The NVA were nationalists fighting under the banner of Communism, and the political commissars looted their victory.

A quick defeat at the hands of the Americans would have been far kinder. Almost a million men would have lived to experience the somewhat corrupt but still preferable capitalist system of the South. Vietnam could have become one of the "Asian Tiger" economies that arose at the end of the twentieth century instead of suffering decades of abject poverty as other nations around them prospered.

As many relatively rudimentary societies discovered two thousand years ago, their best social advancement would come from losing to the Romans and becoming incorporated into the empire. The same would have been true for the North Vietnamese had they lost quickly and gracefully to the Americans so we could have rained money on them instead of bombs. A string of golf and tourist resorts down the length of Vietnam could have allowed them to prosper by catering to newly rich Japanese in the 1980s.

This catastrophe replayed the same scenario of the American Civil War. Had the South not had a fanatically dedicated army and superlative generals compared to the North's inept bureaucratic commanders, the North might have won quickly. That would have saved America hundreds of thousands of war dead, spared Atlanta from being torched, and made Sherman's march to the sea unnecessary.

Who *were* those guys in the North Vietnamese Army? They were a splendid, ferociously capable guerilla army whose prowess, ironically, doomed their country to economic depression while decimating their population. They won the war but lost the future.

A VIETNAM CHRISTMAS, 1971

A Touch of Home

Photo courtesy of the American Red Cross

A Vietnam Christmas, 1971.

Christmas 1971 provided a mental break from the war. In an annual event, the Cam Ranh air wing painted a C-7 with a red Santa Claus face on the forward dome and flew to various bases as a treat for the army troops. I participated on this run but only as a back-up crewmember for the primary pilots. I was not called upon to perform, so I got to play Santa's helper at the various stops. One of the flight mechanics played Santa dressed in an appropriate red suit and fake beard, and a small, half-dozen strong, squad of "Donut Dollies," or female Red Cross workers, played Santa's helpers. We also carried a large stock of liquor and sandwiches for the troops.

I had underestimated the potential poignancy of the event. Bringing the Christmas aura to the trenches of Vietnam unleashed seemingly well-secured emotions that suddenly broke loose in everyone, none more clearly displayed than at the small northern delta army base of Bao Loc, sixty miles northeast of Saigon.

This base resided as close to the pits of Vietnam as you could get. The approach plate for the runway warned: "Runway in poor condition, south end 20% coverage by large, loose rocks. 200' overrun each end, poor condition. Parking area east side and south end, poor condition, partly overgrown."

We pulled onto the poorly conditioned parking ramp, but before we could shut down the engines and open the rear cargo door, a series of large transport trucks appeared on the road to the field filled with troops whooping and waving. They pulled up next to us on the ramp and disgorged fifty or so soldiers in their green fatigues that surrounded the rear of the plane to welcome whoever might disembark.

The rear cargo door came down, and Santa emerged. The troops cheered and whistled. Then the Donut Dollies came down the ramp and the troops went joyously berserk, but not in a nasty or lewd sense. They spun around in the same frantic ecstasy of a pet dog when you pick it up from the vet or when you hold its dinner bowl over its head to make it dance. No group of children ever carried off the fantasy so well. A young soldier shook my hand with tears in his eyes and said, "Sir, this is the best thing that has ever happened here. Thank-you so much!" Maddeningly for my composure, he was about to make me cry, too.

This brought to mind, yet again, the imperative question: "What the fuck are we doing here?"

We carried a bag of letters from school kids in the States for the soldiers. They told of how proud they were of the troops, how they hoped they didn't get hurt, and to come home soon to their families. As I watched the troops reading these simple letters, I did start choking up as they became silent with faces contorted to avoid crying.

As the sun set over the Central Highlands, we flew up the coast past Phan Thiet (Pappa Tango) toward Cam Ranh with the upper cargo door raised and the bottom ramp angled up so we could lie against it and look out the back of the plane. Two or three Dollies joined me gazing out at the South China Sea in wistful contemplation of the day, marveling that in our mid-twenties we found ourselves in such a perplexing situation halfway around the world.

BOB HOPE SHOW

I managed to catch the 1971 Bob Hope Christmas Show at Bien Hoa airfield in Saigon. I will always consider this yearly journey by Hope to entertain the troops as one of the most selfless and heroic actions taken on behalf of the troops of this and earlier wars. This turned out to be his next-to-last trip. Lots of politicians mouth platitudes in support of the troops, but Hope and his entourage delivered the goods, repeatedly and under trying conditions. He made us laugh in an environment that did not encourage laughable thoughts. Comedy, ironically, would be his deadly serious salve on our emotional wounds.

Like a star-struck kid, I waited in line to shake his hand once he put down his ever-present golf club. He worked the line with the professional baseball pitcher Vida Blue and shook as many hands of the troops as he could. I caught him on the tarmac as he walked to his aircraft to depart for some location in the boonies.

His show got everyone's blood pumping. Of course, he cheated, with that sly grin of his, by bringing the hottest babes of the time on stage to play straight babe for his jokes, to include Raquel Welch, Ann-Margret, Connie

Stevens, and others. He would try to dance a little soft-shoe first, as if that is what the troops wanted to see, then, mercifully, let the hotties take over the chore to the berserk delight of the troops. The hottest dance routine I ever witnessed was that of Joey Heatherton on the stage with Hope. I didn't know they made them like that.

Thank you, Bob. Though of another generation, you did marvels for mine.

R&R IN TAIWAN

In December 1971 we qualified for seven days of rest and recreation (R&R). The choices usually were Taiwan, Australia, or Hawaii, but we were assigned Taiwan. Four of us went together—my pilot training compatriot Ed, the previously mentioned Oscar (Ox-cart, or Ox-fart), and Fast Eddie, Ox-cart's best buddy who roomed with him across the quad on the other side of our squadron compound.

We landed in Taipei and headed for the hotel where the first of the three significant trip events took place. First, the bellboy asked if we wanted girls. Hmmm. As a refugee from the war zone, I figured I should at least check out his wares, so to speak. About thirty minutes later, he reappeared with a stunningly attractive Chinese woman about my age. A popular 1960 movie entitled *The World of Suzie Wong* starred William Holden and Oriental bombshell Nancy Kwan as Suzie, who represented the top tier of lusted-for Oriental women. What the bellboy presented to me made Suzie look like a washwoman. I can't remember the price, but I slapped it into his hand and commenced several days of escape from everything.

Unfortunately, as is often the case, Suzie brought more to the arrangement than good looks, and I was soon searching for a VD clinic to banish a pox. I didn't want to risk visiting the military clinic at the American C-130 base at

CCK. The old joke had the flight surgeon addressing sick call by saying: all enlisted men with VD sit over there, all officers with "colds" sit over here, but I didn't trust that would be the case. I didn't need this on my records.

It seems this was a common problem, as an office across the street from the hotel advertised "VD Clinic" in English. *At least the doctor is wearing a white coat*, I thought as I entered. The Chinese doc smiled and said in pidgin English, "Ah, yes, we fix you!" Oh, he fixed me, all right, with two penicillin shots with vaccine tubes so large he had to put them into a metal brace with two curved finger holds to steady the application. I've seen smaller shots given to horses. As I lay on the table, he pumped the first shot into one of my ass cheeks that bulged with the cottage-cheese-consistency liquid. He then put a big cotton swab on the entry point and leaned on it with both hands to disperse it from the site. Then, to my chagrin, he did it again on my other cheek. When I got back to the hotel, I bid a fond adieu to Suzie. She was almost pretty enough to make it worth it, but not quite.

The second event of note happened while we bought tailor-made suits for a pittance at a nearby haberdasher shop. We proved such good customers for our new Chinese friends in the shop that they treated us to dinner and drinks one night. They spoke English pretty well and we were having a good old time when the boss decided he should drink me under the table with sake, a clear Japanese wine. It turned out he could not, since I outweighed him by about forty pounds, but it made for a friendly evening of international cooperation between Americans and Chinese, and both sides departed with fond memories of the other, something that was not always the case. Going to Vietnam provided many corollary educational experiences, and consorting over sake with Taiwanese Chinese proved interesting and did not require penicillin shots to recover from.

The third event evolved when Ox-cart, Ed, and I decided to have some fun with Fast Eddie, an ultraconservative, religious married man. We gave the bellboy ten bucks to send a hot number to Fast Eddie's hotel room, gratis from the hotel. We warned the bellboy that Eddie was very shy but very lonely and the woman should convince him he should let her relax him properly, and not to take "no" as an answer because Eddie *really, really* wanted companionship. We watched from around the hallway corner, dancing in silent mirth, as the woman knocked on the door. Eddie answered and listened to the pitch that she had been sent to make him feel better for free. As anticipated, Eddie refused, but his sternly enforced manners allowed the woman to enter the room, as she insisted he should not worry and let her handle things. The door closed. We left. Later, Eddie swore nothing happened and that we had some chutzpah to try to trick him like that. I don't know what transpired behind that closed door and don't suppose anyone but Eddie will ever know.

CARIBOU REDEPLOY

After R&R, we found the war rapidly winding down. The Caribou force at Cam Ranh would be split, with half the airframes returning to the States and half remaining to be awarded to the South Vietnamese Air Force. Through some arrangement, perhaps to let some of the married guys go home, half the squadron would fly planes back to the States for Christmas and half would remain to continue the mission until the handover to the Vietnamese in March 1972. That meant Ed would depart on the ferry mission and leave the rest of us to carry the remaining mission through March.

The primary effect on me would be maxing out my 120 hours per month flying time limit. It seemed, at times, I was the only copilot left on base. Also, as a senior copilot, I got repeatedly assigned to fly with staff officers who were woefully nonproficient on flying the line. They were good guys, and good pilots, but they had flown very little of late and needed constant monitoring. Some of them let me do all the flying to avoid embarrassing themselves.

During this time, I became very proficient and had several show-off moments to my credit. One neat trick was landing in a crosswind and rolling the upwind tire onto the asphalt seamlessly, so no one would know we had already landed until some little runway bump revealed we had touched down without anyone realizing—a grease job, as we termed it. This seems incredible, especially in a strong crosswind. This actually made it easier because only one tire had to be transacted, not two at the same time, as with no crosswind. Passengers did not realize this, of course, and I didn't disabuse them of their wonder at this feat.

A second moment came on a return to Cam Ranh with a stiff, thirty-knot headwind directly down the runway. With full flaps, this put our inferred ground speed across the runway threshold at only about forty knots and resulted in a very steep final approach. I called "on final" to tower, but the controller said he couldn't see me.

"Look higher," I said. Still he could not see me. "No, higher," I encouraged.

"Oh," he said, "now I see you!"

I touched down firmly and put the engines into max reverse, allowing me to stop in about five hundred feet of runway and turn off on the entry taxiway used by planes starting their takeoff. After pulling off the runway, I told the tower we were clear, and he again could not locate us because he didn't consider checking the approach-end taxiway we were on.

The cadre flying the planes back to the States had unique conditions. Due to its slow cruise speed, the Caribou did not have a long range, a significant problem crossing the wide expanses of the Pacific. To extend the range of the last-leg segment from Hawaii to the States, two large fuel bladders had to be loaded in the cargo compartment and pumped into the fuel tanks with deicing pumps. This gaggle of twelve Caribous departed on Dec. 10, 1971, and flew segments to Clark, Guam, Midway, Hickam, and finally to Hamilton AFB north of San Francisco.

All went well until the final leg, Hawaii to California. This is the longest flight segment of the entire globe, where there is absolutely no . . . place . . . to . . . go . . . if you have a problem, no little islands to land on to save yourself, almost 2,500 miles of nothing but water. At the crucial moment, just over halfway to California, one of the Caribous lost an engine. It could still fly, awkwardly, single engine, but the added drag and lower altitude meant it might not make the California coast before the good engine quit of fuel starvation. The larger C-130 mother ship hovered over the crippled plane as it flew nearly on the wave tops toward the coast. The crew threw overboard everything not bolted down to extend their range. Finally, with the fuel tank reading fifty pounds of gas remaining, the pilot told the mother ship he was going to ditch and at least have power for the landing, even though twenty miles from the coast. The copilot and flight mechanic opened the rear cargo door and held on as the plane crashed into the waves. Once the plane stopped, as directed, the two crewmen launched off the cargo ramp into the ocean and inflated their raft as the plane filled with water.

Unfortunately, the crash caused the instrument panel to fall on the pilot, pinning him in his seat and injuring him significantly as the plane began to sink. A "Jolly Green" rescue helicopter had flown from the coast to meet the crippled plane, and it hovered near the aircraft as it touched down in the water. Two parachute jumpers, or PJs, rappelled into the water next to the plane, swam to it, and began a frantic effort to free the pilot. They pulled the panel off him as his head was about to disappear under the water and dragged him through the overhead hatch onto the top of the fuselage. They then pulled his underarm life preserver units (LPUs) that kept him afloat as the plane sank out of sight beneath him. All crew members survived.[7]

Incidentally, PJs never had to buy a drink in a bar. Any pilot in the area would pick up his tab since the PJ may well pick up the pilot's ass in the future from a hostile jungle or surging ocean.

Those who flew the aircraft to the States got the holidays at home before returning, but they came back with sometimes disturbing accounts. You see, their learned vocabulary in Vietnam had a particular feature that did not play well around the family—the use of the F-word as an adjective, adverb, noun, verb, and every other classification in sentence structure. Had the F-word been eliminated in Vietnam, 50% of all conversations would have disappeared.

In the perfect anecdote, one of the pilots related an incident from around the Christmas dinner table with family and relatives. All he remembered was asking for someone to pass the peas when conversation ceased and everyone stared at him with their mouths agape.

HOW YOU KNEW THE WAR WAS OVER

In retrospect, I saw many harbingers that, despite our valiant effort in Vietnam, our involvement had neared its end. Things were starting to come apart in the ranks, and it had become time to leave.

Discipline collapse provided the most obvious indicator that it was over. The draftee military had lost its edge and its morale. I saw it daily walking the base in uniform as black enlisted troops would cross the street to avoid having to salute me. Other times they would turn their heads, looking away as they approached, a paltry excuse for having not seen me. Sometimes I would force the issue by saying, "Good afternoon, airman," which would get me a lazy, half-assed salute. Other times I just let it go. I knew the system expected me to jump the frame of every soldier who did this, but there were too many of them. I expect things began deteriorating after Martin Luther King was assassinated in 1968. They saw this as a white man's war and themselves as forced labor in a cause many of them could not understand. Having their spiritual leader murdered in the American South by a white man turned their mood even uglier than that of white draftees, who were none too pleased with things, either. By late 1971, discipline and morale had tanked and would take years to recover.

The blacks also developed a ritualized handshake called the dap that involved a patterned series of handshakes and hand slaps that seemed to signal preliminary moves to a wrestling match instead of a greeting. It served as their way of social networking to identify themselves as members of a select subset of the wartime military culture. These hand grasps, clasps, and slaps could go on for five or ten seconds, the not-so-secret secret handshake of the brotherhood.

The second, corollary indicator took place several times in the squadron where I occasionally pulled casual duty when not flying. The Deputy Commander for Operations, or DCO, a full colonel, would stalk into the building and track down the squadron commander. After scowling at him disapprovingly for a moment or two, the DCO would lace into him about lax discipline and especially about the squadron commander's haircut that, while well within regulation, was not short enough to suit the DCO. Unless he had shaved his head, I don't think the squadron commander could have avoided the repeated upbraiding. Senior officers knew discipline had collapsed and spent much of their day in a rage over it while searching for a scapegoat. (You might try SecDef Robert McNamara, sir, for concocting this extended fiasco!) To deflect the blame from themselves, they often took it out on their immediate subordinates. Yes, that's it; the squadron commander's hair length caused the discipline problem. Case closed!

When I saw the DCO striding into the building on his mission, I'd hide in a corner to avoid collateral damage from the firestorm about to erupt. Someone dearly needed to tell that blowhard bastard to shove it, but of course no one could.

"Haircut colonels" are those who, if they cannot lead, can at least scream about haircuts. This DCO was not the first I'd encountered but was arguably the worst I ever saw. The squadron commander was a superb leader who didn't deserve what he was getting. Unfortunately, that is often the case in the military.

RETURNING TO THE WORLD

In one way I had lucked out. The decision to transfer all the C-7s to the Vietnamese, in line with President Nixon's program of Vietnamization, meant I could rotate back to the States after six months in the theater. While I welcomed this, I felt disappointment at losing my impending upgrade to aircraft commander, but I did get credit for a full tour.

The military strategically adjusted such largesse for others, however. Strategic Air Command (SAC) crews had orders cut for 179 days, one day short of combat tour status, so they could be sent back six months later, indefinitely. This led to significant stress on B-52 and KC-135 crew members and their families. It also led to all sorts of hanky-panky at the home base while either bombers or tankers were in Southeast Asia while the other group stayed home, and then swapped out six months later.

My luck ran out on my departure day. I wasn't feeling quite right when I awoke to head to the passenger terminal at Cam Ranh to board the "freedom bird," a commercial stretch DC-8 cattle car used to move as many troops as possible on each flight. As I waited in a long line to be processed, I began to feel much, much worse. When I was fifth in line to process, it hit me. My gut felt like it might explode, and my mouth felt like someone had put two lead fishing weights under my tongue that signaled an impending puke-fest.

I threw my bags in a waiting room chair and sprinted to the bathroom. I blasted open the stall door and found myself in a novel dilemma; I didn't

Photo by John Stymerski

Cam Ranh Bay passenger terminal.

know which end to stick in first because wrenching explosions were coming from each. Over the next thirty minutes, I just managed to swap ends as necessary to avoid despoiling the entire area. I have never been as debilitated in my life, before or since. When I felt the spasms had run their course, for a while at least, I very carefully retrieved my bags and staggered out of the terminal to hail a Vietnamese cab to transport me to the base hospital, where I spent the next week, initially with IVs in my arm to combat dehydration. I had these tubes in me for the first few days, since anything I tried to eat started the volcano in my stomach erupting again.

After this very long week, I returned to the terminal to catch another freedom bird. This proved a mistake because I was nowhere near well yet. On the twelve-hour flight to California, I blew gas from both ends and, though close, the odor coming from my mouth was worse. The poor guy next to me should have passed out from the stench. I couldn't believe he didn't demand a different seat. Upon landing at Travis AFB, I immediately checked myself into the base hospital for another three days until I had more fully recovered. I still have no idea what I had, or where I got it, but I hope never to go there again.

When I volunteered to go to Vietnam after pilot training, my career advisor told me that, upon return, I could have any airplane to any base I wished as a reward. I had not yet experienced the big lie of promised assignments.

When I queried the new advisor, he laughed at my naïveté. "Why yes, Lieutenant." He smirked. "That promise was true, except what you 'want' is a B-52 to Loring AFB, Maine; any questions?"

As the only single person in my R&R group, I alone got a northern tier assignment to this northeastern-most post just below the Canadian border and a five-hour drive north of Bangor, ME. Ed Moreland got McCoy AFB, FL; Fast Eddie went to Seymour Johnson AFB, NC; and Ox-cart shipped to Blytheville AFB, AR. I protested that they already had wives; I did not. How was I supposed to find a proper spouse in Limestone or Caribou, ME, the nearest towns to the base? Milo suffered a similar fate with his assignment to Minot, ND. As the saying went, "Why not Minot?" Besides, the assignment advisors promised with a laugh, there was a woman behind every tree— except there were very few trees on those windswept northern plains. So, bachelors north, married guys south. Life is cruel.

WASHINGTON, DC, VIETNAM MEMORIAL

Photo courtesy of the National Park Service

I've never been to the Vietnam Memorial in Washington, DC. I've gotten near it several times on the Mall but have never had the strength to venture in. There are emotions I've locked securely inside me that I fear will erupt if I enter. I may eventually go, but alone, so no one I know will see me fall apart, Starship Trooper on his knees, sobbing into his hands. So many names, so many dead, and for what? I can only imagine the sorrow felt by those who fought down-and-dirty in the rice paddies who had their compatriots killed next to them, or who came back maimed or horribly traumatized. If I am so fragile at the prospect of visiting the Memorial, I applaud the strength of those, with much heavier burdens than I, who can stand it.

As a group, the reception we received upon our return compounds the angst we feel. I had seen myself as an avenging American warrior traveling across the Pacific to fight the Red menace, and we did the best we could. Yet, upon our return, my compatriots and I seemed to bear responsibility

114

for the calamity the war had become in the eyes of other Americans. I never experienced the reported spectacles of being spat upon or vilified upon arrival at a Stateside airport—because I landed at Travis AFB, CA—but I bear the indirect scars nonetheless.

In 1991, fifteen years after the Vietnam War ended and immediately after the first Gulf War, C-5 aircrews and the troops from many states their aircraft carried received a marvelous welcome home upon landing at Westover AFB, MA. An entire hangar full of local townsfolk, perhaps five hundred strong, formed a hundred-yard long, horseshoe-shaped welcome line as the troops entered to booming cheers and applause. These were not their soldiers, but they received a welcome as if they were. Walking the reception line, they found eager hands reaching for them as if they were Super Bowl quarterbacks. All were very appreciative, but one memorable feature stands out.

It wasn't the younger troops who often broke down emotionally on the line; it was the crusty older troops and crew members, probably Vietnam veterans, who proved fragile. When they reached a group of fiftyish "military mothers," the women smiled, hugged them, and held on for a few moments. That is all it took. At frequent intervals, the older troops would dissolve emotionally at this display of gratitude, shoulders heaving, perhaps from a long suppressed hurt they thought no longer existed until the arms went around them. From somewhere deep within them, the knot of past emotional injury would erupt and not be stifled by any measure of self-control. Some tried to break free from the embrace to escape their rampaging emotions, but the mothers held them fast and, once the struggle ceased, would guide them behind partitions to allow the tears to flow and the wounds to heal. Finally, the jungle troopers had received their welcome home that released twenty years of repressed sorrow. Someone had finally said "thank-you."

I know these incidents happened because I, too, walked that line and felt the arms go around me.

OTHER ISSUES

There are several issues I'll cover quickly because they don't really fit anywhere else but need to be explained.

KENT STATE MASSACRE

On May 4, 1970, while I was flying T-41s in Texas, the Ohio National Guard shot and killed four students during a campus riot—two antiwar demonstrators and two non-demonstrators heading to class who were standing in the wrong place at the wrong time. Campus violence had ramped up once the draft lottery removed college student exemptions; it boiled over at Kent State.

For many years afterward I assigned blame evenly on the guardsmen and the demonstrators because there were some very bad actors in the campus mob that burned buildings, causing widespread damage. This is where I first developed my "playing on the train track" analogy. As our mamas told us, if you play on the tracks long enough, a train will arrive and you may get run over. As college demonstrators demanded to play on the tracks with violent protests, this was bound to happen, I rationalized at the time. Actually, in retrospect, the US government had been playing on the tracks in Vietnam, and Kent State was the train that was bound to show up, and it did.

I was wrong on Kent State, irrevocably wrong. American troops killed four citizens who were not threatening them with lethal force. At the Boston Massacre in 1770 there were at least manslaughter convictions of the British troops who fired on colonists. Here, incredibly, no one was held responsible. The government eventually said it was very sorry, yes it was, even exceptionally sorry. Their rationale for the actions made perfect, plausible sense except for one fact: there were four dead students lying on the ground. The presiding judge in the enquiry said there was not a strong enough case to take forward.

Oh, really? American troops do not shoot unarmed citizens, period. A series of heads should have rolled for this, but none did. The government had to ensure there would be no indictment of the war effort. Inexplicably, it saw this as an unfortunate accident for which no one should be prosecuted despite the *four dead students*.

However, history has correctly labeled this the Kent State Massacre, not the Kent State Unfortunate Accident For Which We Are Really Sorry.

Kent State provided the fourth red flag that we were off-base in Vietnam. The first three occurred in 1968—the Tet Offensive, the police riot at the Democratic National Convention in Chicago, and the My Lai massacre of Vietnamese villagers. These bothered me at the time but seem vividly revealing in retrospect. How many red flags does it take?

Rolling Thunder

When people mention Viet vets as a group, one image pops to mind— Rolling Thunder, a hundreds-strong armada of Harley Davidson motorcycles cruising Washington DC, or other political venues, demanding respect for the now grizzled and gray riders and displaying patriotism. I see this as a response to their having gotten screwed in Vietnam, an experience that wrecked many of them, and I entirely understand. On that score I applaud them. However, I'm not thrilled about my assumed inclusion in that group. I am not a tattooed biker with attitude.

Jane Fonda

A fledgling actress and daughter of movie star Henry Fonda, Jane did some truly unfortunate things, including sitting on a North Vietnamese anti-aircraft gun with a helmet on as if she were preparing to shoot at American planes, and waxing self-righteous in her antiwar views.

However, Fonda has also been accused of something she did not do. According to an Internet fable, Fonda committed an abomination when she met with a group of POWs before cameras to shake their hands. As Fonda moved down the line of prisoners, the bogus story goes, several held pieces of paper in their hand to slip to Fonda during a handshake that confirmed their name and status. Allegedly, Fonda gave the paper slips to the North Vietnamese at the end of the line that resulted in significant punishment for these POWs and one death from torture.

This account is disturbing because none of the POWs in that line will corroborate that it happened. It has become a legend accepted by constant, hysterical repetition on the Internet.[8]

I realize the Fonda issue sends many Air Force crewmembers into a hyperbolic rage of denunciation for an act they consider treason. For many years Air Force urinals had "Not Fonda Jane" stickers on the targeted position of the porcelain trough, stickers more recently replaced with a similar picture of Osama bin Laden.

While recognizing Fonda's actions on that pom-pom gun were unfortunate, I did not view it as most of my contemporaries did. It didn't particularly bother me when she did it, even though I would theoretically be exactly who she'd be shooting at in my B-52, and it doesn't particularly bother me now. Fonda seems to be the poster girl for the troops' anger over the war's unpopularity and represents a lightning rod for the general ire at antiwar protesters, to include the ones who taunted us on our return.

I invoke a version of the sentence Jesus gave on the cross: forgive her, Lord, for she knew not what she was doing. Had this been a calculated exercise planned by Fonda, I'd agree with the consensus. As it is, I cut her some slack for being a naïve young woman manipulated by the NVA. As Fonda writes in defense of her actions, she wishes she had had adult supervision to protect her from the unfortunate situation on the anti-aircraft gun. Amen. She has suffered under this pall for decades despite having categorically apologized for her actions on that gun.[9] It is time to let bygones be bygones; it is time to let it go.

Besides, you cannot let the Ohio National Guardsmen walk free while demanding punishment for Fonda. In retrospect, her viewpoint on the war was correct and mine was wrong, thus my angst at confronting the Vietnam War Memorial. Go in peace, Jane.

CHAPTER FOUR:
STRATEGIC AIR COMMAND

APRIL 1972–JULY 1979

SAC GO CODE

USAF photo by Kevin Bishop

Descending into Armageddon.

My new assignment to Loring AFB, ME, as I returned from Vietnam transitioned me from a hot war in the jungle to the Cold War with the Soviet Union where the stakes could be the survival of civilization itself. Strategic Air Command (SAC) had no sense of humor; it was as sober as a nuclear bomb, the delivery of which was its prepared-for mission as outlined in the Emergency War Order (EWO).

This war order employed codes that would be passed to bomber and air refueling tanker crews, perhaps in tactical orbits over the Arctic. If instructed, the orbiting crews would open their top-secret decoders and validate the "Go Codes" sent by radio from SAC headquarters in Omaha, NE. If the Go Codes were validated, crews were ordered to complete their dreaded missions.

For the tankers, things would probably be short and sweet. They would have to deliver virtually all their fuel to their mated bombers (down to the "standpipe"), which would afford the tankers about enough fuel to coast down to the Arctic Ocean and ditch.

I always thought they might do something else. Since the Go Order would mean a worldwide nuclear war had erupted, and presuming their home base would probably already be incinerated along with their families, they might have favored flying up to 35,000 feet, depressurizing the cabin, and having everyone remove their oxygen masks. The time of useful consciousness at this hypoxia-inducing altitude is about fifteen seconds, just long enough to think of your incinerated loved ones before you joined them.

The bomber crews' ordeal would last somewhat longer. If they could clear their first target by twenty-five miles, they had to proceed with their mission. After that, they could parachute down to the countryside to introduce themselves as the American crew who just nuked the nearby city . . . nice to meet you!

My navigation team assured me, only half-jokingly, that they had the charts to fly us to Rio de Janeiro to "establish the reconstitution force," if I wanted. From one viewpoint, the nuclear weapon threat standoff (mutually assured destruction) would demonstrably have failed, so why continue with it? Completing our assigned mission would only "make the rubble bounce" after our missiles from continental silos had hit their Russian targets, so why bother?

If we had proceeded, I imagine I'd prefer to drop the first bomb and then circle slowly above it until it went off. Or, to climb up well into defense radar coverage, squawk "emergency," and hope a Soviet fighter got us before we reached the target, if there were any Soviet fighters left.

This provides an opportunity to ponder the end of mankind, to be the generation that turned out the lights on our hallowed fifty-thousand-year human experience.

At least the meteorite that wiped out the dinosaurs was not self-inflicted. We would be the first creature to attain self-awareness who, nonetheless, snuffed itself out. With the quantum leap in mental ability came the quantum leap in self-destructive capability. I suppose this mental capability, coupled inextricably with a reptilian brain stem, may have doomed us from the beginning.

It might even be extraordinary that we have lasted as long as we have. So perhaps we could cheer ourselves, ruefully, in the bomber, at the end, for perseverance in the face of a preordained losing hand, for reaching such a high level of accomplishment before our fatal contradiction finished us.

LORING AFB, ME

APRIL 1972–AUGUST 1972

A favorite Vietnam pastime involved reviewing car magazines to select a vehicle to buy upon our return, a present to ourselves for returning from the war. I was torn between a 1972 Pontiac Lemans V-8 coupe with a GTO front and a Ford Grand Torino V-8 with the egg-crate grill. When I got back to Greensboro for leave en route to my first B-52 assignment in Maine, I hit the dealerships to decide which car I would buy. I saw the Torino first, a vehicle made famous about forty years later in a Clint Eastwood movie, *Grand Torino*. I really liked it, but the salesman was giving me the standard "let me check with my manager" dodge, so I begged off the Torino and visited the Pontiac dealership. Fortunately for me, the Ford salesman accompanied me to the Pontiac showroom to make a deal once Pontiac had presented theirs. His presence seemed to energize the Pontiac salesman to close the deal with me for the Le Mans, and I drove the silver beauty home for a mere $4,000.

A joke at the time said that after pilot training, pilots always rushed out to buy a Corvette to drive and a German shepherd for companionship. I settled for the Le Mans, the one and only time I have gone for a full-bore muscle car. It only cost $5 per week for gas and could blow past vehicles driven too slowly by blue-haired seniors. (The blue hair resulted from a popular rinse of the time for gray hair that turned it blue. I am uncomfortably close to blue hair status myself now, alas.) I had been warned that northern Maine winters demanded four-wheel-drive, Jeep-level vehicles. *Screw that*, I thought, *I want a rear-wheel-drive hot rod and I'll take my chances with the snow.* As it turned out, with studded rear snow tires, there were only three days in five years that I could not get on the road.

On the drive to Loring, I stopped by my frat brother's bank office in Hartford, CT. I had roomed with him for six months, three years earlier, waiting for my delayed enlistment to start. I worked as a camera salesman at the now-defunct G. Fox Department store while he began his apprentice training at a bank. Now I found him dressed in his dark banker suit while I wore a long-sleeved Pendleton outdoor-in-the-woods plaid shirt for the drive to Maine. Our roads had diverged in poet Robert Frost's yellow wood (ironically, the poet's name was the same name as my frat brother's) and we were on drastically different paths. He would wear a suit and tie to work; I would wear flight suits and tieless, short-sleeved cotton uniform shirts. We shook hands as I left, and I would not see him again for forty years. We were in different professional fraternities now.

124

I drove north while listening to the music of the time, to include the group America singing "A Horse With No Name" and "Ventura Highway" on the radio. I felt comfortable with the passing landscape until an hour or so north of Bangor, ME. Now the topography consisted of endless bare, brown forests of April just prior to spring shoots arriving. I kept thinking I was a trapper headed into the uninhabited wilderness. During the final portion of the trip, I crossed Aroostook County, a massive area three times larger than my later state of residence in Delaware. I didn't see a moose up close for a year or two, but I expected one to trot out in front of my car at any time.

The Loring AFB main gate lay at the end of a long, straight road that gave me a glimpse of what was coming as I approached the base. Huge, lumbering tankers and bombers filled the local airborne traffic pattern above the forest, and suddenly everything was in noisy motion, on the ground and in the air. The gate guard checked my ID closely since I did not yet have an ID sticker for my car and saluted crisply as notification that everyone on this mission would be deadly serious in their efforts.

I had several months in casual status, however, before I left for initial B-52 training at Castle AFB in Merced, CA. They stuffed me into an office at base operations as the assistant base ops officer. Only two memories remain of those few months, the first of which was the female airman one-striper named April at the main counter. I tried not to gawk at her, but she proved tortuously attractive even with her mild case of acne—blonde, petite, and well formed. I kept humming a top-ten tune of the time called "Pieces of April" by Three Dog Night, imagining a series of those pieces. This was a no-no, however. Officers were not allowed to fraternize, or date, enlisted personnel. All pieces of April were off-limits, so I had to pine in silence. Just as well, I suppose.

The second memory provided a glimpse of the diligence demanded by the command. As a new officer to the base, my boss decided I should test flight-line security. I was given a bogus line badge—which was necessary to be on the flight line—with a crusty old master sergeant's picture on it instead of mine. Some of the faux badges had a picture of the canine TV star, German shepherd Rin Tin Tin, so no one could claim the picture looked like the person carrying it.

As directed, I strolled up to several aircraft on the ramp, spoke briefly with some of the enlisted workers, and then moved on. I got onto, or beneath, two aircraft without being challenged for credentials by maintenance personnel, an egregious security violation. On the third aircraft, a senior worker asked to inspect my line badge. I flashed it toward him at a distance and left. He recognized the drill and began barking into his handheld radio for security. I had arrived at airplane number four when the security police screeched to a halt in front of me, asked to inspect my line badge, and ordered me to spread-eagle on the ramp, under arrest.

I imagined those workers who had failed to check my credentials would be on the carpet in the maintenance colonel's office within the hour. The security officer, who knew of my mission, called off the drill after a few moments and thanked me for my efforts. Over the years in SAC, I would be spread-eagled for real, several times, for crossing a forbidden snow-covered line I couldn't see, and for a nuclear alert crew swap-out violation I'll cover later. Nothing like staring down the barrel of an unlocked M-16 pointed at your chest to get your attention.

I kept awakening in my Bachelor Officer's Quarters (BOQ) room when the sun arose at 0430 due to our far northern latitude. Loring was not as bad as Alaska for endless summer days and short, cold winter days, but it proved vastly different from any previous experience for me. Summers and autumns were marvelous up until November, and we usually got snow by Thanksgiving.

I flew one orientation mission before departing for Castle, an air refueling sortie on a bright sunny morning. I knew nothing of the B-52 and marveled at its huge exterior and cramped interior that seemed barely able to fit the crew of seven, including me as an observer in the pilot jump seat. The aircraft rumbled down the two-mile-long runway with its eight engines screaming to get it airborne. I marveled at the length of the wing and the number of engines, two apiece on four wing pylons.

As we approached the tanker, the IP in the right seat asked if the tanker's boom operator had us in sight. Inexplicably, the boomer said he did not. *This is impossible*, I thought, *I can see him plainly less than a mile away.* The IP paused a moment, then took control of the aircraft and moved slowly to the right of the tanker. It soon became obvious from the red paint on the "tanker's" tail that we had inadvertently rendezvoused by mistake with a commercial Northwest Airlines B-707. This was decades before each aircraft would have the equipment to identify other planes in the vicinity, so we got away with our error. It made me wonder, however, how such a mistake could be made. I would eventually find out, as I made equally boneheaded errors once I was in command.

1969 B-52 Crash

Three years before my arrival, on an Operational Readiness Inspection to test the base operational mission capability, Loring had suffered a horrendous disaster. A B-52 had crashed shortly after takeoff, killing everyone on board and, because it was fully loaded with hundreds of thousands of pounds of fuel, creating a massive conflagration off the end of the runway. The fireball reportedly lit up the cockpit of an airborne Loring tanker twenty miles away. In the insular, close-knit base community, this presented a devastating loss. Over the five years I flew out of Loring, I would see the remnants of the crash site and be reminded of how quickly I could die in this business. Two times in that five years I nearly did die in such a fireball, something I will cover later. One of the incidents closely resembled the situation that killed this crew. I often marvel that I am still here forty years later to write this.

The following comes from a website testimonial for the crew killed in the 1969 crash.[10]

Testimonial website for Loring 1969 crash victims

Here's a picture of the flight crew from the B-52G that crashed after takeoff from Loring AFB on Sept. 4th 1969 (tail#58-0215). My Dad was Capt. Theodore A. Burbank, the Bombardier Navigator. In the picture, he is the 2nd person from the left on the top. Lt. Col. Robert C. Smith, the Radar Officer is on the top right, but I can't put names to any of the others that are pictured.

Beyond the picture, some additional feedback that I could provide is that the aircraft crashed during an ORI (Organizational Readiness Inspection) and that there was some controversy after the crash surrounding whether or not it should have been ordered to take off.

Regards

Kevin Wade
in email 23rd June 2008

On 4 September 1969, during an ORI, I witnessed the crash of B-52G 58-0215 at Loring AFB as a Sergeant in the Fire Dept working at the Crash Station.

As MITOs* progressed my partner and I stood by in our P-6 pickup about 50 yards in front of the alert bombers. 58-0215 was having dificulties with one or more inboard engines on the port wing, so we were radioed to continue to stand by on that aircraft until it taxied to the south end of the runway. We were then to hustle down to the north end and standby there as they took off. After several failed attempts to start and run up the engine, they finally got it going, or so it appeared. During this time I could see the Aircraft Commander and, I assume, the Wing Commander talking and gesturing to each other. Finally I saw the Wing Commander wave them on...to proceed the south end of the runway, and go.

At the north end we observed the aircraft approach on it's take off run. As the plane neared us, it lifted off much farther down the runway than normal. As it passed us, the plane struggled to gain altitude. I believe it never gained more than a few hundred feet of altitude. I did not hear any unusual engine noises, just the usual roar. Finally we observed it slowly disappear beyond the tree line, and after a few silent seconds we heard the inevitable. It was the beginning of a long night.

I was never privy to any official information concerning the accident, but it appeared several ejections were attempted. I do not know the source of the engine(s) problem, or why they were ordered to go, except that it was an ORI**.

One personal thought: I was deeply moved by the loss of those men, and that I was unable to help. That was my job.

Clyde Sikorski
USAF 1966-1974

This crew replicated the scene from the movie *A Gathering of Eagles* that debuted six years earlier where the base vice commander, played by Rod Taylor, ordered a B-52 to take off on an ORI with one engine not giving full power. Later, the wing commander, played by Rock Hudson, and the inspection team general validated Taylor's call to launch the plane since they were simulating wartime conditions. It appears the Loring wing commander used the same rationale to order this crew takeoff with a malfunctioning engine, with catastrophic results.

In August, as I prepared to head to basic B-52 school, I got into a severe row with the command when I was told I would have to burn leave to drive all the way across the country to Merced, CA. If you recall, I had burnt up over a year's leave, stupidly, after OTS and had precious few days to spare. Now I would use almost all of them to drive cross-country if I wanted to have my car for the three-month course. The command sniffed that I could fly out in one day and go without a car if I wished because only one travel day was allowed for TDY assignments. I countered that they had *discriminated* against me, geographically, since I had to drive 2,800 miles while pilots stationed in California could drive to Castle in one morning. I thought sure the whiff of "discrimination" would provide me some slack, but it did not. I suffered the "travesty" of geographical discrimination and crossed the country in four days, bitching at the injustice the entire way. If that had been the worst screw job I got from SAC, I'd have been overjoyed, but even worse screw jobs were to come and will be covered later. The drive did prove enjoyable, however, hot-rod pilot driving hot-rod car on a trek similar to the one in the 1960s TV series *Route 66* (get your kicks, on Route 66) to the balmy state of California.

CASTLE AFB

AUGUST 1972–OCTOBER 1972

Merced, CA, lay in the middle of the San Joaquin Valley in central California, between Fresno to the south and Modesto to the north. While not much of a town, it was bigger than Big Spring and provided excellent access to San Francisco, Sacramento, and Yosemite Park in the Sierra Nevada mountain range. I would attend copilot class here in 1972, aircraft commander school in 1974, and be stationed here as an instructor from 1977 to 1979.

B-52 basic training lasted from mid-August to October 1972, with the first month or so in academics and the second two in flight training. My roommate, Phil, provided a tennis partner and chess opponent, as we closely followed the world championship chess match in Reykjavik, Iceland, between American chess genius Bobby Fischer and Russian champion Boris Spassky. Phil, also single, had of course been assigned to a northern-tier base that SAC seemed to ensure all bachelors would receive, that being Kincheloe AFB located on the upper peninsula of Michigan.

The base buzzed with activity virtually twenty-four hours a day, with KC-135 tankers and B-52 bombers constantly in the air traffic pattern. The standard schedule ran in three-day cycles: day one—mission planning; day two—flying the mission; day three—debriefing the mission. This three-day schedule seemed extraordinarily spread out compared to pilot training, where a student might fly three missions in one day, instead of one mission sequence over three days. The crushing ten-hour mission length dictated the schedule. Each mission would cover all aspects of the bomber mission— refueling, navigation, low-level bomb runs, and transition training with multiple instrument approaches and landings for the final two hours. This became even more onerous on night missions with a 2200 takeoff and 0800 termination the next morning.

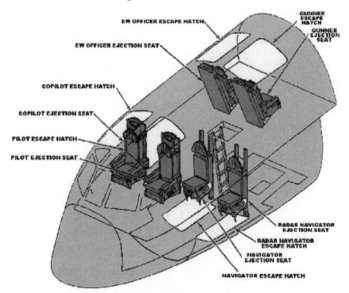

B-52 cockpit alignment.

These training flights tore me up physically. Everything conspired to aggravate. The B-52 had been built to drop bombs, not to make the crew comfortable. The crew compartment consisted of an upper deck with the pilots facing forward and, ten or so feet behind them, a gunner and electronic warfare officer seated backward in a black hole with no windows. The "F" model I trained in as a copilot at Castle, and the "D" model I flew in Southeast Asia, had the gunner in the tail section. The lower deck, reached by a short series of metal steps against the side wall, had the two navigators facing forward, side-by-side, in yet another windowless black hole. During flight, subtle airframe vibrations and extremely dry air took an invisible toll on the body. Besides the cramped quarters, where the only place you could stand up was on the stairs between the two decks, the ejection seats provided a final indignity. Because the seats had ballistic charges under them to explode the seat from the aircraft during ejection, the seat cushion could be no thicker than a half inch. If there were more padding, the ejection seat would have gained such speed while compressing the pad that spinal injury might result. This made for a very lumpy ten-hour flight. As an aside, the navigators had to eject downward to escape the plane and needed the aircraft level and at least four hundred feet above the ground to get even one swing in the parachute before hitting the ground.

THE B-52

The B-52 is nicknamed the "Buff," and those who fly it are "Buff drivers." The explanation of the term in polite company is "big ugly flying fellow," but that is a lie. The term stood for "big ugly fucker," a term of endearment probably applied to the airframe while I was in grade school in the 1950s, when the early B-52s started their spectacularly long operational career.

When I flew them, the Buffs were older than some of the enlisted crewmembers, and that was in the 1970s. B-52H models dropped bombs in the Iraq War of 2003–2010 and remain operational on two bases—Minot, ND, and Barksdale, LA—as this is written in 2013. No other aircraft, even the venerable C-47 cargo plane that served from before World War II to the Vietnam War, has proven so versatile and dependable.

Originally designed to fly at high altitude to drop nuclear bombs on the Soviet Union, B-52 pilots wore the silver space suits of the time to fly to the plane's maximum ceiling of 54,000 feet. However, surface-to-air missile (SAM) technology eventually forced the B-52 mission to go low level to its targets. This remained the SAC mission until after the Berlin Wall came down in 1989 and the Soviet Union dissolved in the 1990s. All Vietnam bombing missions, however, did go in high, above thirty thousand feet.

The "D" model could carry 108 five-hundred-pound bombs in its bomb bay and on wing pylons. (While the bomb bay could accommodate 750 pound bombs, my two bombing missions carried exclusively 500 pounders). It proved the workhorse in Vietnam compared to the "G" model that did not have wing pylons. The "H" model had more modern—and more powerful— fan-bypass engines that required a throttle gate, an adjustable blocker on the throttle quadrant or pedestal that held the throttles, to avoid over-boosting them. They did not participate in Vietnam.

The B-52's modest capability, ironically, has led to its longevity. It functions today as a bomber capable of carrying large bomb loads and as a stand-off platform to launch air-to-ground missiles to do the dirty work it can no longer do. Many faster bombers have come and gone, including the B-58 Hustler and FB-111 Aardvark. The B-1 (the Bone) is much newer, much faster, much prettier, but far less used than the B-52. Though faster than a B-52, the Bone cannot outrun a fighter or SAM; though sleeker and originally designed to fly supersonic, it no longer can, due to modifications. Finally, it cannot carry the payload of the B-52. The B-58 was supersonic but burned so much gas it didn't have the range to penetrate the Soviet Union. The FB-

111, as with the B-1 and B-58, was designed to go supersonic and therefore found itself limited in payload and fuel-carrying capability. So the stodgy, slow, ugly B-52 remains operational while its newer, faster replacements have been retired or are far less frequently used. As I later told my students as a B-52 instructor at Castle, if you ask a ten-year-old kid what an F-4 fighter is, he won't have a clue; but ask him what a B-52 is, and he will know and will be in awe.

I trained as a crewmember on a specific student crew as the copilot. My pilot was a pipe-smoking major who could fly well enough but had a hell of a time refueling. Had I known then what I knew much later, I could have explained it to him, but instead I had to watch him thrash and curse trying to accomplish this required task. He finally got a minimally satisfactory on our check ride, but I hope he got much better, because the time might have come where his wing's ORI score, or his own butt, would depend upon getting the gas.

We flew our first training sortie with a senior renowned B-52 pilot, Lucky Luciano, a Lt. Col. with long B-52 experience. He had Italian movie star good looks and a mild, confident manner that made him a valued senior member of the B-52 community. Regrettably, I tested that mild confident manner on my first landing attempt. Lucky had explained extensively how, because of the structure of the B-52, the pilot must trim the horizontal stabilizer throughout the landing flare. This was necessary because the length of the fuselage compared to the relatively small and ineffective elevators on the tail required that the entire horizontal tail section be moved to provide enough aerodynamic authority to rotate the aircraft into the nose-up landing configuration. As I later explained to students when I was a Castle instructor, you must fly "into the tunnel"; that is, get right down to the runway at the approach end and then hold the plane just above the runway as the aircraft slows and you trim to rotate it to a nose-up landing attitude.

Just above the runway, however, I panicked and forgot everything Lucky had told me. Instead of trimming, I yanked back on the yoke as you would in any other airplane. To my dismay, and no doubt to Lucky's chagrin, the nose hardly rose at all. We pounded into the runway with the front wheel truck and bounced a hundred feet in the air. This put us into a precarious position, since the impact had slowed us down and we didn't have time to redo the flare before stalling and falling onto the runway. Lucky took the controls, growling lowly, "Pilot's airplane!" and shoved all eight throttles to the firewall for the go-around. I pressed my helmet back into the seat in chagrin at my inept performance, shades of my inadvertent no-flap approach in the T-38. Lucky had seen this before, apparently, and let me screw it up so I'd learn. I learned. Eventually I had enough self-confidence to let future students do this to me so they would learn.

Also, on this first training mission, while on a navigation leg at 35,000 feet, the pilot got out of his seat for a break. This left me alone and in control of the airplane. I mentally did a little shoulder dance, reveling that I now controlled this giant bomber! I looked down the long right wing and the four engines on two pylons and got very impressed with myself.

The next segment of the sortie took us low level to simulate penetrating the Soviet Union to drop a string of nukes on the poor Ruskies. This definitely got my blood pumping. We swooped over a ridge on a western low-level route at a few hundred feet above the ground, the desert landscape streaming by us in a blur. Lucky seemed to find nothing unusual in this, so I restrained myself from screaming, "Holy shit!" in rapturous joy at what we were doing. At high altitude, there is little sensation of speed unless clouds are about. Low level, however, the speed, three hundred knots, is very evident. Though overjoyed at what we were doing, I had some apprehension at how close the ground was. When I got to fly, Lucky told me to "keep it low" to stay "beneath Soviet radar," so I took it back down to three hundred feet or so.

USAF photo

B-52 low level. 'Fraptuous joy!' said the Jabberwock.

The ability to maneuver at speed is deceptive. The brain becomes accustomed to maneuvering in the base traffic pattern at relatively low speed. However, the ability to turn while screaming across the ground low level is vastly different. This became apparent flying through the spires of Monument Valley in Arizona, where many John Wayne Western movies were filmed. In my mind, I could snake through them with ease, but the additional speed made this surprisingly difficult. I was moving so fast I had to lead turns far ahead of where I thought I would need to. Of course, I was having a blast doing it. I couldn't believe the American people paid me a generous salary to fly this huge airplane through such picturesque landscapes, to hot-rod across the desert with wild abandon, the throttles for eight powerful engines in my hand.

On another low-level run flying across eastern Wyoming, I smiled broadly as we popped over a ridge line and beheld a broad valley containing a huge herd of black Angus cattle and, on the far side, a rancher on his tractor headed away from us some three or four miles distant. I swooped down on the herd that had all its tails to us. This B-52F had the gunner in the tail with an expansive view of the terrain behind us from his bubble canopy. I approached the cattle at about half the speed of sound, a huge metal monstrosity of a bird screaming up behind them, so they had little warning until we were almost on top of them. They showed no sign of recognition of impending distress as we watched them pass under us from the cockpit. The gunner, however, reported that they broke into panicked flight in all directions after we passed over. If cattle can have heart attacks, I imagine a few of these did.

Next came Farmer Brown on his tractor. We were approaching a right turn in the route, so I swept over him and pulled the plane into a steep, turning climb to the right before diving back down close to the terrain. I don't know if Farmer Brown viewed us with awe, terror, anger, or all three, and I worried we might hear from him for ransacking his herd, but we did not.

Later, on a low-level route out of Loring, I popped over another ridge line approaching Lake Michigan and saw a Cessna-172, like the T-41 I had flown in pilot training, directly in front and just barely above us. He was close enough to detect the pilot's head in the cockpit. We swooshed under him so closely I thought he might come right into our cockpit, obviously with dire consequences for both of us. Regardless of how good a pilot I was or wasn't, this would play out as fate decided. This time it spared us all to fly another day.

The night training missions were body wreckers, completely out of our established circadian rhythm. I found it impossible to sleep during the day before the 2200 takeoff time. I usually liked flying the traffic pattern to do instrument approaches and landings, but I found my body resisted on these night flights. When it realized the sun was coming up and I had not let it sleep, it revolted and shut down. This happened throughout my C-5 career, also after a nighttime ocean crossing. All would go well until the sun started to come up. Then I had to fight my body's attempt to go to sleep in retaliation for what I had done to it.

After the night training missions, I'd sleep five or six hours, wake up for three or four, then go back to sleep at my normal time. While a Castle instructor a few years later, I remember twice receiving calls from Sears about an hour after I had fallen heavily into my bed to ask if I had any complaints with the vacuum cleaner I had bought from them. The first time I tolerated the call, but the second one asking the same question sent me into orbit. After that, I unhooked the phone before pulling up the covers for blissful sleep. I often joked that sleep felt so good, it was too bad we couldn't be awake to enjoy it.

HIPPIE CHICKS

Castle provided many off-base opportunities, San Francisco being the primary one. Milo and I spent many a weekend exploring and carousing on Union Street, down on the Wharf at Ghirardelli Square, and around the rest of the town with its cool, bright days and often marvelous, foggy and misty mornings and evenings. We'd stay at Treasure Island Naval Station on Yerba Buena Island halfway between Oakland and San Francisco. Approaching the entrance walking up the circular driveway, the aroma of eucalyptus trees wafted in the air. The theme song of my San Francisco adventures that fall was "Brandy" by single-hit wonder group Looking Glass.

This late summer of 1972 came about three years after the hippie heyday of 1968 and 1969 when flower children festooned the corner of Haight-Ashbury in all their glory. As a contemporary of the hippies, I viewed them as disengaged druggies who seemed to be having a good time but didn't seem to be going anywhere. My younger brother Greg became one of them and attended the original Woodstock festival in New York state. He and his wife

Suni moved into a log hut in the mountains of southwest Virginia with no running water to escape society. Obviously he and I had taken different trails in the yellow wood and lived in separate universes for several decades.

At any rate, Milo and I discussed how hippies seemed to be getting far more action from hippie chicks than he and I were from non-hippie chicks. So we decided to go "find us a few" in the bars on Union Street one weekend. The follies of youth seem particularly egregious from a late-in-life perspective, and this turned out to be one.

We found a pair dressed like hippies who were actually college girls from Oakland impersonating hippie chicks for competitive advantage in the bars. Mine wore a serape, or a square sweater of sorts with a neck opening in the middle that allowed it to drape down her body. Milo's seemed nondescript and must have been because I remember nothing about her. The girls seemed willing to spend the night with us at Treasure Island, so we imagined, stupidly, that things would be wonderful. Things were not. I discovered my hippie chick wore a serape because she was significantly overweight, something I would not have tolerated even in the dimness of the bar and the dimness of my bourbon-addled brain. Always game for the games once the decision was made, however, I pressed to consummate our relationship, so to speak, but she insisted she would not. Having made the half-hearted offer, I shrugged, rolled over, and went to sleep.

The next morning, Milo, slacker that he was, stuck his head into my room from the shared bathroom and muttered that he wanted *me* to take the girls downstairs for breakfast because he "didn't feel very well." Oh, great! He goes back to sleep in bliss while I take the two faux hippies out in public? So, ever the compliant trooper, I took the ladies down for the marvelous breakfast served by excessively courteous and proper Filipino waiters in the hotel restaurant. The conversation among us was strained and almost nonexistent. Once Milo finished his beauty sleep, we drove our lovelies back to Oakland and dropped them at the dorm.

On the ride back to Castle, Milo derided me scornfully because he had gotten lucky while I had not. He attributed this, of course, to his excessive masculine prowess and to my hopeless ineptitude with women. "Heck," he taunted, "you couldn't even score with a hippie chick, for God's sake!"

I nursed my wounded ego until the next weekend when Milo was watching football on TV with us. He went to the bathroom to download some of the beer we had been drinking. Suddenly I heard a string of sharp half-shouts, half-screams of pain, followed by expletives. It seems his lovely from the previous weekend had bequeathed a VD dose to him that had just now shown up as he pissed firewater. I estimate my date had a similar malady and had shown mercy by refusing to consummate. This validated the saying that what goes around, comes around, and it came around hilariously for Milo.

As a final revelation on this first Castle tour, I for some reason caught a ride to the flight line with an instructor pilot, a major. His car radio was playing contemporary rock—The Mamas and the Papas, I think—and I wondered why senior citizens such as he were allowed to listen to "my" music. I mean, he should be playing the big bands or Lawrence Welk's champagne music or something, right?

HAIRCUTS

Despite my tweaking the college girls for impersonating hippie chicks, the flower child movement had a profound effect on the military. You see, military guys found it difficult to compete for hippie chicks wearing the crew cuts of the 1950s and 1960s, as seen in the pictures of the Loring crash crew. All of us pressed and exceeded the hair length limits, as shown in my picture on the "perfect freeze" lake near Loring in the next section. This change happened in three short years and as a direct result of the hippie movement.

So intensely did we, as a group, press the system that it bent to allow a hair length that old-timers found quite disturbing. Official pictures from 1972 would later embarrass many of us, with our hair longer than it would be before or since. The hippies forced a cultural change beyond their social circle, and hippie chicks ruled the social scene.

BACK TO LORING

OCTOBER 1972–FEBRUARY 1973

Following my crew's check ride, I departed for my second of half a dozen Air Force career–induced cross-country car adventures.

I have only disjointed smatterings of memories of places I passed through on these trips. Here are a few.

Austin, NV: a town that seemed to live perpetually in the 1880s—austere, remote, and a long way from anything. As a former mining town, I have no idea why it is still in business, but I guess it is.

El Paso, TX: a city right out of a Clint Eastwood spaghetti Western, with vast vistas of Western landscapes to include large, bare mountains that trail off into Mexico. The Rio Grande River turns north from El Paso and runs up to Albuquerque, NM, along with the mountain chain. Approaching Albuquerque from the west provides another vast view from an elevation high above the city that, at night, becomes utter isolation once you leave the town, as the landscape becomes totally dark.

Telluride, CO: I visited in 1979 before it became a trendy movie star haven, sitting at the end of a box canyon surrounded by steep cliffs. My father resided there at the time in a fifth-wheel mobile home, and we fell asleep to the sound of a nearby waterfall; very nice. The cowboy bars seemed more rustic and authentic than any I have seen elsewhere.

After the cross-country trip and taking some leave en route, I reported to the 69th Bomb Squadron at Loring. I waited in the commander's outer office to do the official "Lieutenant Lacklen reporting for duty, SIR!" when he came out of his inner office deep in animated conversation with the squadron ops officer. It seemed they needed to provide an "Arc Light" crew to form, train, and depart for the war effort in Southeast Asia in the spring. (Arc Light denoted a B-52D crew. Loring's B-52G crews deployed under the term "Bullet Shot." Arc Light crews that came from "G" model units had to train in the slightly different "D" model at Carswell AFB in Ft. Worth, TX, before deploying.)

Apparently the squadron's nuclear alert and training requirements had strained squadron capability, and the commander was asking the ops officer where they could come up with another Arc Light crew to be ready on such short notice. "Who could we send?" he asked, shaking his head.

"Um, sir, I'll go," I said. The commander looked at me as if to ask who the hell I might be since he'd never seen me before. "I'm Lieutenant Lacklen, sir, reporting in from basic copilot school at Castle."

The commander smiled. "Well, there's one!" he said to the ops officer, and away I would go back to the war.

I soon met my first crew, a hodge-podge collection of members pulled from all areas of the squadron to fill the Arc Light commitment. We would fly as a crew for a few months before heading to Carswell for "difference training" in the "D" model. The aircraft commander would be Danny, a cautious, introspective but friendly pilot whose nickname in college had been the "Mad Mouse," although I never heard why. The navigation team consisted of a navigator from Kalispell, MT, and a radar navigator named Bob who, in retrospect, was one of the most memorable characters from my career. Bob put on a crotchety demeanor and always seemed to be complaining about someone or something but would add a rueful chuckle at the end of his diatribe to show he accepted whatever indignity he had suffered.

Once, in our crew quarters on Guam, I barged through the closed bathroom door to find Bob seated on the throne. As I stopped short, he uttered a single word that I could write an entire chapter to describe. He said: "hi" with the "i" clipped and high pitched like "hai," the Japanese word for yes. This conveyed several messages. On one level it was a casual greeting, saying, "Hey, how's it going?" On another level it asked, "What the fuck are you doing, asshole?" Despite the awkwardness of the moment, I savored his response-of-several-colors and collapsed laughing against the wall outside. He seemed most pleased with his one-word effect on me.

Bob's other significant factor for the crew was his total tobacco addiction. When he awoke in the morning, his first action, before rubbing his eyes or scratching his balls, was to reach emphatically for the cigarette pack on his night stand. His body had been without nicotine for whatever duration he had slept; it now screamed for a fix. I never counted how many packs a day he smoked, but I'm sure this habit must have killed him decades ago. It would be another twenty years before the Air Force outlawed smoking on all flights.

For the next few months, we trained but did not pull nuclear alert. In fact, I didn't pull nuke alert until two years later on Guam because I repeatedly volunteered to return to Southeast Asia, always as an Arc Light crew instead of a Bullet Shot crew.

During this time, I lived in bachelor housing mixed in with family housing on the infamous Tennessee Circle, the first street in the housing area. This street became notorious for all-night parties where families and bachelors had been, perhaps ill-advisedly, mixed. With either tanker or bomber crews gone for six months at a time, half of the husbands were always absent and not to return for the specified deployment period. Things happened. Mistakes were made, and made again. But I wouldn't find myself in this unruly mix until after my first Arc Light deployment.

143

For this first winter at Loring, I roomed with Steve, a brooding, dark-haired New Englander who almost constantly muttered the phrase, "Fuck me!" I'm not sure what oppressed him so, because he had a generally sunny, conspiratorially funny demeanor.

And then there were the two single nurses—"Millie," as I'll call her, and Janet—who enjoyed perhaps the most favorable eligible male-to-female ratio of any females on earth. They were the only game in town, officially, although enterprising wives would soon show up, and they played this for their advantage, usually good-naturedly.

That winter Millie, Janet, and I were guests at the personnel chief's house located on the road to Limestone. He was a heavyset, twenty-year major, probably prior enlisted, and we all knew he would never make Lt. Col. During our visit, he received an unexpected phone call from a female coworker from many years in the past. His face lit up as he took the call, and I could sense tears forming in his eyes as they reminisced about great adventures of their youth at faraway bases, the promise they all felt at the time, and the somber pang that this promise no longer existed as they neared retirement. Even as they would soon be routinely transacted off active duty with little fanfare, they would remember the glory they felt they had earned as young officers in the new Air Force shortly after World War II. As he continued to poignantly embrace this long-ago friend over the phone, I had a disturbing premonition that this identical conversation might take place twenty years hence for some of us, where we similarly would have tears in our eyes over these years at Loring in faraway northern Maine.

We traveled as a young officer group on several weekend skiing trips that winter, usually to Sugarloaf Mountain west of Bangor, or to Mont-Sainte-Anne in Quebec. I cut an un-dashing figure on the slopes, since my only winter jacket was my Air Force–issued parka with its fur-encased hood that I left unzipped and lying on my shoulders. Also, I couldn't ski worth a damn. I took lessons the first day at Sugarloaf and managed brute-force turns (instead of lifting my weight off the skis to make the maneuver effortless) just barely within the sides of the one-hundred-yard-wide bunny slope.

That is when Steve did a number on me. He convinced me to take the chairlift to the mountaintop with him for my first run. I objected that I didn't really have the hang of this yet and maybe I'd better take the T-bar to a lower, easier run.

"Naw," he insisted. "You'll do fine; it's easy. Let's go!"

What a prick! We disembarked at the top, and he swooshed off somewhat competently, leaving me staring in terror at what lay before me.

"See you at the bottom!" he shouted as he disappeared down the slope on a trail that was thirty yards wide, while the bunny slope I had barely managed to negotiate was over three times wider. To compound my dilemma, the slope was three or four times steeper than the bunny slope.

I'm fucked! I thought, but not half as fucked as Steve would be when and if I got my hands on him at the lodge, providing I didn't have a cast on my leg or arm.

My only recourse, since I couldn't possibly turn in the tight trail parameters, was to streak straight down the course and to fall at the maximum speed I thought I could stand without injuring myself. Once I did fall, I had to laboriously reattach my skis to the boots in knee-deep snow. I repeated this maneuver about twenty times before reaching the bunny slope at the bottom.

Steve found my dilemma hilarious despite my threats to castrate him on the spot. "Hey!" he exclaimed, "you're in one piece, aren't you? Chill out and have a drink."

In some measure of revenge, Millie, who would marry him years later, paired off with me that night in the bar. Ski that one, Stevie!

We usually stayed at a raucous roadhouse hostel named the Red Stallion that had a bandstand/restaurant directly below the overhead second-floor rooms, which meant no one got any sleep until the band quit for the night. By Sunday afternoon, when we started the five-hour drive north to Loring, all of us were totally whupped, having skied all day and not having slept well all night, and had difficulty staying awake.

One Sunday night we drove home in a developing blizzard. I approached the sharp left turn just prior to Houlton, ME, to head north an hour to the air base as the storm intensified and blew relentlessly with wind-whipped snow falling at a forty-five-degree angle. The entire world seemed a very dark blue, often evident in snowstorms.

On the far side of the turn, a yard light, about the size of a street light, tried hard to illuminate the area between a house and a barn, a task it was not quite accomplishing. The dark blue of the storm and the swirling thickness of the snow made it seem the light could not possibly hold out much longer, as the storm threatened to overwhelm it.

I often think of that scene in bed as I settle in for the night, regardless of where I am or what the temperature is. I succumb to the power of the snowstorm, pulling the covers up tightly and cocooning myself in bed as wolves or dogs do in such a storm by letting the snow cover them, creating their own personal cave around their body and shielding them from the wind.

From the warm coziness of my cave, I can mentally marvel at the beauty and power of the storm and release all concern about the yard light losing its battle to illuminate the yard. I capitulate to the darkness of the snow-covered landscape and allow the storm a total victory as I drift off to sleep. Of course, this certainly didn't help me stay awake for the remainder of that trip.

On another weekend we stayed at the Red Stallion with a larger group of young officers. I remember this one because, besides Steve, there was another B-52 copilot sniffing around Millie, which put me on high alert. He was devastatingly good looking and seemed smoothly confident with women, just what I didn't need as competition. *Who invited him along, anyway?* I thought grumpily. I glared at them as they sat laughing over beer in the bar, helpless before whatever would transpire.

I mention this because tragedy enveloped Mr. Smooth. He later visited Canada one weekend, which we found easy to do since we only needed to show our military ID and didn't require a passport. On this trip, however, he was parceled out of the line of cars for a detailed inspection by the Canadians. In his glove compartment, the border agents found traces of marijuana. He explained to them, apologetically, that he had loaned his car to his college-aged sister and someone must have transported some of the illicit weed in the compartment. They assured him this would not be reported to American authorities.

Unfortunately, that promise was not kept, and the Office of Special Investigations pulled him in for interrogation on the matter, charging him with a career-ending drug felony. Total disaster. As I have said, SAC had no sense of humor on such matters and gave no weight to his explanation of the incident. I never knew if his explanation was true or not. Tragically, soon thereafter, he blew his brains out with a gun. What a waste.

THE PERFECT FREEZE

One November Saturday at a small lake near the base, nature presented me with a perfect freeze that solidified the entire lake six inches thick overnight. As the first significant freeze of the fall, the ice took on a deep, dusky purple hue and lay perfectly smooth across the entire square mile of the lake. I walked gingerly onto the surface with scores of others who had discovered this marvelous event, trying not to slip but venturing farther and farther out, looking deeply into the ice that reflected my image in near-mirror quality.

My experience with freezes as a child in the mid-Atlantic region had made me wary of early ice that would groan and then crack loudly, sending a spider web of fissures out from my foothold. Often it would then break beneath me, leaving me wet to the ankles. But this Maine lake held as solidly as a parking lot and supported me without apparent effort. I had never seen such a sight—a solidly frozen expanse of water with a surface as smooth as a pool table, showing nary an imperfection.

As more people discovered this perfect freeze, there was a sudden run on ice skates at local sporting goods stores. I managed to find a pair that fit prior to the shelves emptying and hurried back to the lake.

The lake soon became a mass of Southern boys wobbling around on our new ice skates, our ankles collapsing out and then in, as we wind-milled our arms in an attempt to stay balanced and try to maneuver in this new environment.

The locals glided effortlessly across the surface and even skated backward! *How is this possible?* I thought. I could barely stand and move slowly in one direction, but the locals went backward as fast as they did forward!

By the end of the day, I had managed to skate slowly while falling only occasionally, a stupendous achievement in my view. I couldn't wait to get back out on the ice the next weekend, perhaps to play rudimentary hockey if I were fortunate in my improvement.

Photo by Janet Stone

Millie and me and the perfect freeze. See my buddy's reflection in the ice.

But this was not to be. As I discovered, the perfect freeze had been a special and precious event. By the next weekend, there had been a brief thaw and then a refreeze. The thaw allowed the lake ice to buckle and warp, leaving sharp upward thrusts in the surface and producing undulations that spoiled the perfectly level pool table I had found on that first day. The color had also gone from the deep purple of the previous weekend to an opaque milky white as air had been trapped within the ice during the thaw.

The perfect freeze had been made possible by a steep temperature drop that froze the lake deeply and quickly from a fully liquid state. It could not have happened if the freeze had been less severe or had taken effect gradually; it had to be steep and quick.

Now we would have to put up wooden siding around an impromptu hockey rink and fill it with water to freeze smoothly, a bothersome effort I had not anticipated. Winter snows also had to be cleared from the ice in small rink-sized patches. The entire lake would no longer beckon skaters as it had after the perfect freeze; we would have to make do with the small patches.

Never again did the lake provide the perfect freeze of that first day. Only now, nearly forty years later, can I appreciate what a special event I was watching at the time.

LINEBACKER II

From December 18–29, 1972, while my crew awaited its "D" model training en route to Southeast Asia, the Air Force suffered the most horrific loss ever of B-52s over North Vietnam in a bombing campaign named Linebacker II. President Nixon had decided to crack North Vietnamese resolve in the continuing negotiations to end the war by bombing Hanoi and Haiphong every night for eleven days, a terrible regimen for the North Vietnamese and for the bomber force sent against them.

Bombers from U-Tapao AB, Thailand, and Andersen AFB, Guam, saturated the sky over North Vietnam and dropped twenty thousand tons of bombs on military targets.[11] Ten B-52s were shot down by Russian SAM missiles provided to the North Vietnamese, and five more were lost after severe damage that caused them to crash over Laos or Thailand. Loring suffered one lost aircraft that had seven of its eight engines shot out. It limped toward U-Tapao until it crossed the Thai border, where the crew bailed out without serious injury. Thirty-three B-52 crewmembers died during the operation, and thirty-three more were captured and sent to the Hanoi Hilton, the prison used for Americans.

Some B-52s simply exploded in the sky from direct, or nearly direct, hits. Morale sank as SAC planners sent the bomber formations into the target area on the same heading and at the same altitude night after night. The North Vietnamese would send MIG fighters up to the bomber formations, not to attack, but to record altitude, heading, and airspeed so SAM operators on the ground could fire the SAMs up to explode in the vicinity of the formations. This often proved close enough to take down some of the bombers. By the end of eleven days, the NVA had no SAMs left (the Russians complained the NVA shot off the SAMs like firecrackers), and the bombers had no remaining valid targets, having obliterated every one. This intense bombardment brought the North Vietnamese to the bargaining table and led to the 1973 armistice signed by Secretary of State Henry Kissinger. The final bombing halt was called in March 1973, after I had flown my only two Arc Light missions from Guam.

One bit of humor arose while the captured B-52 pilots were under initial interrogation. The North Vietnamese interrogators apologized to the bomber pilots that they would have to share cell space with captured fighter pilots and, while possibly improper, would that be permissible? The implication that bomber pilots were the top of the pilot pecking order seemed to be the NVA concern, and they thought bomber pilots might be insulted by having to room with fighter guys. Maybe this is a bomber pilot fairy tale, but I really like it.

BACK TO SOUTHEAST ASIA

FEBRUARY 1973–MAY 1973

In mid-February 1972, our crew left for Carswell AFB, TX, for "D" model difference training enroute to our three-month deployment to Guam. This was mostly procedural because flying this slightly different version of the plane was virtually identical to the Loring "G" models.

Several of the systems, however, were quite different. First, the copilot-controlled electrical panel consisted of four generators that had an infamous recovery process for total electrical failure. Each generator had three switches: the generator switch that started the generator, the generator bus switch that connected each generator to its own bus, and the bus tie switch that connected all four individual generator buses to the common main bus. Although I can't remember which way the mantra went for total failure, the two options were all four generator switches up, all four bus tie switches down, all four main bus tie switches up, or up/down/up. Actually, it might have been down/up/down, but I do remember that if you did down/up/down instead of up/down/up, you'd fry the generators.

The "D" also used very high pressure pneumatic air. The emergency procedure if this system sprung a leak proved the most severe I have ever encountered in any airplane manual. It warned that a pneumatic leak "constituted an impending disaster."

The copilot also ran the fuel system, routing fuel from a series of fuselage and wing tanks into the engines. This had to be done in a specific order or the plane's center of gravity would move too far forward, or aft, which could lead to loss of control. If improperly done, it could also flame out the engines from fuel starvation. The copilot ran a fuel log to discover if a fuel leak existed. Once an hour, he would plot the fuel remaining against a graph of expected fuel remaining for comparison. If the total fuel was not close to the projected line, a fuel leak had to be investigated. I never heard of anyone having a fuel leak, but I suppose it happened sometime before my tenure and prompted the procedure.

USAF photo

Perfect level-wing balance, a copilot's pride.

After landing, copilots would madly transfer fuel to level their wings during taxi, a matter of copilot pride. At light loads, any imbalance would tilt the heavy wing down and the light wing up. This was an art, since the transfer must be stopped the instant the high wing starts to drop or else it becomes the down wing and the balance is lost. Copilots assiduously monitored other copilots' prowess on getting this right after landing.

Since we flew with light fuel loads in training, I had never run the full fuel load sequence that would be needed to fly from Texas to Guam. In a frightful scene at base operations, I had my instructor go over the full load sequence with me again to be sure I had it down. This did not build confidence in either of us—a rookie copilot about to launch on a sixteen-hour mission having never run the full load sequence. I'm sure the instructor did not sleep that night, waiting to hear that Lt. Lacklen had flamed out the engines due to fuel starvation over the Pacific. However, the sequence worked well and we made it to Guam.

Andersen AFB, Guam

Andersen got my jungle fix back with its tropical climate and dense, if low, jungle cover. Located an eight-hour flight west of Hawaii, it lies at the south end of the Northern Mariana island string that includes Saipan and other smaller islands.

Guam has an interesting history. In 1521, Ferdinand Magellan landed on the island on his initial circumnavigation of the globe. He was apparently glad to find this island, since he had exhausted his food supply after departing the Tierra del Fuego of South America before launching across an ocean of whose size he had no concept. By the time he and his crew reached Guam, they had been reduced to chewing leather fittings as their only sustenance.

As a US territory, Guam has a representative in Congress, although its citizens cannot vote. Guam also, at the time, had the largest McDonald's fast food restaurant in the world. Most of the large hotels were Japanese and provided a closer alternative than Hawaii for Japanese tourists. The island held two major military facilities, the naval base on the western bump of the island and Andersen about fifteen miles away on the northwest end.

Andersen is built on an up-sloping volcanic escarpment that ends abruptly at a five-hundred-foot cliff. This cliff proved popular with bomber and tanker crews, since if they experienced engine failure late in the takeoff roll toward the cliff, they could limp off the end and have an immediate five-hundred-foot altitude above the ocean. Landing over the cliff could be interesting also, since you had to studiously ignore the ocean far below as you approached the runway on a proper glide path. The runway formed a bowl shape that played fun and games with crews. Taking off to the north, toward the cliff, airspeed would increase quickly as the plane rolled down the hill toward the bottom of the bowl, about a third of the way down the runway. Then, however, the uphill grade of the far side of the bowl would drastically reduce airspeed acceleration, leaving crews wondering with

154

increasing concern if they would reach their rotation speed prior to the end of the runway.

USAF photo

Approaching runway over five-hundred-foot cliff.

In the early 1970s, the "G" and "D" models proved underpowered for their loads, even with eight engines, due to the high temperatures that reduced thrust. The "H" model, with more modern fan-bypass engines, was more capable but was not used in Southeast Asian operations. Most B-52 takeoffs from Guam were white-knuckle affairs, where the plane ate up most of the runway before getting airborne. Several "G" models saved themselves when their engine water injection system failed near rotation and they dove over the cliff to use the five hundred feet to gain airspeed.

KC-135 tankers seemed to have it worse. They were saddled with the antiquated "A" model engines that struggled to get these fully loaded tankers off the runway. I watched several limp into the air and disappear below the top of the cliff as they dived to gain airspeed. In later years, these KC-135s would get upgraded "E" and then "R" fan-bypass engines that gave them all the thrust they needed. But for Southeast Asian operations, they had to live and die with the "A" model engines.

USAF photo

Taking off toward the cliff on Guam.

The operational pace on Andersen was frantic. Scores of bombers and tankers launched and recovered every day, and the base teamed with personnel to keep the mission moving. In later years when I flew through Guam, the base seemed a pallid version of its Vietnam War self, with skeleton crew operational levels compared to the "glory years" of the late 1960s and early 1970s.

One day standing on my cement barracks' second-story balcony walkway, I watched the huge base indoor movie theater let out from an early evening showing shortly after my 1973 arrival. Gradually, a huge river of humanity began flowing beneath my perch, hundreds of military personnel heading for their quarters farther inside the base. It seemed like a large university hourly class change, but instead of everyone heading for their next class in various directions, the entire combined flow passed beneath me.

This overflow of personnel put barracks space at a premium. Our six-man B-52 crew had a single suite built for two officers. This area was separated by freestanding closets used to divide the room in two, with two pilots on one side, the two navigators and electronic warfare officer on the other side. The gunner lived separately in the enlisted barracks. I thank the gods I flew only two bombing missions because those two, with their twenty-hour days, almost finished me physically.

Up to now, bombing missions had been training affairs and theoretical exercises, but now that we had deployed, they became deadly earnest reality.

BOMB RUN

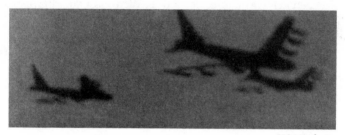

USAF photo

Three-ship B-52 bombing cell.

When asked if I killed anyone during the Vietnam War, I have to answer that I don't know. I may have, and probably did, since my B-52 bomber crew dropped several thousand pounds of bombs on the Cambodian jungle, but I will never actually know.

I only flew two live bombing runs in March 1973, before President Nixon's final bombing halt prior to the negotiations that ended our involvement in the war a few months later. But the first mission captured all the terror, anticipation, wonder, and angst of flying into a war.

The mission began after dark as the crew bus dropped us at the hot loading zone on a far corner of a field, a remote location that would provide some protection for the base if something went wrong while loading over fifty thousand pounds of bombs in the bomb bay and on wing pylons of our B-52D.

A full moon painted the bristling black war bird in a ghostly light, a formidable metal dragon that would righteously drop explosive mayhem onto America's enemies, or so I thought at the time. I paused and slowly put down my flight bag to stare in awe. Was I really a part of this? What was I about to do?

Six hours after takeoff, we approached the target area over the Parrot's Beak region of Cambodia as one of a half-dozen three-ship bomber formations. Each cell was named for a tree. We were Oak Flight; others were Pine, Maple, and Birch.

As the lead aircraft copilot for my cell (for some unknown reason, I got to be lead on my first mission), I had to announce the impending bomb drop on "Guard," the international radio frequency all-aircraft monitor. This would allow aircraft in the vicinity to vacate the area and avoid the "rain" of our falling bombs. (As an aside, this is the same rain referenced in the Creedence Clearwater Revival song "Have You Ever Seen the Rain?")

I had been warned to switch my radio toggle from the interplane frequency to the Guard channel before transmitting the warning. Being a raw rookie, however, I gave the entire two-minute spiel on interplane, to the great amusement of the other copilots. "Hey, lead, want to try that on Guard?" they snickered on the interplane frequency.

Then the bomb run began in the early morning darkness over an Asian jungle. Our three-abreast, triangular-shaped formation banked steeply, ominously, onto the bomb run heading. The radar navigator, who would throw the switch to drop the bombs, informed the crew we were approaching the IP, or Initial Point, to begin the run.

Just as we passed the IP, a male Asian voice began transmitting in

Cambodian on our radios. He sounded as if he were babbling in an opium den, and his voice disturbed and frightened me. I feared he might be an apparition warning us off our task, a voice of doom giving a last opportunity to save ourselves, or a soon-to-be victim in the target zone making his last hopeless statement to his slayers. He continued talking, as if relating a story to a fellow opium smoker, while our formation approached the target. No matter what I did to my radio controls, I couldn't make the voice stop.

In the near distance 33,000 feet below us, the ground glowed red, eerily, from explosions from preceding bomber formations. A mist hung over the terrain that gave the area the look of a graveyard in a horror movie.

The radar navigator began the countdown, "Ten . . . nine . . . eight,"—the apparitional voice continued his drunken soliloquy on the radio—"Three . . . two . . . one . . . *bombs away!*"

The aircraft shuddered lightly as the bombs unhooked from the wings and dropped from the bomb bays of our three aircraft in a ten-second release sequence that would obliterate an area equal to three football fields and unleash a shock wave that would kill any unshielded creature within half a mile. North Vietnamese soldier and author Bao Ninh later wrote that the immediate aftermath of such a strike resulted in "a rain of arms and legs dropping before him on the grass."[12]

We waited as the radar navigator counted down to detonation, about fifty seconds for the bombs to fall 33,000 feet, "Three . . . two . . . one . . . *impact!*" The thin clouds around our aircraft reflected hundreds of small bursts of light from below. It was done.

The radar navigator announced the closing of the bomb bay doors.

We flew on in the darkness in silence as I pondered what we had done. I ponder it still.

Gear coming up, pylon-mouted bombs waiting to come down.

On the following morning of this first bombing mission, as we flew east over the Pacific toward Guam into the rising sun, the utter exhaustion began to show. We were lead aircraft with #2 and #3 echeloned loosely behind us. Looking out my right window, I discovered #2 was slowly drawing abeam. I waited until he started getting ahead of us to start calling him. My calls went unanswered. For a while, both we and #3 tried to raise him on the radio without success. Both #2 aircraft's pilots were dead-ass asleep, with the plane on autopilot. Finally, about ten minutes later, #2's wings began to dip left and right, as the pilots had awakened and were looking for the rest of us, hoping they were still in formation and could get away with having both gone to sleep. No such luck. We ribbed them severely as they moved back into the formation. My policy, that I would instruct my students to follow when I became an instructor, demanded that you always inform the other pilot if you were going to take a nap. Sleeping was approved, and necessary, but not for both pilots at the same time.

USAF photo

Nav team downstairs, bombs away!

The first mission lasted thirteen hours, and I was so tired I couldn't see straight when I finally got to bed in the crowded barracks room. Then, twelve hours later, we got the call that we had just gone into twelve hours' crew rest for our second mission. This proved disastrous. The twelve-hour alert call woke us up from twelve hours of sleep. There would be no way we could get any more sleep in the next twelve hours before our alert. I wondered what moron scheduled us for this back-to-back mission travesty.

The second mission lasted fourteen hours because we had to divert to the "Pearl Seven" air refueling track off Okinawa to get enough fuel to get back to Guam. When I got off the crew bus on Guam to walk to the room, I tried to talk to the other pilot, but I was so tired, my addled brain couldn't form words. I emitted a slurred set of moans that conveyed nothing. I thought, *if this sequence repeats itself, I'm not going to make it.* I then slept fourteen hours, the longest sleep period of my life. I didn't know anyone could sleep that long. Three cheers for Nixon's bombing halt that saved me from the possibility of another twelve-hour alert after fourteen hours of sleep.

B-52D delivering 'scrap iron' to North Vietnam. Was this terror bombing?
Bomb-bay bombs falling in a row, random bombs from the wing pylons.

LIFE ON GUAM

With the bombing cessation and the armistice, there wasn't much to do operationally. We flew a few hokey practice bombing runs on small islands near Guam, but the pace dropped to almost zero for the rest of our three months on the island. This allowed time for golf on the base course and exploring the island.

A recreation briefing convinced us to do two things when swimming in the ocean—wear sneakers and stay inside the reef. Several fish could do fatal harm if stepped on, especially the stonefish. I solved this problem by never going in the water, although some of the crew ventured into the surf inside the reef at Tumon Bay down the western side of the island.

The golf course had its own problems, also. First, its grass covering proved very thin, and sharp, tough volcanic pumice lay underneath this minimal grass carpet. That is why everyone used rental clubs, because the pumice would nick and dent the striking surfaces of the clubs.

The second problem lurked in the jungles that lined the outside of many of the fairways. Club workers warned us not to pursue balls hit into the jungle lest we encounter the exploding population of brown snakes. These serpents had been inadvertently imported from Australia in shipping containers and, with no natural predator present on the island, had overwhelmed the local ecosystem. This included devouring most of the island's bird population.

The snakes average about six feet in length, but some have approached ten feet. While poisonous, the toxin is no more than a nuisance for an adult human but can be dangerous for children or pets.

Due to the pervasiveness of the snake population, they occasionally invaded homes on the island, especially during storms that flooded their habitat. In May 1976, Typhoon Pamela scored a direct hit on Guam as the slow-moving eye passed directly over the island. In addition to 135-mph winds that damaged 80% of the buildings on the island, thirty-three inches of rain fell that drove snakes into many dwellings in base housing. This often proved more problematic than the typhoon and left "the night of the snakes" seared into residents' minds.

Guam seemed a more primitive, less developed Hawaii—at least in the early 1970s. There were two or three fairly fancy Japanese hotels, such as the Dai-Ichi on Tumon Bay, but most of Guam was rural, covered with scrub jungle and undeveloped. Native Guamanians, or Guacamoles as we sometimes called them, bore close resemblance to Hawaiians but seemed to lack the implied royal stature of Hawaiians. Car trips from Andersen to Agana or the navy base traveled an antiquated two-lane blacktop road with the low jungle foliage on each side. The cars we drove were termed "Guam bombs" since they were old and rusted but still ran well. Sometimes a squadron would purchase one for its crews to hand off to each other, and other times a crew would buy one for three months, then sell it to a new crew.

The navy base had a larger BX than Andersen and also had the best stereo equipment at the best prices. The brand names of the time were Pioneer and Sansui. I had bought a top-line Sansui outfit in Vietnam, so I was already set until my four four-channel speakers, each two feet tall, were stolen from my apartment in Merced, CA, in 1979.

The navy base also had a first-rate officers' club (O'Club) that made the slow journey down the island worth the trip. At the time, we could get away with parking in slots reserved for "captains," meaning Navy 0-6–type captains equivalent to Air Force full colonels, not lowly Air Force 0-3–type captains such as us. In the intervening years, the military changed the labels to "0-6" designation to foil Air Force captains. On another note, the Navy O'Club presented the final straw for me with Officer Wives Clubs (OWCs).

Officer Wives Clubs (OWC) and O'Clubs

OWCs, I suppose, served some purpose, but whatever their laudatory aspects, I felt abused every time I encountered them. They also played a pivotal role in the demise of the O'Club concept.

In pilot training in 1970, the local military community coalesced around the O'Club, which served as the primary restaurant and bar for base personnel. Everyone paid dues to be a member of the Club because they wanted to belong, not because they were coerced, as would later be the case.

Within one twenty-year military generation, however, the military clubs for separate ranks faded into consolidated messes that could barely keep themselves in business. While clubs at the more isolated bases struggled on and broke even due to lack of competition, those in larger metropolitan areas made so little money that other recreational centers, such as the golf course and recreational rental stores, had to support the clubs.

This degradation happened for two primary reasons—the OWCs and the social shift encouraged and embraced by the military services—which militated against smoking and drinking.

When I ventured into the Webb Officer's Club during my first weekend in pilot training, it pulsed with activity in all areas—the bar, the lounge, the restaurant, and, most enticingly for me, the stag bar, the nemesis for the OWC.

The stag bar, the smallest yet most densely populated club area, operated under the rule that women were not allowed through the door and were not allowed even to contact their husbands or boyfriends within the bar. If any wife should try to contact one of the pilots barricaded within the premises, that pilot would have to buy the bar an expensive round of drinks. This attempt at contact would be obvious in these days before cell phones, because the call had to come in through the bar phone answered by the bartender.

While pilots drank, sang, laughed, postured, and performed simulated aerial maneuvers with their hands inside the stag bar, their significant others fumed outside the door. Dinner reservations were missed, babysitters earned overtime, and women grew increasingly frustrated waiting for mates who had seemingly forgotten they were there.

I often found myself placed uncomfortably in the middle of this angst as a single officer. When I would venture out of the stag bar to see how long I had to wait to be seated for dinner, one or more wives would accost me sternly, instructing me to tell captain so-and-so to "get his ass out of there right now" because their name had been called for seating.

I would assure them I would do so and would then disappear back into the forbidden zone with the message.

Often, captain so-and-so would be in the middle of a self-promoting recitation of one of his incredible flying exploits and would not want to be bothered by a lowly student delivering an unwanted message. This also gave the captain a chance to display to his peers that no woman could tell him what to do!

"Tell her I'll be out when I'm good and ready!" he would slur, to the cheers of his compatriots.

I could not deliver this message as dictated, of course. I would tell the wife he was in the middle of a professional discussion and would be out soon. This would only work once, however. The next round trip would be somewhat terser. I would only hold up my hands in self-defense and tell the wife that I had told him and there was little more I could do.

This pilot safe zone in the stag bar allowed the O'Club to break even all by itself. Liquor of all descriptions flowed freely and profitably for the bar from four in the afternoon until well after midnight. The (eventual) spillover to the restaurant allowed clubs to prosper.

Go-go girls provided the final straw for the OWC. I had first encountered this phenomenon at the OTS bar in San Antonio just weeks before. As the band played on a large stage before several hundred officer trainees and their instructors, two young women danced the frug, the watusi, and the twist on circular pedestals in front of the stage. As the girls pranced and twisted in their bikinis, tassels and fringe swaying and thrashing about, males who had suffered significant sensory deprivation for weeks and months at the school would surround them, offering rapt attention to their efforts. As I stood within easy reach of one of these sensuously writhing females, I had to use the utmost self-control to avoid doing something truly unfortunate.

The OWC finally went to war on go-go girls and stag bars. The hands that rocked the cradle could also rock the male establishment, starting with the wing commander's wife pulling the chain on the commander. No more impenetrable safe zones for drunken pilots, no more go-go girls. Nirvana, from the pilot's perspective, *denied!*

The OWC created even more carnage in collateral areas. The Navy OWC on the naval base on Guam decided one of the most spectacular ocean views in the Pacific from the hilltop club location should be blocked with a row of tall evergreen bushes for "privacy and intimacy." When I saw this and got that explanation, I wanted to tear down the bushes with my hands. Banning go-go girls was bad enough, but blocking this million-dollar panoramic vista was an abomination and soured me forever on the OWC.

Perhaps more significantly, societal shifting against smoking, and especially drinking, put the final nail into the O'Clubs. Draconian, and probably proper, punishment for drunk driving arrests slowly depopulated the O'Club bars. No one could risk such an infraction.

In the next generation of senior officers, a DWI would result in immediate dismissal from a command position. At a naval conference in Hawaii in 1993, the secretary of the navy was forced to resign after drunken navy officers groped two female officers in a hallway. The sense of humor for drunken escapades had evaporated, as had profits for the O'Clubs.

The military fought back against what it, and the OWC, had wrought by *demanding* officers belong to, and pay dues to, clubs they no longer frequented. Senior officers would hold commander's calls, or mandatory briefing formations, at the club and challenge everyone at the door for their club card.

The running joke at the time said the base would close the club and cut the dues in half in compensation. The escape maneuver designed by innovative clubs allowed any officer, at any location worldwide, to belong for only $10 per year in dues. Suddenly officers sporting a club card from Boondock AFB, Korea, would strut into commander's calls, smiling smugly.

A standard maneuver used even at the OTS club in 1970 involved busing in women from local colleges to the clubs, presuming that if you provided the women, the pilots would show up. This had limited success, since often the women who showed up were those who had not been asked out otherwise. Today, a growing percentage of pilots are now women themselves, who bristle at the double standard and wonder when men will be bused in for them.

The club on Guam, however, had about everything we could want except the go-go girls—a large dining area, a large indoor bar, and a cabana bar/ grill with at least a limited ocean view. Its claim-to-fame sandwich, the "He-burger," provided half a pound of hamburger with a mountain of fries for clientele from the golf course as well as the club. No pilot would dare order the smaller "She-burger." In later years, these names were changed to a "C-5" or "C-17" burger. I believe this made the She-burger the predecessor of the C-17 burger, much to my delight since, as a C-5 pilot, I often took a dim view of the newer, smaller, most-favored-by-the-brass C-17. But that controversy is for a later book. The C-17 is an adequate little airplane.

The main bar could hold, perhaps, several hundred patrons and make money like mad. Here I would first confront the dice game: 4-5-6. Each contestant would roll the dice as a sort of poker hand with a 4-5-6 on the dice being the highest hand and 1-2-3 being the lowest. From my few forays into this madness, I began to refer to the game as 1-2-3, since that is what I seemed adept at throwing. Hundreds of dollars would trade hands in these games, a large sum in 1970 dollars, and many a pilot blew his entire combat pay allotment and more in these drunken dice games that lasted long into the night. I presume this provided a tension release from the 179-day continuum of bombing missions.

After a few months back at Loring, I volunteered for a second Arc Light tour as a copilot, something that would help me build enough hours to upgrade to aircraft commander. My aircraft commander for this tour was John, another Air Force Academy pilot who seemed an ill fit for aircraft commander. While solid as a pilot, he showed great frustration as a commander. If the slightest thing went wrong with the plane or his interactions with the command structure, he would fly into a spittle-flying rage, cursing the plane or the command. In later years, I would cite such inappropriate anger to students as a prime indicator a commander was in over his head.

The glorious confirmation of this maladjustment happened in the main bar of the Guam O'Club one night during our three-month stay. After a long night of drinking without bothering to eat dinner, John leapt over the bar and hugged the large ship's bell, which, when rung, would proclaim someone was "buying the bar" (drinks all around for everyone at someone's expense). He then began frantically beating the bell with his Academy ring, which brought patrons racing from every corner of the club for free booze. His bar bill had to be in the thousands of dollars, all the result of massive built-up frustration with his aircraft commander task. I hope he got into staff work quickly to keep his sanity.

Another interesting event from this second Guam tour happened during one of the nuclear alert tours we began pulling as the Vietnam War ceased for us. When the alert Klaxon went off one day, one of the crews' copilots could not be found. (If this happened, the crewmember was directed to find a bathroom stall to hide within. Further, he should stand on the toilet seat so inspectors who might sweep the facility would not perceive him hiding behind the locked stall door.) The crew raced to the airplane but did not have a full crew. Since they did not have to really fly the mission, or even start engines, the aircraft commander put the gunner in the copilot's seat, so when the commanders drove down the ramp looking at the cockpits, it appeared the plane had a full crew.

Two other features of note happened on my three-month tours on Guam as a copilot.

Miles was an aircraft commander on another crew and bedeviled me at

Loring and on Guam. His favorite ploy was to use jovial, kidding ridicule to belittle his associates. If I blew a crucial shot on the tennis court, he would put on faux concern at my dilemma and say, with insincere friendliness, "Hey, your game is really improving; that was only out by a little, so if you keep practicing you might . . . stand a prayer of beating me!" This aggravated the hell out of me because I was a better tennis player than he was; I knew it, he knew it, but he kept beating me. Being the perceptive devil he was, he knew just how to effectively goad me on this failing.

His demeanor masked something else, I suspect, although I'm not sure what. When he and I first played golf at Loring with his wife, he muffed a putt on the second green and flew into a rage, slashing his putter wildly through the air followed by several expletives. He seemed to harbor some insecurity that drove him to ridicule others as he feared he might be ridiculed himself. He was very good at it as a result.

The second episode of note happened on the base tennis courts. Four of us copilots were playing doubles when a sky-cop truck pulled up. One of the cops walked to the court and asked to speak to one of the other copilots. After speaking, the copilot got into the truck and left. We never saw him again. It seems his wife, for reasons unknown to me, had attempted suicide with a revolver. I didn't know her, and barely knew him, but obviously something significant must have happened to drive such drastic action.

Our crew did get one ferry mission to U-Tapao, Thailand, on this tour that provided a few days to see Bangkok, a marvelous opportunity. As I tell my pilot training simulator students forty years later, they really got screwed on theaters of operation. They must put up with a Middle Eastern tan, sand universe with women who wear veils and are off-limits anyway. My generation got the lush tropics and legions of LBFMs (little brown fucking machines) flirting with the GIs at every turn.

The bellhop at the Chau Pia hotel in Bangkok asked the standard question on the way to the room, did I want a girl. Well, sure, I said, and about ten minutes later, he returned with one. I was not impressed with the product; she was about eighteen, slightly overweight, very shy, and did not display the standard hooker's brassy demeanor—a far cry from Suzie in Taiwan.

Nonetheless, we transacted business unenthusiastically. As we got dressed, I handed her a tip and got quite a surprise. She immediately fell to her knees and bowed her head in gratitude, holding my hand tightly and crawling after me as I tried to back away. Apparently the money she had just received would save her, or someone close to her, and she was profoundly grateful. She seemed a novice at such things and had probably come in from one of the provinces in desperation. I wish I had known that; I'd have given her the money gratis and found a more suitable candidate for my intentions, and everyone would have been happier.

Returning to Loring at the end of 1973 from the second Guam Arc Light tour, I found myself promoted to standardization/evaluation copilot as a member of crew S-03, or stan/eval 03, the third-ranking crew of the bomber crew force, behind crews S-02 and S-01.

From my pictures of the time I thought I was hot stuff, and other copilots from lower-rated crews would acknowledge me warily as I passed. I was now the dreaded enforcer, the emergency procedures test administrator and publications inspector. From this exalted perch, I splattered ignominiously and learned a valuable lesson.

TAKING A HIT

Everyone takes a hit, or screws up, many times in a career. Some hits are small in the grand scheme of things; some are large. For all but the most egregious, unrecoverable hits (airplane crash, caught in bed with the wing commander's wife), I learned that the most important factor in taking the hit is how you react to it, not the hit itself. Superiors will watch your response closely because this will provide them with a glimpse of your soul. Their rapt attention is not about your sin but about your reaction. They, too, have made numerous mistakes, so the fact that you made one is not their major concern; they want to judge the integrity of your response. I found this imperative: you must take responsibility for the fiasco and explain, perhaps, the flaw in your procedures, personal or professional, that caused the lapse. Then you assert you will correct that lapse with a vengeance. That is what your superiors and contemporaries expect and demand of you; weak excuses or trying to shift the blame inappropriately can finish your promotion potential. The OTS imperative rears up again: no excuse, sir.

My first hit came on a Combat Evaluation Group (CEVG) flying inspection from higher headquarters to see that crews were following command directives on their missions. As a stan/eval crew, we were one of the first crews "jumped" by an inspector, as we knew we would be. My hit came as I busted the check ride before we even became airborne. As we pulled onto the runway, my right seat belt anchor connection to the seat came loose for the only time in my two thousand hours in the B-52. The evaluator in the jump seat pointed this out to me as we pulled onto the runway for takeoff. I struggled frantically to reattach the belt but, in so doing, failed to arm the engine water activation switches required for this takeoff. As the pilot started the throttles forward, the evaluator said: "Copilot, water switches." Game over, busted. The rest of the ride went well, so my corrective action was to activate the water switches in the simulator for the chief of stan/eval.

172

This fluke equipment failure seemed fairly easily explainable, and the heat was not severe for it. It could have happened to anyone, seemed to be the staff's attitude.

The next hit, however, would be inexplicable.

I had returned from leave and, due to poor planning, had not taken my "closed book" emergency procedure exam that was due the day I returned. I went directly to the squadron to take the test. I thought of checking my vertical-file folder for any new publications or advisories that had been issued during my absence, but I decided to knock off the test first, a fatefully disastrous decision.

While I was on leave, the command had, for the only time in my B-52 career, added a Bold Print emergency procedure, one that had to be committed to memory. There is absolutely no excuse for busting a Bold Print, especially for a stan/eval copilot. But as I opened the exam, I saw to my horror that one of the common emergencies that had not been Bold Print before I left had been elevated to Bold Print status. I knew the first three steps of this procedure very well, but I had no idea how many of those steps had been made Bold Print. I guessed two, but the correct answer was only the first.

I explained the situation to my fellow stan/eval copilot who had administered the test, but he seemed perplexed by the dilemma. Would he be seen as cutting slack for a fellow stan/eval pilot when he would not for a squadron pilot? He took the issue to the stan/eval chief, who took it to the deputy commander for operations, who made the call to bust me.

I suppose that was a correct decision, but it put a very damaging torpedo into me. The wing commander would have to explain to the SAC commanders why his stan/eval copilot had busted a Bold Print, for God's sake! I, in turn, would get to stand before the wing commander and his staff to explain how I could have failed to know a Bold Print.

Fortunately, the wing commander was a slow-talking, laid-back country boy who seemed to appreciate how this could have happened. I wasn't stupid or negligent; I just failed my due diligence prior to the test. He read me the riot act, softly, about how stan/eval copilots should never bust a Bold Print. I had to stand there, take it, and offer no excuse. They knew the excuse, but I couldn't invoke it. I had to eat the shit sandwich, slowly, before the wing staff.

I recall another example of a pilot invoking inexcusable excuses for a performance. Years later, a C-5 copilot had excused his poor descent from altitude, his instrument approach, and subsequent landing as a result of being tired, as if that would get him off the hook. It did not. If he had crashed the plane, could he tell his dead passengers at the pearly gates it was no big deal because he was tired? If he were debilitated and unsafe, he should have given the plane to another pilot to fly the approach. Being tired is not a sufficient excuse for killing everyone on the plane.

Because there could be no excuse, I had to make sure my personal processes were stringent enough to avoid such a dilemma. Better than any excuse was to stay prepared and not to need one.

Despite these travails, I still received my class date for Aircraft Commander training at Castle for the fall of 1974. Instead of driving, I flew out commercially and bought a 1964 Ford Fairlane for $400 to serve as my transportation for the three-month school.

B-52 AIRCRAFT COMMANDER SCHOOL

SEPTEMBER 1974–DECEMBER 1974

My IP for the course was "John," a senior captain. Although an effective instructor, he was also an alcoholic. On classroom days, he would down a few beers at lunch and head directly for the O'Club bar at the end of the afternoon. As soon as his dedicated bartender, June, saw him enter the bar, she would line up three martinis for him to down as the beginning of the

174

evening's activities. Most days his eyes were bloodshot. Disturbingly, John was just like me in many respects, except alcohol had taken over and was slowly wrecking his life. He remained contentious when we flew, but his preparation and paperwork had declined badly. On a CEVG inspection the year before, he knew some of his paperwork might not be up to standards, so he opened the copilot window in flight in the traffic pattern and threw it out so it could not be inspected afterward.

We made a good team, since I upgraded successfully, but there were moments.

On an early night ride with my student crew and instructors, we were taxiing down a long row of revetments, or U-shaped parking spots you could taxi into but not out of. The standard parking procedure had you park the plane on the taxiway after the flight and let a tug back the plane into the revetment. Alas, taxiing down the revetment line in the dark, I turned short of the exit taxiway and into one of the revetments. That meant it would take us thirty minutes to have a tug back us out again. John had been writing something on his notepad as I started the turn. When the taxi lights lit up a revetment instead of a taxiway, he shot forward from the IP seat and screamed "Noooooo!" Two of his buddy IPs, who were his seniors, and one of whom was Lucky Luciano, were taxiing ahead of us for Minimum Interval Takeoff (MITO) training. John now had to admit, on the command radio, that he had allowed me, his dolt student, to pull into a revetment and everyone would have to wait for us to be tugged out.

On a less distressing note, on an overwater navigation leg over the Pacific off Oregon, I wondered who had won the Ali/Foreman heavyweight boxing championship that night. I thought Ali the most gifted boxer of the time but one who didn't always go for the kill and often showed off by dancing around and taunting his opponent instead of dispatching him. Foreman had a devastating punch but was not an exceptionally gifted boxer. However, he did have the killer instinct and had decimated several fighters, Ken Norton and Joe Frazier, who had given Ali problems. Therefore I thought Foreman would probably prevail. I asked Oakland Center who had won the fight, unsure if he would have any idea. He did. "Ali by KO in eight," he said. I found that incredulous, but it was true. Ali didn't so much knock Foreman out as let him punch himself out, so Ali pretty much just had to get out of the way and let him fall.

SOCIAL TANGLE, MOTHERS AND DAUGHTERS

On the social front, I again found myself in a conflicted tangle while at Castle for this course.

There I was, as pilots say, minding my own business, dropping by the O'Club for dinner shortly after arrival at Castle. The very second Frieda, the waitress, walked into the room, my libido radar locked onto her and refused to let go. She was long, slender, blonde, and utterly attractive, an Aryan goddess from a Hitler propaganda film.

After small talk over a few dinners as she waited on me, I asked her out and she smiled so agreeably I began to melt in my chair. True, there would be an age difference; I was twenty-eight and she was nineteen, but that didn't seem an impediment to either of us. It seemed I'd been dating nineteen-year-olds since I was nineteen. I got older, but my dates never did, somehow. This proved curious since I had always been attracted to older women, but I'll get to that complication shortly.

While things seemed about standard at this point, they soon got dicey. Frieda's father worked as a chief master sergeant on the flight line, something that didn't have to hamper things but would. Frieda's mother, a German by birth, brought Frieda into the world from an out-of-wedlock relationship with a German Air Force pilot in post-war Germany. Ostracized for this, Frieda's mother married a man who she might not have otherwise, but she relented due to his willingness to accept her and her daughter by another man. His acceptance of Frieda flagged over the years, and eventually she became a constant reminder of her mother's transgression.

As I approached their on-base quarters one night to pick her up for our first date, I heard a male's voice angrily and unyieldingly berating someone. I stood for a moment, listening to the tirade, then knocked on the door. The tirade immediately ceased. Shortly thereafter, Frieda's mother answered the door. Frieda threw a short good-night over her shoulder and shot out of the house. She said this was one of her father's standard screaming matches about what a no-good child she had been. Apparently he had sometimes physically slapped her around in his rage.

As the fall progressed and the tirades continued, I told her that to protect herself, she should challenge him with a violation of the HRP, or Human Reliability Program, a regimen designed to identify out-of-control personalities whose job could put them in the vicinity of nuclear weapons. From Frieda's reports and my experience listening to one of the tirades, her father would definitely be in danger of crossing the HRP line. I didn't know if the threat to report him would give him pause or, rather, cause him to completely lose it with her. She used it on him once with no apparent change in his demeanor—no better but at least no worse.

Her father's main influence on her now was to drive her to get out of the house as fast as possible for her sake, and her mother's. Mom had to survive positioning herself somewhere between her daughter and her husband. The relationship seemed to be tearing up all of them, and getting Frieda out on her own seemed the best alternative.

And, then, alas, there was my libido's constant lock-on to Frieda's mother. I had often lusted, unsuccessfully, after older women since I was in junior high. I remember protesting to the gods when fourteen that I didn't want to wait until I was twenty-five to cavort with a twenty-five-year-old woman; I

177

wanted to cavort with one *now*, when I was fourteen. This didn't happen.

To digress, I nearly scored a victory on this front at sixteen. My family had hired a twenty-three-year-old Swedish nanny for my ten-years-younger twin brothers. I had just blossomed into the youthful trim attained free of effort at sixteen, and never to be attained again regardless of effort. I had lifted weights in preparation for high school football and looked as trimly muscular as I ever would. Slowly, Swedish nanny began hanging around my weight lifting sessions in my basement room. Even in my clumsy naïveté, I perceived I was about to get lucky and got weak-kneed thinking about the possibilities. She'd have to teach me *everything*, oooooh, yes! One day I thought I was about to mount the stairway to heaven, so to speak, sitting on my bed with her when my mother appeared at the door with the angry visage of a she-bear who fears her cub is in mortal danger. Mom fired the Swedish maid that night and she was gone the next day, to my berserk consternation.

Years later, I unloaded my ire on my mother for this; how could she have deprived me of my desperate teenaged dream? My God, a Swedish maid, could it get any better than that? Mom countered by suggesting that when my first daughter, then two, reached sixteen, she would hire a Swedish man to educate her similarly. Argh, no fair, Mom! This left me holding an egregious double standard that, somehow, I did not find unreasonable despite appearances.

Now I found myself halfway between two libido targets, one about ten years my junior and one about twelve years my senior. Frieda's mother displayed a demure, reserved personality and still had a slight German accent I found very appealing.

One day, driving toward their quarters on base, I saw the mother walking home from the convenience store. She still had six or so blocks to travel, so I stopped and asked if she would like a ride. She paused just long enough to suggest she thought this might not be a good idea, but I suppose the distance remaining convinced her to accept. She got in and sat rigidly with both feet planted in front of her and never moved or spoke. Although I had made absolutely no move on her, her pause suggested she too recognized a potential mutual attraction and wanted no part of it.

She was right, of course. Such an illicit liaison would blow our little world to smithereens! It would be a toss-up as to who would be more enraged at such dalliance, Frieda or her father, and both would be volcanic in their rage. I knew by even thinking about such things that I was playing with fire, but the damn libido radar would not relent. I fantasized about telling her that if she wanted to get even with that tyrannical jerk husband of hers, I'd provide her a delicious method if she wished. Immediately after such a thought, I'd chastise myself for stupidity; had I lost my mind? Her husband would get the Air Force to boil me alive!

I greatly enjoyed my time with Frieda and briefly considered marrying her, and perhaps should have, but left for Loring after my course completion, having avoided acting on any of my destructive imaginings with her mother, something that would have been a ticking time bomb in a long-term relationship.

Thirty years later, as I found myself in divorce proceedings, I pondered who from my past I might have married if I had it to do over again. I selected Frieda and two old high school flames. As if by magic, Frieda and the only one of the two flames available showed up and got me tangled in another triangular mess before I married the flame, Eleanor. I had chased all over the world looking for the right woman and only belatedly realized, in hindsight, I'd passed up the best ones early in the process.

LORING: MY CREW OF DESTINY

DECEMBER 1974–MARCH 1976

I flew back to Loring, leaving my clunker car for my brother, Drew, who lived in Missoula, MT. Unfortunately, he took several weeks to get to San Francisco and had a several hundred dollar parking fee to pay to spring the car loose, and it only cost $400 in the first place. Great plan.

Naturally, once back at Loring, I immediately informed the squadron commander that I'd like to form a crew to return to Southeast Asia, something he was only too glad to accommodate. Now a captain, they awarded me four 1st lieutenants and an airman basic, the most junior of all crews on base and none of whom had been overseas before. Our designation in the crew pecking order, R-14, or Regular crew 14, was the lowliest on the crew board, a crew where everyone was new to their job after initial training.

This would be my crew of destiny, one that would excel, astonish, and nearly die twice in our B-52: nameless copilot (who is still mad at me almost forty years later for the wrong reasons), Electronic Warfare Officer (EW) Buddy, radar navigator Boonie Bill, navigator-to-remain-nameless for obvious reasons, and gunner Fonzie.

As cited earlier, I will always remember pausing to board the crew bus after my first flight in command at Loring and looking back at the B-52 I had just flown "solo" as an aircraft commander. A flamboyant end zone dance would have been in order. I wanted to spike a football emphatically into the turf and turn a cartwheel followed by a back flip, but settled for taking an indelible mental picture of that huge, ugly, wonderful airplane that had finally validated the history major as a pilot.

First ORI (Operational Readiness Inspection)

We had just come out of training status in early 1975 when the twice-a-year ORI hit. The scenario dictated that a certain number of crews fly the ORI mission according to the number of airframes assigned to the base. For Loring, that meant fourteen crews, and we were the fourteenth, the tail-end Charlie, the last of the crew batting order.

The ORI had a maneuver they pulled to try to surprise the target base. Being one of a half dozen B-52 wings in 8th Air Force, Loring would monitor KC-135s launching from headquarters at Barksdale AFB, LA, to the eastern bases that comprised the 8th, and track them closely. The ORI team would board the tanker and file for a given base but divert en route to drop in unannounced at the target base. Since every SAC base command post would track the tankers, the selected base would get about thirty minutes' notice that the inspection team was on the way and they were "it."

Once the team landed, there would be a Klaxon alert scrambling the alert crews to their aircraft to start engines and perhaps to taxi (elephant walk). For a taxi exercise, all the alert bombers, fully armed with nuclear warheads, would have to cross the runway hold line within fifteen minutes from the time the horn sounded and then return to their parking spots. This usually meant four bombers on alert at Loring.

For the next week, the ORI team would scour the base, checking publications and manuals and testing the crews and maintenance personnel for procedural knowledge. Then, finally, the wing crews would fly the designated ORI mission to include an on-time takeoff, air refueling, navigation leg, and low-level route that would culminate in a bomb run to drop a string of simulated weapons on designated targets.

All these tasks had to be completed to specification: fifteen minutes of contact in air refueling with no more than three disconnects from the tanker, a navigation leg within geographic and time parameters, the low-level route flown without violating the corridors of the route, and, the grand finale—dropping the simulated weapons on the targets within distance specifications. The "bombs" were mere tones over the ORI radio frequency that would be matched to the plane's radar location to determine where the bombs would have hit. As an aside on this issue, I never flew with nuclear weapons on board, a practice that ended years before I arrived in SAC.

USAF photo

ORI Klaxon alert and 'elephant walk' to cross the runway hold line
in fifteen minutes.

The ORI would be career life or death for the command colonels. If a wing failed an ORI, those colonels would pack their bags and leave shortly thereafter, fired from their positions. They had been trusted to train the crews to be capable of flying the ORI and their real-world nuclear mission successfully, and if the ORI didn't go well, they were gone; no questions, no excuses (the OTS "no excuses" mantra again). The crews would suffer retraining and have to fly a make-up ORI, but they would remain at the base; the top brass would not.

So when the mission day arrived, we filled in as the final crew. Before the launch, the wing staff would bet on which crew would get the "best bombs" award. Selecting by seniority, with the wing commander going first, they bet on their estimate of the best crew. My crew fell, by default, to a lowly Operational Plans major who had to take the last remaining crew—us, R-14. Most of the crews above us in the pecking order had thousands of hours of experience, including copious amounts of combat time and months together as a "hard" crew that had flown extensively as a team. We, however, had flown only a few dozen hours together, and my two copilot bombing sorties in 1973 were the full extent of our combat time. The other crews had also flown many ORIs and knew the ropes well. We didn't know shit-from-Shinola except for what we had studied.

What no one knew at the time, including me, was that I had perhaps the best radar navigator/bomb dropper of his generation. Affectionately known as "Boonie Bill," suggesting he often threw his bombs into the boonies, or far off target, which he did not, he would earn great renown as a radar nav and would instruct at the schoolhouse at Castle AFB for many years. He was my magic man. I hadn't selected him or done anything to deserve having him on my crew, but that is how it turned out.

As you may have guessed from the buildup, we, the lowly R-14 crew, dropped the best bombs on this, our first ORI. We astounded the staff, drove the premier stan/eval crew, S-01, into apoplexy, and surprised ourselves as much as anyone. In the final scoring, the ORI team calculated that S-01 had a marginally better navigation leg than we did, so they weaseled the overall best crew award from us, but the best bombs accolade was ours. Cock-a-doodle-doo!

There was no need for an end zone dance; the word of our coup spread almost as rapidly as had my Bold Print exam bust that was now forgotten. While previously we had been invisible to the more senior crews, they now nodded to us as we passed to acknowledge their acceptance. Yeah, baby! I don't know if we, as a crew, were really that good, but Boonie Bill certainly was, and he made a stupendous reputation for himself with that one bomb run. As the bomb scores came in, the ops plans major chortled as he swept up all the bets for his outstanding "selection" of our crew for best bombs.

With the ORI successfully completed, we headed a few weeks later to difference training in the "D" model at Carswell in preparation for our tour to U-Tapao, Thailand, the only one of my three tours that would not be on Guam.

Our course at Carswell ran from January to March 1975. It was old hat for me since I'd taken the course twice already, and I relaxed and enjoyed the base golf course a little. Spring had started to arrive as we graduated and prepared to fly our "D" model to Guam and then on to U-Tapao. On a bright March morning as we prepared for takeoff, the air held the same hopeful fragrance of new grass I had experienced five years before at OTS down the road in San Antonio. The genre of rock songs on the radio had progressed from The Beatles' "Here Comes the Sun" in 1970, to The Animals' "We've Gotta Get Out of This Place" in Vietnam, to "Philadelphia Freedom" by Elton John.

The rooster rose in me again as I advanced the eight throttles and roared down the two-mile-long runway with my own crew on a magical mission halfway around the world to the land of dragons and silk with "Philadelphia Freedom" ringing in my mind. One of my wistful images has me watching seven-mile-high contrails coursing westward off the coast of California headed for marvelous destinations, because in that direction, every

USAF photo

Headed for the land of dragons and silk.

184

destination is marvelous. About three hours after takeoff, we were making those contrails ourselves as we crossed the coast of California near Los Angeles, headed southwest for Guam.

The arrival at Guam had an interesting wrinkle. On the descent from altitude, all our cockpit windows except for the copilot's fogged over due to a window defog system malfunction. I had warned the copilot that the bowl-shaped Andersen runway was challenging, but now I told him he would have to make the landing since I couldn't see anything. He did so without missing a beat and beamed in pride as we rolled out to the end of the runway. The next day we took off for Thailand and our three-month tour.

U-Tapao Tour

March 1975–May 1975

Arriving at U-Tapao, about sixty miles south of the capital, Bangkok, I found the mission greatly reduced. Since the armistice had ended hostilities in 1973, not much was happening at U-Tapao except occasional training missions. Mostly we just sat waiting for a possible reignition of hostilities, which did not happen, and which was fine with me.

We lived in house trailers lined up in long rows just south of the American O'Club, with four to a trailer that was divided into two sections by the bathroom. Upon awaking, we would walk the short distance to the O'Club for breakfast and argue over what we would do that day. First question, should we have lunch at the US O'Club and dinner at the Thai O'Club down the main boulevard, or vice versa? Once we settled that, the next discussion centered on what activity we would pursue that afternoon— sunbathing, racquetball, or a three-mile run along the perimeter? The final discussion would involve our weekend trip plans, Pattaya Beach or Bangkok? These were our weighty wartime decisions.

USAF photo

B-52D landing at U-Tapao, Thailand, during the war.

Usually we chose the Thai O'Club for dinner. They had a $5 lobster thermidor so tasty I would have paid $50 for it. The Thai waitresses flirted with the customers as they delivered Singha and Amerit beers. Once, Milo, also pulling a tour there, told a small gaggle of waitresses that we were going to Bangkok that weekend. One of them twittered: "Snake go Bangkok, find many holes!" This brought uproarious laughter from the other waitresses. In weeks after that, we would stroke our chins in serious contemplation and say: "Snake must go Bangkok again."

Milo had a girlfriend at the local brothel, "Swan Lake," a gaudy complex next to a small lake near the base. Once, when he headed to Guam for an alert tour, he loaned me the girlfriend, "Wanna," for the duration of his TDY. I dare not guess how she got that name. Wanna knew the GIs well and, although in her late twenties as we were, played sage advisor and mother confessor in addition to her, ah, standard duties. This perplexed. One of the

186

most astute personalities I would encounter at U-Tapao would be this Swan Lake hooker. The bothersome revelation: I was born lucky; Wanna was not.

PATTAYA BEACH

The trip to Pattaya or Bangkok required taking one's life in one's hands. Thai taxis were small Japanese imports such as Datsuns and Toyotas that could accommodate three of us, at most. The payment for the trip would be $10 or, more preferably from the driver's viewpoint, a $3 fifth of Gilbey's gin from the military Class Six store.

The most junior officer had to ride in the front seat and spend most of the trip with his eyes closed, praying. The narrow two-lane road had to accommodate bicyclists, motorbikes often carrying two people, taxis, large industrial trucks, and, finally, dragon wagons. These were buses garishly adorned with colorful dragon depictions that provided basic transportation for most Thais. The crucial fear factor in this mix resulted from repeated games of chicken among all the vehicles. Several times per trip, our taxi would try to pass a motorbike or other car with not nearly enough space to complete the maneuver before coming nose to nose with a truck or dragon wagon. As the front seat occupant would gasp or scream at the situation, the taxi driver would pull back into our lane at the last second, laughing at the lack of fortitude of his passenger. Incredibly, I never heard of anyone dying in a crash on the Bangkok road.

Pattaya, which we pronounced Patty-ah, and the Thais pronounced Pa-TIE-ah, lay about thirty miles up the road toward Bangkok. In the early 1970s, it remained a sleepy little beach resort that had not yet been discovered by European vacationers in great numbers and still held a quaint charm. When we turned off the Bangkok road down the short one-mile or so narrow two-lane road to the town, the field to the right had a water buffalo foraging, so primitive was the landscape it still enjoyed. By the time I next returned

187

during the Desert Shield in 1990, it had become a full-blown European-style resort with large swank hotels and concrete buildings even where the water buffalo roamed in 1975.

The beach had the usual umbrella vendors and small tour boats, but we usually went for the long, narrow outboard motors to take us to the island about a mile off the beach. The motors on these "klong boats" had long drive shafts connected to a small propeller that spun far behind the boat and just beneath the water so it could travel in very shallow depths. After renting basic scuba gear at beachside shops, we would hop into the Klong boats and pay for the trip to the island with small transistor radios from the BX, a boat captain favorite.

Although none of us were certified in scuba diving, the water around the island was never more than six or seven feet deep, so we couldn't really get into trouble. Of greater danger, we foolishly took spear guns down with us to skewer poor helpless little fish. Somehow, we managed to avoid skewering each other in the process.

After heroic snorkeling activities, we'd repair to the thatch-roofed beach huts on the far side of the island, where the boats docked, to drink Singha beer and have lunch.

BANGKOK

On alternate weekends, we'd go to Bangkok, a marvelously busy and boisterous city much like Saigon. We did have a crew dust-up prior to the first trip, however. The two navigators, Nameless Navigator and Boonie Bill, decided they would rather stay at U-Tapao and write letters to their wives instead of venturing to Bangkok. The copilot and I thought they had lost their minds and that it must be some sort of navigator thing. "You'll see your wife every day for the rest of your life; you might not ever see Bangkok again,"

I said. But they were determined, so we left their sorry asses and jumped into the taxi.

We did get them there on a subsequent weekend, however. I had told them of a marvelous bar atop a hotel I had visited on my previous tour, the "Bora, Bora" room. The process was very easy, I had told them. You and other customers sit on chairs around the edges of the dance floor. Then the girls come out on the floor and dance with each other. You review the choices and make your selection, or selections (ho, ho, ho).

When I got them to the night club, however, something seemed drastically wrong. There were no girls to dance for us. I collared the manager and asked what had happened and where the girls were. He said the club had changed things and you had to bring your own girl.

"What?" I protested. "I came here to find a girl. If I already had one, I wouldn't need to come here, you moron!"

This opened me up to unending ridicule from the rest of the crew. "Oh, yeah, the great Bora, Bora room, hey? Dancing girls, you said; sure!"

I got my ass handed to me similarly on a later Bangkok foray, this time when I went out alone. I signed up for the floating market tour of the sampans on the Chao Phraya River that flows through Bangkok to the Gulf of Thailand.

The river contained a veritable city on boats and skiffs, some that remained anchored and others that were rowed among the anchored boats as merchant vessels to sell or buy various commodities, from food to flowers. Motorized tourist boats also plied the waters, some with the same bizarre motors I saw at Pattaya that had a five- or six-foot-long drive shaft that extended to the small propeller far behind the boat.

The tour was very interesting and colorful, but also proved disgustingly enlightening. As we rounded a residential sampan, we saw, on one side, a smiling boy brushing his teeth in the muddy brown river, and on the other side, a floating dog carcass.

But I digress; my embarrassment occurred before the tour.

A limousine would travel to five hotels to pick up tourists for the tour. My hotel was the first stop, and I got in. At the second stop, an attractive Oriental woman about my age joined me, sitting opposite me on the circular bench seat at the rear.

Being a suave man of the world, in my estimation, I decided to impress this young lovely. Judging she was Japanese, I said hello: "konnichiha." That was all I said as I gave her a smile, presuming she would be impressed with my smooth international savoir-faire.

She looked at me for a few seconds and said, in perfect British-accented English, "Are you a GI?"

In those few seconds, she had deduced that I had misjudged her as Japanese instead of the Hong Kong Chinese she actually was (a terrible faux pas!) and, in turn, had correctly deduced that I was not European or Russian or South American or any other possible form of Caucasian moron, but that I was an American, and some sort of military grunt to boot. She was right on; I had missed by a million miles.

As I grasped the import of what she said, I slid down in my seat, mortified and defeated. I did not relish spending an entire floating market tour with someone who now knew me as an American hayseed idiot. How could I converse with someone who had so thoroughly blown me away, who had confirmed that I "can't tell any of those Orientals apart," but she can pick out an American military man from the many choices of available white boys after hearing a single Japanese word spoken by me?

Fortunately, the woman, Helen Chen, my non-Japanese seatmate, quickly turned the page on our relationship and gracefully allowed me to escape my embarrassment. We enjoyed the tour and even corresponded for some months afterward.

SAIGON FALLING

Mayhem broke loose over U-Tapao on April 30, 1975.

As I left the squadron building, I heard the air-tearing shriek of a fighter jet overhead. Since fighters were not stationed at this B-52 bomber base, this seemed curious, and I watched the single-seat F-5 flying over the runway at 1,500 feet. At midfield, however, to my utter amazement, another F-5 whizzed past the first jet in the opposite direction at the same altitude, barely averting a midair collision.

I wondered what fool in the control tower had put two planes on a collision course over the runway. This was unimaginable!

What quickly became apparent to the tower, to the base command structure, and to me, was that *no one* was directing those aircraft. No one was talking to them; no one was controlling them. As Saigon fell to the North Vietnamese, the South Vietnamese Air Force had fled in their aircraft, often with their families in the cockpits, and had arrived unannounced and without communication.

These two fighters were soon followed by every stripe of aircraft we had given the Vietnamese: fighters,

CORBIS/Bettman New York Times

Panic to escape from Xuon Loc.

cargo aircraft, jets, props, helicopters, everything. The U-Tapao traffic pattern became a frantic, unregulated swarm of aircraft desperate to land and communicating with no one.

The overwhelmed supervisor of flying raced to the runway to attempt to direct each landing aircraft off the runway to make way for the next desperate arrival. Amazingly, there were no collisions, and soon, the south end of the airdrome, where the aircraft were sent, looked like an impromptu air show with a dozen types of aircraft parked in all directions and without order.

I raced down to the chain-link fence on the airport border to watch the spectacle, along with most of the rest of the base. The aircraft began to disgorge an incredible number of passengers. A family of five—pilot, wife, and three children—deplaned from a single-seat F-5 fighter. An A-1 Skyhawk, a slow-flying prop ground support fighter, landed with three people in the cockpit and two people clinging to the gear struts in the wheel wells. An entire village, it seemed, flooded out of a C-130 cargo plane. In all, 167 South Vietnamese aircraft landed on U-Tapao on April 30th.

Now the second "Chinese fire drill" began—hundreds of foreign nationals were loose and unsupervised on the airfield with more unannounced aircraft inbound. Security police frantically corralled this distraught, disoriented mob into a fenced containment area near the passenger terminal. They stood, in shocked stupor, with barely room to move or sit, several hundred newly minted refugees who had, on short notice, abandoned their country, their homes, their valuables, and even their families to flee, irrevocably, for their lives.

I stood within arm's length of the fence that held the refugees and viewed them with bewilderment and helplessness. Terrified children clung to their parents; terrified parents clung to each other as the condition of their plight sank in. Most had nothing but the clothes they wore and had forsaken their previous life for an unknown fate. For all they knew, we would ship them back to Saigon.

I found a Vietnamese Air Force pilot and motioned him over to me. He recounted the day in Saigon, the collapse of South Vietnamese resistance, anarchy, and the frantic efforts to escape under constant bombardment of the air base. He then looked at me forlornly and said he had no idea what would happen to him and his family now. I wanted to give him some reassurance, but I didn't have any idea what would happen, either. The next day, the Air Force sent twenty C-141 cargo aircraft to airlift the refugees to a camp at Andersen AFB on Guam.[13]

This was months before the refugees would need sponsors to escape refugee camps in the United States after having spent months on Guam. I wished later I had given this officer my name so he would have a sponsor, but none of that structure had yet been established.

Many months later, I did volunteer to sponsor and received four South Vietnamese sailors who had turned their boat around in the harbor and escaped to an American destroyer offshore. They were not the family unit I had requested, but none of those were available at the time, so I told the Lutheran placement agency to send me what they had, and four sailors is what I got. I explained to my father that I supported the war, so I supposed I should help clean up the mess. The group, one officer and three enlisted, lived with me for about six months in northern Maine before integrating into various communities from North Carolina to California. I will cover this more later.

I recall glancing up at that first fighter over the U-Tapao runway, and marvel at what it portended.

MAYAGUEZ

USAF photo

Marines deploy on Koh Tang Island, Cambodia.

No sooner had the refugee issue been resolved at U-Tapao than the Mayaguez incident put us back in the thick of world news.

The Cambodian Khmer Rouge had seized a US merchant ship off Koh Tang Island on May 12, 1975, claiming it to be a spy ship. This was probably a lie, but then, what was a US merchant ship doing in the vicinity of Cambodian territorial waters? Regardless, the Cambodians seized the ship and removed the crew as hostages.

I knew none of this at the time, but I did know something was up. On May 14, large CH-53 helicopters started arriving at U-Tapao to upload at least several dozen Marines of D Company, 1/4 Marines from U-Tapao that had flown in from the Philipines. The operation consisted of 179 of them, but I don't know if they all came from U-Tapao or also from ships off the coast. I

194

watched the Marines with their rifles and backpacks, fully loaded for action, line up and board the choppers that then lifted off and headed southeast for the approximately three-hundred-mile trip down the coast to Koh Tang.[14]

The operation got hopelessly muddled in execution. The Cambodians released the crew from the mainland as soon as the attack started on the island, but the Marines did not know that. Meeting stiff resistance, they suffered fifteen killed, three missing, and fifty wounded. Twenty-three were also killed in a helicopter crash, all in an effort to rescue the crew that had already been released. The Marines remained overnight on the island, as hostile fire and nightfall precluded extracting them until the 15th.

The Marines that disembarked from the helicopters returning to U-Tapao two days later looked far different than those on their loading prior to the engagement. Medical personnel removed several on stretchers with IVs attached. Others hobbled toward ambulances, their heads covered in bandages, leaning on the shoulders of their comrades. I marveled that some significant action had torn up the force I saw deploy. The Vietnam War was over, but I now saw the aftermath of Cambodian action that displayed more carnage than I had seen in Vietnam.

PLAYING ON THE TRAIN TRACKS AGAIN

In SAC, you always had to keep your actions between the lines or disaster could ensue, or as previously described, playing on the railroad tracks could eventually get you run over by a train. During this third and final B-52 Southeast Asia tour, I strayed outside the lines and onto the tracks.

We had to pull a few alert tours on Guam during our three-month U-Tapao tour. One of the cement dorms had been surrounded with razor wire and declared to be an alert facility. We studied China missions, the logical destination from Guam.

On one of those tours, I arranged to have nurse Millie, previously at Loring but now stationed at Tachikawa AB, Japan, fly down to meet me on Guam. She took up residence in a BOQ room situated immediately next to the outdoor movie theater, about halfway between the alert facility and the O'Club. (The last time I visited Andersen in 2003, the theater had been replaced with an F-4 monument.) This juxtaposition of theater and BOQ proved too tempting. One evening, my crew and I took the alert vehicle down to the outdoor theater. As they settled into their seats at dusk, I told them I would be across the street and would be back in an hour. Ill-advisedly, I didn't tell them in which room I would be. While I left the alert radio with the crew, I would be able to hear the alert siren on the pole next to the theater if it went off.

The visit went well and provided a marvelous break from alert duty. What could go wrong? After about an hour, I opened the curtain to see how the movie was going. As the curtain motion revealed the theater, I suddenly screamed, "*Oh, FUCK!*" A rain shower had swept over the base, the outdoor theater had stopped the movie, and everyone, including my crew and the alert vehicle, was gone.

This put me way out of bounds if the Klaxon went off. ("Your plane failed the alert because you were *where*, captain?") I frantically threw on my flight suit and hopped around the room, trying to don my boots and gather my wallet and line badge simultaneously. I bid Millie a quick farewell, sprinted from the building, and headed for the alert facility half a mile away in a walk as brisk as I dared to avoid bringing attention to myself. As I approached the alert facility, sweating like a pig from the tropical humidity, I slowed to make it appear I had just been strolling outside the facility for a few minutes. The entry guard eyed me suspiciously, but my line badge matched the aircraft commander of an alert crew, so he let me in. The train missed me.

CHAPTER 4: STRATEGIC AIR COMMAND

PUTTING OUT THE ARC LIGHT

At the end of May, the B-52 Arc Light mission ended as the final three-ship cell, with our crew in the lead, departed U-Tapao. For many years, SAC crew members had joked about "putting out the Arc Light for good," and here we were about to do just that. I had only flown two actual Arc Light bombing missions in 1973, and the rest of the crew had flown none, but we got to put out the "Light" for the thousands of crewmen who had flown the tens of thousands of hours over the previous ten years. They had done the heavy lifting; we had done little for the time we were at U-Tapao, but we got to take it home for good.

We would fly in cell formation until we reached the coast of California, then "two" and "three" would leave the formation to land at March AFB, CA, and we would continue on as a single ship to Carswell AFB, TX, a sixteen-hour mission.

We had an indignity to suffer before takeoff, however. The staff told us to report an hour early so we could string up a room full of rattan furniture in the bomb bay to deliver to the deputy commander for operations at Carswell. This did not sit well. We faced a tortuously long mission without any extra duties, and this was an absolutely unnecessary task. No doubt one of the commanders at U-Tapao garnered a significant kudo for shipping the colonel's furniture for free, but we were the ones providing the service. We hoped to be required to cycle the bomb bay doors en route over the Pacific, one final rattan bomb run.

(On a similar mission during Gulf War 1 in 1990, I had to personally deliver two live lobsters sent by General Colin Powell from Massachusetts to General Norman Schwarzkopf in Riyadh, Saudi Arabia. Getting them there alive was my assigned mission. I await my grandkids asking what I did during the war. Why, I babysat two lobsters!)

197

When the time came, the three B-52s sat behind the runway hold line awaiting permission for the final B-52 takeoff from U-Tapao. Then tower cleared us for takeoff. On interplane frequency, I said, "OK, guys, let's take our Buffs and go home," and with that we took off. As we climbed out over the Gulf of Siam, U-Tapao fell silent for the first time in a decade and would largely remain that way.

At cruise over the Philippine Sea at 42,000 feet, two interesting things happened. First, a jet contrail passed over us. This was unusual because we were already at our max altitude over eight miles high, and the other plane's contrail was so far above us I couldn't see the aircraft. I decided it must be a U-2 or SR-71 spy plane because I didn't expect to encounter any aircraft higher than we were, much less so far above us I would be unable to see it.

Next, a US Navy ship broadcast on guard channel asking if any American military aircraft were in the area. We answered that we were, and he asked if we could go "cipher" mode, or the scrambled, secret mode on one of our radios. The ship said they had an unknown target apparently shadowing them and asked if we could drop down and take a look. I said I'd have to get permission to do so because I couldn't make my destination if I used the extra gas to chase a shadow. Shortly thereafter, the ship said they had resolved the issue and we wouldn't be needed. I thought, briefly, we might find an excuse to cycle the bomb bay doors to rain rattan on the mysterious shadow, but it was not to be. The Carswell colonel would get his damn furniture. As the final indignity, neither colonel met us at either end to thank us for our efforts.

RETURN TO LORING

JUNE 1975–JULY 1977

No longer able to escape to Southeast Asia, I returned to Loring with my crew for my final two years at the base. This period would include two near-death episodes in the airplane, half a year living with Vietnamese refugees, and the bizarre social entanglement described in the book prologue.

VENUS FLY TRAP

As I recounted in the prologue, after blasting nav wife on her unacceptable offer to have an affair, she destroyed my position in a few choice phrases, explaining the affair was her husband's idea. I'm reminded of a salesman who listens to a prospect's objections and then says: Well, if I convinced you these objections were not valid, would you be ready to sign on for the deal? That is where I found myself. My primary objection, refusal to betray her husband, lay in shambles at my feet.

Unfortunately for my purpose, nav wife closely resembled actress Elizabeth Montgomery of the current *Bewitched* TV series, a female my libido lusted for. Nav wife smiled at me with an enthusiastic let's-get-to-it smirk while I sat frozen with eyes wide and my mind thunderstruck at what I had just heard. My brain whirred rapidly as my good angel and bad angel fought it out. Nav wife had prepared the battlefield well and knew, when she sat down, every detail of how this would transpire. As she anticipated, my mind used the few days between the two phone calls to orchestrate the speech for why this could not happen, while my libido marinated in delicious possibilities of erotic mayhem with her, an option now authorized, incredibly, by hubby. My stern, proper, logical fortitude crumbled, and a deeper imperative arose. The bad angel prevailed. I slowly returned her let's-get-to-it smile, and we did.

Of course, my bad angel left a crucial question unasked and unanswered. What was the price of this free, bountiful offer? I had always marveled at the clueless stupidity of the house fly enticed into the Venus fly trap plant with nectar seemingly easily and freely available. Once inside the plant, however, the fly finds it is trapped and about to be devoured. How could the fly be so stupid? Nav wife proved to be my Venus fly trap, and I succumbed as cluelessly as the hapless fly. I will say, however, that I enjoyed being "devoured" much more than the fly did.

The next day during mission planning, the navigator and I stood separate from the crew at a chart rack, searching for an appropriate low-level chart. I thought surely he would say something subtle to acknowledge what had transpired the night before, but he did not. He acted as if nothing significant existed to be discussed, with no hint that he had unleashed his wife on me without strings, apparently. This totally confounded me.

But, confounded or not, I lusted for round two. As in a boxing match, the first round of preliminary feeling-out was over, and each of us prepared to start throwing haymakers from the opening bell of round two. My mind had trouble concentrating on anything else.

And then . . . and then . . . nav-wife revealed the price I would have to pay. The nav had provided the first-round freebie to leave me dying for round two. Nav wife seemed mildly distraught about the price herself, as she explained it to me, but she too had been awarded round one to encourage compliance with the withheld rule that, if obeyed, would allow continued frolic.

Each of us receives prewired sexual predilections we do not choose but gradually become aware of. If the mind is a house, one room is draped and adorned with each individual's assigned sexual furniture. As the years progress, we become generally attuned and comfortable with this furniture. But often, there is a dark closet attached to the room that can contain strange and frightening demons whose low moans and cackles from behind the closet door simultaneously warn us not to open the door while also compelling us with a siren song to do so.

Nav wife now opened the closet door and beckoned me to follow her inside. She explained that round two would be at their house, and while hubby would allow ten or so minutes for us to get warmed up alone, he wanted to quietly enter the room to silently observe the rest of the festivities. I was aghast, but not quite aghast enough to refuse, due to the delicious rapture of round one. He had hooked me and seemed to know I would answer the bell for round two.

I was now meeting the "cuckold syndrome" that I had no idea existed. This mystery syndrome from the closet provides an erotic rush by observing a mate's ravishing by some perceived superior force that can elicit an exponentially heightened sexual response from the spouse. This would be no wife swap, obviously, since I didn't have one, but would provide a purposeful, voluntary, tacitly humiliating conquering of the husband and ravishing of the wife with the consent of all participants. Nav hubby would eagerly await that enhanced response, silently, in the dark.

We would be fooling with dangerous emotional dynamite in this scenario, yet it proved irresistible. As the "superior force," the navigator's boss, I already could not resist. I cannot perceive any imagined superiority I possessed other than my military position. Nav and I were a close match in looks and physique, and my single level of authority over him seemed the only factor sufficient to provoke the syndrome, to the extent I understand it. Although perhaps any "stranger" would do, I don't know. My lame rationalization for doing this read: "Hey, this wasn't my idea, this isn't my wife, and I have permission, so what's the problem?" I'd eventually find out.

A few days later, we commenced round two. None of us could escape the pull of the scenario. I left the bedroom door ajar that let in sufficient light to somewhat illuminate the room, which obviously would be necessary, would it not? The festivities did not start well, as nav wife and I were both apprehensive at the situation, but things were rolling along acceptably when the light in the room increased slightly as hubby entered and sat on the floor a few feet from the foot of the bed (at least that is my best guess of where he was since I was otherwise occupied).

201

With hubby now observing, nav wife began to noticeably stifle her aural responses, I suppose to mask her enthusiasm to protect his feelings, an action at odds with the prescribed scenario for which we were all there. When I recognized her now demure demeanor, some primordial awareness, perhaps from my reptilian brain stem, took over and I instinctively knew my assigned role. I learned just enough from round one to know what nav wife could not resist and I employed that knowledge. I started throwing the haymakers. Quickly the aural responses reignited and shortly thereafter all three of us got what we had come for.

The relationship with nav wife trailed out sporadically for the rest of my time at Loring and proceeded as one might expect. When hubby was flying or on alert with his subsequent crew, I would visit. I think he knew this would happen and let his imagination run wild with the possibilities, sensing, correctly in my view, that the imaginings in his head would be significantly better than the real thing became.

Just as I thought I had gotten away with this improper dalliance, the Air Force, in one of its clumsy efforts to do the right thing, dropped me directly into the Venus flytrap and wrecked my dream crew, as I no doubt deserved.

One-Two-Three OER

The ludicrous military efficiency report procedure, as I related in the Vietnam section, made a sham of the ratings. At the time, these were termed the Officer Effectiveness Report, or OER. If done properly and with integrity, these reports might have performed their desired purpose, to rank officers by ability and potential, and to provide valuable feedback to encourage improvement. But since no rater wanted to risk ranking his subordinates and thus unleashing rank-ordered animosity among them, the system inflated rapidly to where most officers received the highest rating in performance as well as potential, which negated the entire exercise.

This should have dictated the demise of OERs and accompanying Airmen Performance Reports, or APRs, that had similarly inflated. But, no, the Air Force required the sham system give the appearance of having rating system integrity. This also made a joke of the Air Force's self-righteous admonition of "Integrity in all we do!" Yeah, except for efficiency reports, that is. I gagged every time I wrote my own OER, as all raters required. They didn't have time to write them, and they were nearly irrelevant anyway, so why bother—have the ratee do the work and make a few changes if necessary.

This ridiculous charade prevailed long before I came on the scene and has persisted to the present-day Air Force where I recently saw an *Air Force Times* article citing the need for integrity in the APR system. Left unsaid was that this would be for the "Integrity first!" Air Force.

So in 1975–76, the Air Force devised a method to put some integrity back into the OER system. The system would be converted from high ratings of "9" to making a "1" the highest rating. Then, by edict, every rater would have to award no more than 25% "1"s, 25% "2"s, and the remaining bottom 50% as "3"s. Or, as the designers insisted, these would be "promotable threes," another laughable stipulation. Since I had four 1st Lieutenants to rate, a copilot, two navigators, and an EW, I could award one "one," one "two," and two promotable (ho, ho, ho) "threes."

The award of the "one" rating would be easy. Hands down, it had to go to Boonie Bill, dropper of best bombs on our first ORI. But then it got very dicey. The EW generally would not be competitive due to his relatively minor role on the crew (unless hostile fighters were about, of course) and Buddy wasn't staying in the service anyway, so it didn't matter if he got a "three." This left the toss-up between the navigator and copilot for the "two" rating.

Do we see the problem here? The nav had been a primary producer of the ORI success teamed with Boonie Bill, but the copilot had saved our lives low level (to be covered shortly). And, the vital complication, I was cavorting with the navigator's wife, and the copilot's wife knew it, since she had made the initial approach to me. That meant the copilot probably knew, or would for sure once his wife found out if he got a "three" while the navigator got a "two." I'm unclear if the copilot's wife knew of the navigator's complicity in the festivities, but that would not matter on this issue. I was "doing" the navigator's wife, and that irrevocably tainted any rationale I used to award a rating. The Venus fly trap was feasting on me now.

There were other objective considerations, however. The copilot often displayed a contrary negative attitude toward the Air Force and its strictures. His favorite expletive for something he disliked was "mo-ther humping!" While we all had some heartburn with the system, the copilot delighted in carping about it, something that would not serve him well as an aircraft commander and did not help my efforts to keep the crew tuned up for the mission. I would have to mollify the crew after the copilot had gone on a rant about something we had been tasked to do unfairly in his view. The nav had proved much more compliant with the system and had produced well in his position. I thought he, too, would make an excellent radar navigator when it came time to upgrade (and he did). The navigator, my cuckold buddy, got the "two" and the copilot got the "three." And then all hell broke loose.

This hell would be compounded by an additional problem beyond the self-inflicted one from my relationship with nav wife. The wing swore it would hold all aircraft commanders to the strict rating percentages demanded by the Air Force. Each aircraft commander's integrity would be tested by this task, and he'd better meet the rank-ordered standard, commanders insisted. This, of course, was a lie. This vaunted attempt to instill integrity into the system could not survive even a single iteration before collapsing. While I met the standards, almost every other aircraft commander did not and awarded all his ratees "one"s without repercussions. Almost every one of those lying bastards said their crew really was the best there was and deserved all "one"s.

Oh, I retorted, you've had best bombs on an ORI? I seem to have missed that. Just what did you do that would trump that, especially since I met the OER standard and you ignored it?

There were other problems the designers did not allow for in their standards. Some units, such as test pilot squadrons, had all top-rated performers; that is why they were there. They were an all-star team that would have to rank-order the all-stars like everyone else, something that would be destructive and prove an impediment to recruiting test pilots, since 50% of them knew they would get screwed on their OER. If they stayed in a standard line squadron, they'd get a "one"; if they dared to join a test pilot squadron, they'd stand an excellent chance of getting a "three," especially on their first rating.

So great was the hue and cry from the force, that the "One, Two, Three" OER inflated to all "one"s in three years. I got two "one"s during the effective two-year run, one for my crew's first ORI performance, and one for being a stan/eval pilot the next year. Fortunately for me, the system reverted to a completely inflated joke by year three, when I fell to the bottom of the seniority ladder as a new instructor pilot at Castle AFB, CA, where I surely would have received a "three" as a new guy.

Back on the initial rating period with my first crew, I was not only a goat with the copilot for not "looking out for a fellow pilot," but, in addition, with my entire crew, since all their contemporaries had received "one"s from their frigging low-life aircraft commanders who folded on the integrity front and gave all top ratings without repercussions. (I did not make my initial mistake the second year; it was all "one"s for everyone.) So incensed did the copilot become, toward me and toward the navigation team that "stole his 'two' rating," that the crew could not function effectively and suffered acrimony just beneath the surface during each flight.

Mercifully, the wing soon promoted me to S-03 with a new stan/eval crew. My former copilot, if he knew the score, had shown mercy on me by not revealing my conflict of interest in the ratings. I thought, and still think, I rated as I should have, but there would be no explaining cavorting with a ratee's wife, regardless of the license I had been granted by hubby. I'd have been hung from the yardarm.

NEAR-DEATH EXPERIENCES

Around the time my two pilot training IPs died in aircraft crashes, I nearly did, too—twice.

The first episode took place on a routine takeoff from Loring and proved a near replay of the 1969 crash described earlier. As we rolled down the runway, we barely made our acceleration check, a certain speed that must be reached by a certain elapsed time or the takeoff must be aborted in order to stop in the remaining runway.

This alarmed me because we usually beat the time easily. After eating up eight thousand feet of the eleven-thousand-foot runway, we remained thirty knots below rotation speed and were barely accelerating. Something was terribly wrong. I had pulled several of the throttles back slightly to match the prescribed takeoff power setting, but I now shoved all of them to the firewall. At least they'd know we gave it everything we had if we didn't make it.

I looked down the remaining runway at the pine forest off the end, where it seemed we were about to meet a fiery and apocalyptic end. At this point, my mind began going haywire. Viewing the remaining three thousand feet of runway, I thought, in rising panic, that I could easily stop my car in this distance and perhaps I should try to abort on the runway. Fortunately, I also recalled an imperative John, my Castle IP, had impressed on me: "When in doubt, continue the takeoff." John's advice saved us, because if I had as much as touched the brakes, we'd have died horribly in that pine forest.

206

As the end of the runway approached, I experienced my life flashing before my eyes — in an odd form. I pictured my family members and Boonie Bill's dogs for some crazy reason and marveled, almost serenely, that I now knew where I would die—right off the end of this runway. At the last possible second, I pulled the yoke back hard into my stomach, not knowing if the plane had enough airspeed to respond. It did. We blew all the dust off the overrun and limped into the air barely above the treetops. I briefly considered ordering the crew to bail out since I still didn't know what was wrong or if we could gain airspeed and stay airborne, probably the same dilemma that confronted the aircraft commander in the 1969 crash. But I realized the navigators, with downward ejection seats, did not have enough altitude for a successful escape. No, we would all make it or not, unless we approached a stall. At that point, I'd have to try to save the four of us upstairs, at least, and order the bailout.

When we turned onto the seventeen-mile arc as per the departure procedure, we were only 2,500 feet above the terrain. We should have been at ten thousand. The copilot's eyes were wide as saucers when I dared to look at him. We had both thought we were dead. I aborted the mission, burned down my fuel to the maximum for landing, and put it on the deck with a demand for maintenance to meet us at the parking spot.

Upon later inspection, it turned out maintenance had mistakenly trimmed the four outboard engines to produce about 5% less than their full power. We might have caught this, but we normally concentrated on the two center-engine instruments that showed proper settings. The reduced outboard engine thrust was just sufficient to make our acceleration check but not enough to make our rotation speed before the end of the runway. Fortunately, the engines provided just enough power to save our skins.

That night, I visited the pizza restaurant not quite a mile off the end of the runway and just off the extended centerline. I sat down at the bar in my flight suit, but before I could speak, the owner exclaimed loudly to me that some idiot pilot almost tore the roof off the place that morning. I told him, yes, I know, and I knew exactly who that idiot was.

The second episode happened on a night low level over South Carolina. Things started on a shaky note. As the crew bus pulled up to the aircraft, I noticed the Deputy Commander for Maintenance (DCM) standing in front of the plane. This meant he would probably try to talk me into taking some maintenance problem they couldn't fix. Sure enough, that is what he did.

He explained the plane had experienced runaway nose-up trim, where pitch controls ran to the upper limit, un-commanded, resulting in a sharp aircraft pitch-up while low level on its previous mission. He said they had replaced every part they could think of, but they never discovered what the problem had been, a classic C&D (could not duplicate) write-up. At any rate, would I take the plane? I thought a pitch-up would not be catastrophic, even low level. Besides, they had probably fixed the problem, since they could not duplicate it. Sure, I said, we'll take it.

The B-52 has a large, striped trim wheel by the aircraft commander's right knee to make it obvious when the wheel is turning and the trim control device is running. The wheel often rotates steadily during configuration changes, such as putting down the flaps or landing gear. Having been warned that the trim flight controls might incorrectly run to the full nose up position, causing the plane to suddenly climb steeply, as it had before, I watched that wheel for unanticipated motion throughout the thirty minutes of the low-level run and on the first simulated bomb run. Nothing unusual happened. I mentally declared the problem solved, relieved to be done with it. I gave the copilot the plane for a climbing turn to the racetrack pattern used to set up for a second bomb run.

As the aircraft climbed from five hundred to eight hundred feet above the ground, I later vaguely recalled the trim wheel moving steadily. This was not unusual since we were slowing and climbing, and that would require a trim change. I did not notice that the trim was running the wrong direction, nose down, instead of the proper nose up. As the copilot leveled off at eight hundred feet, and I was busy reviewing my low-level chart, the aircraft suddenly snapped nose *down* ten degrees, a horrendous and panic-inducing loss of control that promised to kill us all in about ten seconds as the moonlit pine forest below us filled the windscreen and rushed toward us.

Reflexively, I grabbed the yoke and pulled, but nothing happened. It felt as if someone had poured concrete on it; it would not budge. That is because the copilot had already pulled the yoke to the full nose-up position and it could not move any farther. The low-level autopilot mode, which approximates power steering in a car, had tried to compensate for runaway nose-down trim. When it could no longer cope with the severe out-of-trim condition, it abruptly disconnected, allowing the out-of-trim condition to take effect and allowing the nose to drop precipitously. The horizontal stabilizer on the tail, having trimmed full nose down, could not be overcome by the relatively less effective elevator controls that the copilot had already pulled to the full-up position. Our inability to raise the nose resulted from the same B-52 flight characteristic that prevented me from rotating in the flare during my first attempted landing with Lucky Luciano.

From the deck below, the navigators fairly screamed in the interphone, demanding to know what was wrong. They needed four hundred feet above the ground and level flight to get one swing in their parachute before they would hit the ground. We were now diving at the ground and closing on four hundred feet. By my command or not, they would have to eject shortly to save themselves. I tried to get my index finger to the interphone toggle on the yoke but could not manage it because I was pulling so hard on the immovable yoke. Even if I had been able to transmit, I couldn't have told them anything, because I didn't know what was wrong. Not knowing the copilot had already pulled the yoke to the full up position, I tried to grasp why the yoke would not move. Within a few seconds, I'd have to give the bailout command.

Fortunately, the copilot recognized that the trim was probably the problem since he was flying the aircraft when it ran away. He immediately began running his trim button nose up against the runaway nose-down command from the trim system. Slowly, he managed to overcome the erroneous command and to raise the trim to a slight nose-up position. As the aircraft nose rose above the horizon, I disconnected the automatic trim system for the remainder of the flight. From then on, I would trim manually with the trim wheel by my knee. Fool me once, shame on you.

The copilot, having saved our bacon, now hit the panic button and started shouting, "Mayday, mayday, mayday!" on the air traffic control frequency. I tried to stop him because I now, a few seconds belatedly, realized what had happened and knew we were OK once I killed the trim system.

Unfortunately, every aircraft and air traffic controller for a hundred miles started asking us for our situation. I couldn't just say, "Oh, never mind," so I explained we had suffered a runaway trim situation low level but we had now disconnected the system and seemed to be OK. Several aircraft continued to query us, apparently indignant that we had invoked the mayday distress code if we didn't need help. I explained that the call was justified but that we had regained control, so no aid would be required. This would be the only "mayday" call I heard in thirty-three years of flying, and it was my aircraft that made it.

I called Loring on HF radio and told the command post that the aircraft stood us on our nose, low level, but we seemed to have it under control and were aborting the mission and RTB-ing (returning to base). The DCM got to meet us that morning for our landing at 0400 to apologize for the aircraft he gave us. I'm sure he had the wing commander's footprint on his ass.

COLONEL PATTERSON, EXEMPLARY LEADER

My Loring DCO from 1975 to 1977, Col. Ken Patterson, wins the award as one of my three commanders over thirty-three years to win best in show. Patterson could don the insufferably superior full colonel aura as well as any for a stern commander's visage, but his normal demeanor was friendly, good-natured, and with a mischievous sense of humor. He treated subordinates as intellectual equals during discussions and never used his rank to bludgeon us into obedience. He carried a small notebook with a spiral wire on the top in which to take notes and develop his to-do list. This was decades before Day-Timers became ever present in the force.

Patterson kept this demeanor despite being ensnared in the 24/7 pressure cooker that was a SAC command position. There was no escape from this asylum. If you were awake, the command post had you on a short leash every minute of every day. If you were asleep, they could wake you up at any hour to put you back on that leash. If any crew or crew member screwed up, it would be Patterson's screw up, and he would suffer for it. Unfortunately, he served under an imperious jerk of a wing commander (to be dealt with shortly), yet even this did not despoil his bright, optimistic personality. I'd have followed him anywhere and done anything he demanded of me.

While trapped in the alert facility, we kept constant watch on the parking lot a hundred yards outside the facility's front door, across the street on a small hill. When a white-topped staff car arrived and parked there, we got our tip-off that the Klaxon was about to blow to send us scrambling to our aircraft. One of the colonels would observe the scramble from this optimum vantage point. One day, Patterson's staff car pulled into the lot, and the word spread rapidly throughout the facility. Sure enough, a few minutes later, the Klaxon blew and away we went, racing to our alert six-man pickup trucks.

For this particular exercise, the aircraft were located on a temporary alert pad used while the regular pad was being resurfaced. This area of the ramp had been surrounded by a chain-link fence, and this would be the first Klaxon alert with aircraft in this area.

An alert engine start is all frantic motion and noise, somewhat like a NASCAR pit stop. Each crew's alert vehicle speeds to the pad through the main guarded entrance and pulls in next to their aircraft behind one of the wing tips. The crew scrambles out of the truck and races to the entry hatch beneath the fuselage while the crew chief runs to pull the wheel chocks. Within seconds of the pilots disappearing up the hatch, the engine start sequence begins. Gas cartridges are exploded into the two center engines—#4 and #5— to spin them up to speed as they gush gray cordite smoke that envelops those engines. As soon as these two engines reach power, the other six engines begin to spin simultaneously as bleed air from #4 and #5 surges through the wing ducts to reach them. In quick succession, engines from all four to six bombers on alert begin screaming in unison. The senior crew is supposed to taxi first, but if any other aircraft is ready to go and lead has not moved, they can call on command post frequency that they are taxiing. ("Bongo-Three is rolling!") Then the elephant walk commences to make the fifteen-minute timing to cross the hold line before taxiing back to the parking spots.

This particular alert would not be a "mover," just an engine start. That proved sufficient for drama, however. First, the copilot had an incorrect switch setting for the cartridge start. All eight engine starter switches on his side panel had to be turned off when we left the plane. His imperative first step upon his ass hitting his seat was to flick all eight toggles up to the "start" position. He had not done this when I fired the cartridges. If the two inner engine starter switches were not up, the engines would spool down after the cartridges had discharged and we would miss our timing waiting for a power cart to start, a blasphemous error that would have me chewing carpet in the wing commander's office. The copilot caught the error just in time, ramming the switches into position as we held our breath to see if the engines would continue to accelerate or reverse course and start to spin down, catastrophically. They caught, continued to accelerate, and we were saved.

After the engines were all at idle and we had established our timing, Col. Patterson's staff car came creeping down the centerline of the pad toward our aircraft. He stopped in front of us and came up on the command post frequency. "Capt. Lacklen, you've blown down the fence behind you; what are your intentions?" I didn't yet know Patterson well enough to know he was mischievously pulling my chain. I wondered if he wanted me to send my crew out to fix the fence.

"I, ah, guess we'll put it back up, sir," I said. That is when he laughed and said that would not be necessary, and I knew he was playfully toying with me, rare humor in a command usually devoid of humor.

An alert crew change-out went dreadfully wrong soon after. At the end of a seven-day alert tour, the off-going crew meets the oncoming crew to swap control of the aircraft and nuclear weapons.

As the oncoming crew, we reported to the aircraft currently under control of the crew commanded by Capt. "War Eagle" (an Auburn University grad who repeatedly informed everyone he was a war eagle). War Eagle seemed irritated and in a hurry as we discussed airplane problems on the ramp next to the plane.

Once we finished our discussion, my crew climbed aboard and began our acceptance preflight of the aircraft and weapons. The nav team inspected the thermonuclear weapons in the bomb bay, four silver cylinders about eight feet long and two feet wide, the B-28FI (Fusing Internal) four-pack alignment set at 1.1 megatons each. For comparison, the atomic bomb dropped on Hiroshima, Japan was about 15 kilotons.

The copilot and I climbed up to the cockpit for our preflight. This included pulling closed the silver nuclear flash curtains across the cockpit windows and inspecting them for light leaks. On the nuclear bomb mission low-level route, only the curtain in front of the pilot flying would be opened to prevent any nuclear detonation flashes in front of the plane from blinding the crew. The pilot flying would also wear an eye patch so he'd lose only one eye in the flash from such an explosion.

The pilots would also have to place a canvas cover over the windscreen to keep snow and ice at bay since there would be no time to clear the windows in an alert. One of us would have to sit on the side window ledge with our torso outside the cockpit to throw the cover across the front windows, pull it tight, and close the side windows on the canvas flaps. For an alert, one of us would have to madly pull the frozen, snow-encrusted canvas into the cockpit before we could taxi. Just throwing it off onto the ramp was not an option since it might get sucked into one of the engines. This preflight inspection took about thirty minutes.

When we were done, I told the crew chief to tell War Eagle we were ready for the switchover. The crew chief said the words I knew meant we were in trouble: "The other crew is gone, sir."

"Oh, shit," I said on interphone. I now instructed the crew to get off the aircraft and into the truck quickly because we were illegally on the plane if our crew orders had not been delivered to the aircraft sentry.

Everyone made it past the guard but me. The guard looked at my name tag, then at the authorizing order he held in his hand. I was not on the orders. "Halt!" he commanded while lowering his M-16 rifle at my chest. "Raise your hands, sir, and order your crew back here!"

When War Eagle departed before our orders had arrived, he left me illegally on *his* aircraft. He got away; I did not. The sentry keyed his radio and shouted, "Helping hand! Helping Hand! Alert Spot one!" Helping Hand means a possible nuclear procedure compromise has occurred, and the entire base security community goes into action. The base gates are closed, the wing staff alerted, and a small army of security police are dispatched to the area. As that small army arrived, the sentry had my crew aligned in front of him with our legs spread and our hands in the air. The shift supervisor, a master sergeant, listened to the guard's explanation and looked at War Eagle's orders. He knew this was just a screw up and not a true emergency, but he decided to conduct a training exercise for the half-dozen troops he had brought with him and to assert his temporary authority at my expense. This meant a weapons search of the commander—me—as a demonstration. As he prepared for this, Col. Patterson and the supervisor of flying arrived to observe.

The sergeant stepped behind me and kicked my right foot instep firmly, causing me to "spread them" even more, something he probably dearly loved doing. He then patted me down for weapons. That demonstration completed, he walked back in front of the crew and ordered us face down on a snow-packed ramp between my aircraft and the next alert bird.

Col. Patterson's face contorted in an attempt to suppress laughter. He apparently found humor in one of his crews face down in the snow for a procedural screw up. Now Patterson got on his radio to tell the command post that Capt. War Eagle needed to report immediately to his alert aircraft because his premature departure had precipitated a Helping Hand.

War Eagle had reportedly just gotten to his base quarters and dragged the wife to bed when the phone rang. The command post chief read him the riot act and told him Col. Patterson awaited him at the aircraft to explain why Lacklen's crew was spread-eagled in the snow. War Eagle now replicated my frantic dressing routine when I was caught "off base" on alert on Guam. Mercifully, Patterson terminated the Helping Hand and let us get up, dust off, and return to the alert facility. My only regret is not being in the room when Patterson confronted War Eagle. As an aside, War Eagle was one of my fellow aircraft commanders who claimed inappropriate justification for awarding all "one" ratings to his crew.

215

I got a small measure of revenge on the security master sergeant. On a later alert tour, my aircraft security guard went bonkers, jammed his M-16 barrel-first into a snow bank, and began a snowball fight with the guard on the adjoining plane. I decided to try to save the security police a wing-level incident and called the command post to have the master sergeant report to the alert pad immediately. A moment later, the command post relayed that the sergeant would not come out unless I explained why it was necessary. Idiot. He should have read between the lines of the message, kept his mouth shut, and sprinted out to us. Having given him the opportunity to avoid a professional disaster, I explained exactly why he needed to be out here. Soon the small army arrived to cart away the offending guards and to explain this inexcusable lapse to the wing commander.

My next encounter with Col. Patterson would not be quite as humorous.

SAC ALERT STANDUP

SAC had a demanding regimen. In the days of mutually assured destruction, it had to; civilization depended upon it.

One of these regimens proved powerfully effective: alert crew standup, which put all the deputy commanders, ops, maintenance, and base commander under the gun in front of the alert crews. This situational reversal revealed many problems that otherwise would not have surfaced.

On a designated day, the wing commander would stand before the crews on a raised platform or stage and ask a simple question: Does anyone have any mission-related problems?

Arrayed in front of the wing commander were the three deputy commanders, who also faced the crews. When a crewmember raised a question, the appropriate deputy commander would explain to the crews, and to the wing commander, what he was doing about this problem. This reversal of the chain of command, where the crews got to grill the deputies in front of the wing commander, got the job done.

The day prior to the alert standup, the deputies would ask the salient question of their troops to discover the problems, to avoid having some issue sprung on them unexpectedly, and embarrassingly, in front of the boss.

In most cases, there were few questions for the wing commander and no surprises because the threat of embarrassment drove the deputies to root out and deal with the issues before they became public. Mission accomplished.

However, with my crew, this method exploded all over me at one standup. Col. Patterson, chomping on his cigar, gathered us together the day before the standup to field questions to avoid being blindsided in front of the wing commander. There were a few, but none that would cause a problem. Operations was good to go, Patterson and I thought.

At standup the next day, the wing commander asked all the alert crews sternly if there were any problems. To my utter astonishment, I saw a hand rise to my right, down the row where my crew sat.

Col. Patterson and I both did a double take to see *my navigator* rising to ask his question, a question he did not seem concerned about the day before.

"Sir," he complained, "why are we planning so much wasteful deadhead time into our missions?"

AAAAAAH! This was a nuclear-tipped torpedo shot straight into Patterson! I saw his cigar bob up and down aggressively as if he wanted to stub it out on my navigator's forehead. Instead, he gave a plausible answer about constraints that had to be met and progress he had made reducing such "wasted" time.

After coming to attention as the wing commander and staff departed, my navigator's face turned ashen as I stalked down the row with my hair on fire to find out *what the fuck he thought he was doing*, and if it was so fucking important, why didn't he ask it the day before? I told him I now had to face Patterson's wrath for an out-of-control crew member, and thanks, you frigging moron! This would be the first of only a handful of times in thirty-three years I would lose my temper in the Air Force.

Patterson, in his marvelous manner, took great glee in my distress and let me fluster on for a few sentences of apology before he started laughing. This seemed a penchant of his.

LIFE ON NUCLEAR ALERT

An alert tour lasted seven days, to be followed by four days of "C2," or C-square, time off. For the entire week, beginning on Thursday, my crew and I would be confined to the alert facility except for officially sanctioned excursions outside the facility on the base. These would include offices or training facilities, the BX, or the base theater. We had to be prepared to react immediately to a Klaxon, either by the siren going off, or even an official saying the words, "Klaxon, Klaxon, Klaxon!" Once notified, we had fifteen minutes to have our plane started up and taxied across the runway hold line. If we were standing in the alert facility in our flight suits, this could be done fairly easily. If we happened to be asleep in our beds, or in the shower with shampoo in our hair, things got dicey, especially if it was −20°F outside.

A number of times the Klaxon went off at inopportune times, such as at night, and things did not go well. When the ear-shattering horn went off and bright red hallway lights began flashing, crew members would leap out of their beds, not realizing where they were, and run into the closet, the wall, or each other in their panicked haste to meet the timing. Uniforms would be laid out in easy reach for quick donning, but even then this could slow down the process, as I had discovered in the BOQ on Guam.

One afternoon, when I was not on alert, I heard the Klaxon sound as I left the personnel center. An alert crew had just pulled up in their truck and had not heard the Klaxon. I ran to them and told them the Klaxon had gone off and to respond to their plane. They stared at me in terrified bewilderment, unsure of the official certification of the notification due to the method of delivery. Seeing their confusion, I shouted: "I'm Captain Lacklen. Klaxon, Klaxon, Klaxon!" That was all they needed, and away they went.

Seven days trapped with your crew could prove irritating, even among friends. After several episodes of playing a crew game of "Risk," where everyone moves their armies around a map of the world attacking other forces, I had to outlaw the game. Various crew players made side agreements not to attack each other only to have one renege on the offer and attack anyway. More than one board had been flipped into the air in rage by an offended player, and that soured the entire crew.

In the middle 1970s, this facility had a lame excuse for a family visitation area, a room about the size of a large office. Kids rampaged noisily, babies cried, and spouses tried to conduct family business above the din. I would occasionally eye-lock briefly with nav wife as I walked by, but I seldom had to enter since I wasn't married and didn't have a family.

There was separation of the species, with tanker crews on one side of the facility and bombers on the other. The facility connected through double doors to the bomber and tanker squadron areas, so alert crews often hung out in the squadron for most of the day working on their additional duties. This also meant if stan/eval wanted to test the crews, there was no escape. As the daily 0800 briefing concluded, a stan/eval member would advise the crews to remain in their seats for emergency procedure testing, and everyone would grimace. As on many other inspection items, the best you could do was break even by passing, and I would be forced to recall the nightmare of my Bold Print bust as a stan/eval copilot two years before.

Another mind-numbing exercise involved a page count of the Dash-1, or B-52 flight manual, in its five-hundred-page length. Updates to the manual came in piecemeal over the year with specific dates on the specific pages replaced. About once every six months, the alert crews would go through the entire manual, page by frigging page, having a stan/eval pilot up front reading the page and date: "Page 3-103, 2 Aug 71; page 3-104, 15 Sep 69;" and so on for all five hundred pages. Now, in 2012, the whole mess is going electronic. Thank the gods.

About twice a year, we would have to certify our nuclear mission before the wing commander and his staff. He would listen and ask questions if necessary as we explained all the facets of our mission that would strike targets in the Russian heartland. Each crew position took its turn. Generally we had been well briefed by the current ops officer, who was responsible for getting us ready for presentation and for questions the commander had asked in the past. I remember that the laid-back country boy commander when I was a copilot occasionally fell asleep as the crew briefed. We just pressed on as if he were awake and realized he'd be hard-pressed to ask questions on material he had missed.

C-square provided a welcome break, but often we would be restricted to within a certain mileage of the base if we had not yet flown the semi-annual ORI so the wing could have all its crews available. Since we were located an eight-hour drive north of Boston, this meant traveling to see parents or relatives was impossible until after the ORI.

Second ORI

A subsequent ORI proved nearly disastrous for my crew, the wing, and for Col. Patterson. The wing commander at the time, a strutting, egotistical jerk, nearly wrecked the entire inspection. His preening self-confidence and arrogant self-assurance played well with the headquarters brass but grated on the crews that would write his report card on the inspection.

The ORI route created for this inspection wound through the flat eastern portion of Nebraska. This made it difficult to find easily identifiable land formations for the navigators to work with. Several wings busted their ORI on this route, the worst carnage I had witnessed on such an inspection.

An unsatisfactory rating had severe repercussions, as I outlined previously. Shortly after a wing received a failing grade, the wing commander, ops commander, and maintenance commander all packed their bags and left the base, fired and disgraced. No questions, no excuses; you fail, you are gone, and your career is over.

This ORI started catastrophically. The first crew, S-01, with the assistant ops group commander (ADO), a Lt. Col., in the jump seat, got lost in the route. The nav team reported to the aircraft commander that they were disoriented, and could the pilot team help by looking for landmarks to help the navigators relocate their position.

As a backup, pilots studied the route for visual clues for such an eventuality. This method seldom proved reliable, but in a pinch, might help.

The ADO, feeling he knew what needed to be done, took command and ordered the crew to turn at his direction. Unfortunately, he didn't know where they were and directed them out of the route corridor, an egregious breach seen on radar by the inspectors, who flashed a "four zulus" message to the base command post. A code zulu meant the S-01 crew had violated route boundaries and had been "shot down," all their bombs now counting as bad.

Back in the command post, the news of four "zulu" bombs caused a spectacular and unconscionable reaction from the wing commander. With four bad bombs from the first, and supposedly best, aircraft and crew, the unit could have only one additional bad bomb in the following thirteen airplanes to pass the ORI. It appeared the show was over in the wing commander's estimation, so he went out blazing.

He first took his "brick" (hand-held radio, at the time about the size of a brick) and threw it twenty feet against the back wall of the command post, shattering the device to pieces. He then angrily fired everyone in the command post, including Col. Patterson, standing nearby, everyone on the S-01 crew, to include the ADO, berated everyone in earshot for "disloyalty" and for ruining his career, stomped out of the building, and went home . . . in the middle of an ORI. Once home, his anger at this perceived betrayal not quenched, he called on a landline, now hysterically angry, and fired everyone again.

The gods on Olympus could not have orchestrated a better dénouement for jerk commander. There were no further zulu bombs from the rest of the force, and we passed. Celebrations were tempered with scorn for the commander who bailed out on us when the going got tough. Even his later contrived groveling before the crews could not save him from his outrageous betrayal of the team in the command post. The crews and the base bailed out on him for his sacrilege.

Two years later, in a rare example of Air Force poetic justice, the wing commander and Col. Patterson vied for the numbered Air Force command at Barksdale AFB, LA. The board selected Patterson over the wing commander who had "fired" him two years previously, a perfect comeuppance for the prima donna abandoning the wing and crews in the middle of the ORI.

I did not escape damage on this ORI, either, as I erred in a similar manner to the jump seat lieutenant colonel's error on the S-01 crew. In ORI preparation, the pilots study the route and especially the target locations so, if required, they can drop the bomb visually in case of a bomb system radar failure. On this particular route, our visual pictures of the first target showed it directly over an open mine shaft that had scaffolding next to it. You couldn't miss it, and I didn't.

As we approached the first target, Boonie Bill said he had it wired and took control of the aircraft heading with his equipment to drop the "bomb." Approaching the target, however, I saw the mine shaft and derrick a few hundred yards to the left of the course we were flying. I asked Bill if he was sure he had it because I saw the target left of our course. He assured me he did have it locked with no problem.

I then violated crew rule number one for bomb runs: you never take aircraft control away from a radar navigator who says he has it locked, especially from Boonie Bill. I said, "We're missing it to the right, pilot's aircraft," and I banked left and called the drop directly over the mine shaft. We then went time and heading to the second bomb release. I thought either method would be reliable, but I wanted best bombs again and, my God, the target was right there!

Except, sadly, the target was not "right there." The intel shop officer who plotted the target had winged it and only provided an "estimated" position, something they did not explain as they gave us the pictures to study. On replot, the target was right where Boonie Bill said it was and not over the mine shaft. In violating rule number one, I had dropped on a bogus target. Yes, both bombs were "good," but we had the worst bomb scores of the entire wing (save the poor S-01 crew), heroes-to-goats in one ORI, thanks to me and the bonehead intel officer who didn't warn me he was winging it on the bomb plot picture.

The stan/eval crews now smirked at us at the post-ORI party at the club. "Beginners' luck" they claimed for the previous ORI, and I had to eat yet another shit sandwich for Boonie Bill and my crew, who had to suffer the slings and arrows of their compatriots for our poor performance as a result of my error.

A Son's Salute

During the summer of 1975, I got a chance to salute my mother with a flyby, of sorts, near her childhood home of Somerset, KY. She had returned home to be with her mother in my grandmother's final days, and I happened to be flying a mission on the Richmond, KY, bomb site on a route that circled Somerset. I thought a minor flight plan deviation would not ruffle any feathers and would provide a richly deserved tribute to my formative parent.

My mother harbored a lurking insecurity since marrying my father. She came from a small town and had two years at a nearby junior college, while my father had a master's degree from Stanford. It seemed she spent her married life trying to measure up by neutralizing her Kentucky accent, expanding her vocabulary, and pushing to get her kids accepted in ambitious social circles. The marriage had failed some years before, and she feared this had damaged her children.

Years later, I told her that, had I become a POW in Vietnam, I'd have warned my captors that they would have to flee for their lives when my mother found out they had me, that she would rip the scraggly hairs off Ho Chi Minh's chin to get me released. She protected us as a mother bear would her cubs and would throw herself between us and any force she felt threatened or endangered us. She didn't have a master's, but she had moxie and determination, and some of that rubbed off on me. She deserved a salute from her firstborn, and I planned to give her one.

I told her I might be overflying and that I'd have the local flight service station call as we approached. The flight service station controller seemed to be getting a kick out of arranging things, and air traffic control approved our slight diversion as we exited the route.

We flew at three thousand feet, high enough not to rattle windows, but low enough to be clearly seen. Suddenly, flight service had hooked me up to the house phone and said, "Your mother is on the phone, Phantom Six-Zero, go ahead."

Dumbfounded, I could only think to blurt out, "Hi, Mom."

She asked how soon we would pass over, and I said in about three minutes. She said they had to walk up the street to the top of the hill to see through the trees, but she would be there on time.

Three minutes later we overflew the edge of town, and I dipped the wings slowly left, then right. A few seconds later, I pushed up the throttles, the engines roared, and I started the climb out of the route.

I like to think she felt some measure of awe, pride, and wonder, remembering her little boy—who had played with toy trucks in the corner by himself, been horribly shy, wet the bed, and stuttered—and had just flown over her in a giant aircraft to pay homage to the mother bear who had protected him, prepared him, and allowed him to soar.

DANCING WITH INTERCEPTORS

One of the few times we got to maneuver forcefully at high altitude was during intercepts by Air Defense Command interceptor fighters, which included the F-102 and F-106 from the USAF, and the F-14 from the US Navy. Later, in the C-5, I had intercepts run on me, without maneuvering, by NATO fighters that were usually F-16s or British Tornadoes as we flew across Europe. I enjoyed the American intercepts in the B-52 because we got to "dance" with the fighter boys. As the interceptor checked in on frequency, I would tell him we were ready and "had our dancing shoes on."

As the intercept began, the EW would call the range and clock position of the fighter, such as "eight o'clock, ten miles," so I would know where he was and when to maneuver. The F-102s and F-106s proved the easiest to shake. They would come smoking in on us at high speed, but below Mach 1, and line up directly behind us at our six o'clock position, which is the missile launch or cannon firing position. I would push our speed up to three hundred knots or so to keep him at high speed as he approached. When the EW called his position about three miles at a high rate of closure, I would roll into forty-five degrees of bank, pull the throttles to idle, and raise the speed brakes. Then I would pull hard, putting the bomber into a tight decelerating turn. This would invariably cause the F-102 or F-106 to badly overshoot, since with swept wings, designed for high speed, they had greatly degraded turning capability. The long B-52 wings and spoiler deployment allowed a far tighter turn than the F-100 series fighters could manage, and we invariably "lost" them with this maneuver.

The Navy F-14, however, flown by "nasal radiators," kicked our ass. The Tomcat could sweep its wings forward to nearly seventy degrees from its swept-wing, high-speed configuration and match my best turn, which infuriated me. Most incredibly, the Tomcat, of the movie *Top Gun* and "Maverick" fame, got immediately on our "six" despite coming at us head on and having to turn 180 degrees for his initial approach, while the Air Force interceptors had arrived from behind to begin with, a great advantage. As the F-14 swung behind us and approached, my EW, Buddy, called his position as "six o'clock, three miles." Going into my maneuver, I racked the B-52 into a steep turn, groaning at the g-forces I put on the plane. The EW, however, made the maddening call, "Target six o'clock, one mile," repeatedly from the time I broke into the turn until I rolled out, defeated. The Tomcat stayed in perfect formation with me one mile behind in perfect shooting position. At this point, had I been in a B-1 perhaps, I could have gone to afterburner and left the F-14 far behind. The standard complaint for the F-14 was poor acceleration from low speed, as the wings were swept back for high speed from the extended position. The ratio of relatively low power to relatively high aircraft weight made acceleration an all-day thing in a dogfight. The added weight was necessary to provide beefed-up landing gear structures for punishing carrier landings, but it hampered acceleration from low speed.

But for purposes of this combat exercise, the F-14 would have shot us down easily, had our gunner not shot him down first. If he used a missile from ten miles or so behind us, he'd have nailed us; if he had to come into cannon range, however, our fifty-caliber rear cannon might have nailed him first. This is another reason why we knew we would fly our nuke mission low level, so the fighters would have a difficult time even finding us against the ground clutter.

Minimum Interval Takeoff (MITO) Training

One of the most insane maneuvers we practiced in SAC was the MITO, where we would take off fifteen seconds behind the preceding B-52 to practice our wartime departure procedures. We all had to get into the air within fifteen minutes, so this type of takeoff was necessary. However, it led to frantic thrashing of the yoke and rudders to maintain some semblance of control in the direct jet wash of the preceding plane. I clearly recall having full right turn commands with the flight controls and still rolling hard left as the vortices from the preceding plane put us temporarily out of control.

USAF Photo

MITO takeoff, hold on for dear life!

Fortunately, after a few seconds, we would escape the jet blast and recover control of the plane. We would then adjust our heading to fly a path different from the preceding planes to avoid subsequent interference. Once in the air, it was imperative to get away from the base as fast as possible since, for the actual wartime takeoff, one or more Soviet ICBMs would probably be en route to obliterate the home field in a nuclear detonation. We could assume that everything we had left, including our compatriots and families, would be irrevocably gone soon after our departure and there would be nothing left to return to.

ARK ROYAL/FALKLANDS WAR

In 1976, my crew flew as three-ship cell lead across the Atlantic to train in a mock scenario with the British aircraft carrier *Ark Royal*, their sole carrier, which would gain fame six years later in the British/Argentine Falklands War in the South Atlantic. This war displayed that America is not the only civilized country that can stride into a conflict half-cocked and for prideful reasons. In retrospect, I can't imagine what the Brits and Argentines were thinking at the time. However, I can't imagine what the two sides in the American Civil War were thinking, either.

Reality seized the Falkland combatants when, over two days, the Brits sank the Argentine light cruiser *General Belgrano* with submarine torpedoes, and the Argentines sank the *HMS Sheffield* with a long-range Exocet missile fired from an Argentine fighter. The burning *Belgrano* killed 320 Argentines, and the sinking Sheffield claimed twenty Brits. Both populations recoiled in horror that their easy little war had produced such carnage. They seemed aghast that their macho posturing in this little war game resulted in sailors from both sides burning to death horribly in their stricken ships. Both militaries seemed almost apologetic for what their oh-too-cool weapons had done to fellow first-world citizens. Again, the human reptilian brain stem coupled to high intelligence wreaked carnage on other humans.[15]

But this event happened years later; in 1976, the *Ark Royal* was the pride of the vastly reduced British fleet that once ruled the waves for Britannia. A small ship by American standards, it could not catapult-launch state-of-the-art fighters but instead relied on launching vertical takeoff/landing Harrier fighters off an up-sloped ramp.

We were supposed to fly to the eastern Atlantic near the British Isles to fly approaches to the *Ark Royal* as a training exercise. This proved a physically taxing mission.

The initial briefing took place at 0300 at Loring for the three bombers and four tankers that would refuel us over Newfoundland to allow us to make the double oceanic crossing with added time for the exercise. Knowing I had to arise at 0200 made it impossible to get to sleep, as I went to bed at 2100. I kept calculating how much sleep I would get if I fell asleep immediately, which discouraged me and prevented me going to sleep until about 2300. In the future, it seemed the three hours' sleep I finally got was my minimum for maximum crew days. If I got the three hours, I could hack it, I decided.

The briefing room crowd resembled an alert force briefing in size, and a gaggle of every colonel on base hovered around the briefing with concerned frowns on their face. This would be a very high-visibility mission, and SAC would be judging them by our performance. As lead B-52 aircraft commander, I briefed the assembled crews on takeoff, rendezvous for refueling, and the actual refueling prior to our departure across the ocean. My brain kept asking why we were doing this at 0300, and I had to tell it repeatedly to shut up and take it.

We managed to get all seven aircraft airborne on time, but conditions soon deteriorated. The weather on the refueling track over far eastern Canada initially did not allow sufficient visibility—two miles clear of clouds—to refuel. This threatened to terminate the entire mission. In addition, I had a deuce of a time trying to keep the tanker and bomber formations together while we searched for a break in the weather. At the beginning of the air refueling track, the four tankers were stacked up directly above my bomber formation. Buddy, my EW, had the only educated guess to exactly where they were with his electronic warfare equipment. It seemed a hopeless tangle as to who was where. Finally the weather provided the required two-mile visibility, and we formed our echelon line, the other bombers to my right and behind and below me, in line with my wing tip. The four tankers loomed before us in a similar formation.

I told the tankers we had them visually and requested clearance to the pre-contact position fifty feet behind them. As briefed, I would go first to tanker #2, and my bomber mates would begin on tankers #3 and #4. After fifteen minutes, we would drop back and move to the next tanker on the left. After I made the request, tanker lead cleared us in. That is where disaster almost struck. We all concentrated on our tanker as we closed, but #2 bomber was closing on the same tanker I was. This precise error had killed many previously, and would in the future. Blundering into another refueler aircraft probably killed my pilot training IP, John Booker, and also caused a horrendous C-141 accident in the 1990s. In the latter case, two C-141s maneuvering behind the tanker collided and tore the tail off one of the aircraft. During the nightmarish spiral into the ground from twenty thousand feet, the crew knew they would die for several minutes before they did. The plane's cockpit recorder contained the almost unbearable screams as the crew berated the pilot for having killed them.

There were two chances for us to escape this catastrophe. Either the tanker boom operator would see the two planes converging on each other, or my nameless copilot would catch the other plane out of the corner of his eye. The copilot again saved the day, as he realized #2 was rapidly closing on us. He called, "Knock it off!" and brought everyone to the realization of what was about to happen. After wiping the sweat from our brows, we reengaged and took the gas.

Approaching Ireland, however, I started losing oil pressure on my #1 engine and had to eventually shut it down. Not only would I not get to play with *Ark Royal*, I would have to land in England since, with the inoperative engine producing nothing but drag, I would not have enough fuel to return to Loring. SAC Headquarters directed me to land at Upper Heyford, England. I passed command to the #2 bomber's aircraft commander and left the formation before they descended. I slept like a dead man at Heyford.

I did get chances to chase ships, however. Twice I drew oceanic intercept missions, one to buzz and harass Russian spy trawlers over international waters, and one to fly approaches to a naval task force in the Atlantic. I suppose we were getting even with the Russians intercepting our planes over the Pacific or Alaska.

Nothing particularly interesting happened as we buzzed the Russian trawler. I'm sure they were infuriated, but we couldn't tell. The unusual aspect happened when I called Santa Maria Oceanic Control for my clearance back to Loring from a few hundred miles off the Portuguese coast. Santa Maria claimed they didn't have any clearance on me. I told them I would orbit at ten thousand feet and wait for them to find it. Five minutes later, they still claimed they didn't have one. That's when I pulled out my trump card. I told them if they didn't find that clearance in the next five minutes, I was declaring "Due Regard" and proceeding on my filed flight plan regardless of lack of clearance. I had to do this because I had just enough fuel to make it back to base. Being a B-52, I couldn't just land somewhere else for gas since everyone would think we had nukes on board and would freak out. I was going home with or without the clearance. Magically, Santa Maria immediately came up with my clearance!

I got in more trouble buzzing American ships in roughly the same area on a repeat mission. Before we buzzed the USN vessels, I asked how high their top mast was above the surface so I'd know how low I could fly on my radar altimeter. Surprisingly, they didn't know. I guess it depends upon how much fuel or cargo they are carrying and how low they are riding in the water. At the end of the exercise, the helicopter carrier at the rear of the formation asked us to fly slowly over the helipad on the back of the ship. To fly slowly, I put the flaps down, a bad idea because if they malfunctioned and failed to retract, we wouldn't have enough gas to make it home. I didn't think of this until afterward, but fortunately they came up. As we approached the helo-ship, I noticed ten guys facing us, standing in a line across the landing pad. As we approached, all ten turned, dropped their pants, and mooned us. Navy guys, what a hoot!

INSTRUCTOR PILOT SCHOOL, CARSWELL AFB, TX

In the fall of 1976, I spent a few weeks in Ft. Worth, TX, at B-52 IP school. The most startling challenge started immediately after takeoff a minute behind a KC-135 tanker. My instructor informed me I'd have to hook up in air refueling formation with the tanker in the climb out and stay with him to level-off altitude and beyond, turns and all. I thought this insane; no one can do that! But, sure enough, I found myself closing to contact position shortly after takeoff as we climbed out from Carswell. I fancied myself a pretty good refueler, and I seemed to be hanging with the tanker pretty well.

My instructor knew what came next, but I did not. Already at my capability limit—I thought—he took me beyond that limit to the next level. "In thirty seconds, I'm going to lock your throttles in position," he said calmly.

What? I can't move the throttles, I thought. *Is he insane?* This would require precisely, and I mean precisely, matching the tanker's speed with the proper power setting. The tanker, by prior agreement, would not touch his throttles until level-off, where we would back out and then hook up again with the same demand once the tanker had a new power setting. At level flight, however, the tanker would also go to forty-five degrees of bank, more than the standard thirty degrees, just to make it interesting.

I astounded myself by successfully finding the precise power setting before the IP locked the throttles. This was his intent, and it taught me a valuable lesson I used for the next twenty-five years and taught to several generations of air refuelers. You must encompass the entire tanker with your peripheral vision so you sense his mass moving toward or away from you precisely the millisecond it begins to happen. If you can detect movement that precisely, you can use small throttle movements to adjust until you have him nailed on power setting. When I returned to Loring, I became an air refueling god who delighted in showing up my less astute compatriots, much to my delight and to their chagrin. This would carry over to the C-5 in my reincarnation as a cargo pilot in the C-5 as a reservist in the 1980s and beyond. I could smoke almost every other air refueling pilot on a given night and did so without saying a word. I let my rock-solid control say everything for me.

Also, as I have said previously, this refueling capability probably saved me and a C-5 full of marines in the First Gulf War in 1990 when I had to take the gas in a developing typhoon north of Guam, where I did not have enough fuel left to reach land had I not been successful. I thank that Carswell B-52 instructor for giving me that capability by ratcheting up my standard.

BUD HOLLAND, ROGUE PILOT

A B-52 pilot contemporary of mine, Bud Holland, provided the textbook example of the dangers a rogue pilot can represent. Although it seems I should have known him, since we overlapped for several years in the

SAC force in the late 1970s, I do not recall him. I had been about three years ahead of him in seniority.

In June 1994, while practicing for an upcoming air show at Fairchild AFB, WA, Lt. Col. Bud Holland tried to maneuver outside the capability of his B-52H and crashed on the field, killing the four crew members on board. (This information is presented as described in *Darker Shades of Blue: A Case Study in Failed Leadership* by Anthony T. Kern.)[16]

Holland had dead-ended his career as chief of stan/eval, not an uncommon occurrence, but had a troublesome penchant for flying beyond regulation limits, either flying too low, too fast, or on the edge of the plane's capability. Worse, he got away with repeated aerial outrages that should have permanently grounded him on several counts. His shenanigans proved doubly egregious since his position demanded he set the standards for other wing pilots. Yet none of his commanders took the imperative step of grounding him for cause, a drastic but necessary step in this case. Holland had only months left until retirement, and successive commanders hoped he would behave himself until that time.

Apparently Holland fancied himself the best B-52 pilot who ever lived and took pride in displaying his prowess in inappropriate, irresponsible ways. Or maybe he skirted the limits in retaliation of not being promoted; I don't know. At a previous air show practice, he had blasted over the field and the crowd at much too high an airspeed and then overbanked the aircraft during his pull-up, against the agreed parameters for the maneuver.

One of my current fellow simulator instructors flew as one of Holland's copilots and offered at least a partial explanation for his flying. Holland had attended a special course that explored edge-of-the-envelope maneuvers to be used during war. Holland seemed to feel that they would not have taught him these things if they didn't expect him to practice and use them. In films I watched of his air show warm-up in the days before the event, however, he seemed to have lost his mind. I would never have dreamed of trying to pull off the maneuvers he did over the field. He could have crashed into base housing and greatly multiplied his eventual disaster.

So legendary were his flying excesses that many squadron pilots and crew members refused to fly with him in fear for their lives, according to the analysis written afterward. By the time of the fatal air show practice, his squadron commander insisted that he alone would fly with Holland to keep him in check. Obviously, that plan failed, as Holland attempted too steep a turn very close to the ground, stalled the aircraft, and caught a power line with his wingtip before cart-wheeling nose first into the ground and sending a towering fireball into the air. This took the funerals from closed-casket to no-casket affairs and surely required use of the pilot training footprints to identify the crewmembers.

Holland's story became a primer for Air Force commanders in dealing with potentially rogue pilots who had to be clamped down upon to avoid catastrophes. Holland's wing commander on the day of the crash has the same name as one of my pilot training classmates, but I don't know if it was the same man. I don't want to know. All base command heads rolled over this, as well as the heads of previous commanders who failed to rein in Holland. Pilots face enough danger from conditions conspiring to kill us through no fault of our own to have us go looking for trouble.

VIETNAMESE REFUGEES

The Vietnam War aftermath proved discouraging and depressing. After the North Vietnamese overran the country in the spring of 1975, our entire effort seemed to have been for nothing. We squandered hundreds of billions of dollars and 55,000 servicemen's lives in a war we failed to win, and we saw the ally we supported succumb to Communism. We didn't technically lose the war, but our policy had been defeated, and in that sense, we lost. In one of the war's famous quips, an American general insisted to North Vietnamese army commander General Giap that the Vietnamese had never defeated the Americans in a single major battle. True, Giap was reported to have said, but that is irrelevant.

Ever since I had talked to the Vietnamese pilot behind the fence at U-Tapao the day Saigon fell, I wanted to rescue him, or someone like him, from one of the four refugee camps in America where the refugees had been brought from the camp on Guam.

The Lutheran Church ran the camp nearest Loring at Ft. Indiantown Gap in Pennsylvania. In the summer of 1975, I began negotiating with them to sponsor a refugee family. In preparation, I bought a house at 13 Huggard Ave in Limestone, about seven miles from the base, with three bedrooms so the family and I could live together. However, the Lutherans insisted they did not have any families available for sponsorship. Instead they offered four Vietnamese sailors—an officer and three enlisted men. Initially I refused, hoping for a family to appear in the future. The Lutherans reported the four sailors had been severely disappointed by the rejection, but the agency would continue the family search. I pondered this situation for a day and then called back. I told them I desired to serve the cause and they could send me what was best for them and I would live with it. This was about the refugees, not about me. The four sailors were elated, and within a few weeks I met them at the Presque Isle airport.

The officer, Kien (Ken), introduced his subordinates: Nguyen (Win), Chuan, and Hoa. They were very polite and deferential, which I suppose was to be expected, but also remained upbeat and friendly despite their circumstance. They spoke little English, but I already knew their story. The day Saigon had fallen, they had been on the river in their boat. There had been no time to return home for family or belongings (Ken and Chuan had families); they had to flee or surrender. They fled, maneuvering their boat

236

Presque Isle News photo

Meeting the refugees: L to R: Hoa, Nguyen (hidden), Chuan, Kien, Me, Phung. Presque Isle, ME, airport, September 1975.

out to the American fleet offshore and abandoning it. Now fate had put these four Vietnamese men, who had never seen snow or a hardwood forest, into the middle of a near-endless hardwood forest that would soon be chest deep in snow. They were ten thousand miles from a home and families they would probably never see again.

I have failed to mention a Vietnamese woman who was on the scene prior to my refugees arriving. Phung T. Nguyen, nicknamed "Teeny," had fled Saigon shortly before the surrender. She had worked for the American military headquarters in Saigon, and they had evacuated her with as many of their workers as they could. Single and college educated, she spoke excellent English and, by some stroke of fortune, arrived to play interpreter for me and my new roommates. I'd have been truly lost without her.

237

The boys insisted on cooking our first meal together, rice with scrambled eggs mixed in. After the meal, they informed me they were throwing out the La Choy soy sauce.

"Number ten," Ken said, holding up the La Choy bottle; then, "Number one," holding the Kikkoman.

"OK, Ken, you're the expert," I said.

The Lutherans had provided funds for initial clothing purchases, and we soon had the guys outfitted for their new requirements. They insisted on doing all chores around the house and all the cooking and cleanup. I graciously let them.

I wanted to find some work for them to take their minds off their loss and bewildering new environment. The upcoming potato harvest seemed a good fit, since English would not be required. They had never seen non-tropical soil, but they were about to. I would also find a revelation in the fields. I have never been a farmer or known the bond that binds them to the earth, but I got a glimpse of it during the potato harvest in the chilly October days.

Seasonal workers gather at dawn in the Maine fields to harvest the potatoes newly turned up by plows. In the middle 1970s, the farmer would parcel out wooden barrels bearing tags throughout the field to allow pickers to identify with their name as they filled them. The pay was 25 cents per barrel, which was large enough for most workers to crouch within.

I delivered the four guys before I went to work on the base, picked them up afterward, and hung out briefly to watch the process during the two-week season.

Standing next to the field, awkwardly, in a flight suit, I caught the earthy aroma of the newly turned field and began to grasp what binds farmers to their land. I would gladly seek that odor every waking day of my life, a deep humus smell rich in possibilities for nurturing and growth, a partner

Photo by Paul Cyr

Northern Maine potato harvest.

in nature to provide food, income, and solace for whatever this life might demand of me. I wanted to embrace the fields, preparing them in the spring, tending them in the summer, and harvesting them in the crisp, gloriously bright, colorful autumn days as I saw them now.

Shortly after I picked up the guys to return to town one day, a huge orange harvest moon burst over the horizon, seeming to demand we sit on a porch, sip cider or beer, and discuss the day's picking, which we did. I could not join in this properly, of course, and I envied the guys their camaraderie as they stretched their tired muscles and joshed about the day's events with their hands wonderfully dirty from the precious earth that had mesmerized me standing on the field's edge that morning.

My life has been metal airplanes, office cubicles, synthetic fabrics, air-conditioned rooms, and processed, homogenized food. In a significant way,

239

I am the poorer for my advanced modern life that has deprived me of an imperative connection with the earth and its soul-restoring power.

Aside from these personal insights for me, the guys had earned their own money doing honest work, and their quiet silences decreased as they had, to some small degree, taken charge of their lives.

There would be no complete escape from their situation, however. Chuan, especially, felt the loss. I noticed small, round welts on his forearms. After a while, I asked Teeny to ask him what these might be. She reported back he had been burning himself with a cigarette as self-punishment for having abandoned his family. He had suffered in silence except for this self-mutilation that gave voice to his despair.

Ken escaped his torment with beer and often went off the rails on beer binges. Not only had they abandoned their families, they also had no way to contact them, as South Vietnam had been locked down and dissolved into the new state of a unified Vietnam. The next ten years would find most former South Vietnamese military members suffering reeducation in camps run by their former adversaries. While draconian and personally debilitating, there were no reports of mass killings or extensive physical abuse by the NVA, although news from the country would be sparse for years.

The real savagery took place next door in Cambodia, where the Khmer Rouge took the country to "Year Zero" and murdered or took actions that resulted in the death of perhaps two million of their countrymen. Between 1975, when they ascended to power, and 1979, when they were overthrown by the Vietnamese, the Khmer Rouge ran as frightening a regime as the world had seen in the twentieth century, to include the Holocaust and Soviet pogroms against the kulaks.

I suppose I will always wonder if our carpet bombing, which I participated in, pushed these meek and mild-mannered people to go berserk and fratricidal. We bombed far more extensively in Vietnam, and the Vietnamese

240

did not come unglued, but the Cambodians did. As I have opined before, our use of B-52 bombing cells constituted terror bombing, since there would be no warning that bombs were coming until the entire world exploded on those in the target area. Our Southeast Asian strategic bombing was the Nazi V-1 terror bombing on massive steroids, although we did not purposely target civilians. In the future, our leaders need to appreciate the repercussions, both positive and negative, that may result from such tactics.

During the Cambodian bombing operation, the Air Force suffered a horrific disaster when a B-52 cell inadvertently dropped its entire bomb load on the only "friendlies" within one hundred miles at the village of Neak Long. The lead aircraft radar navigator was supposed to use a "wet snow" beacon, located in the village, as a reference point to drop the bombs on a target on a specific radial and specific distance off the beacon. In a tragic error, the radar navigator forgot to throw the switch to drop on the offset target and instead dropped directly on the beacon in the friendly village, obliterating it. An armada of white-topped staff cars awaited the plane when it landed on Guam, a nightmare scenario for any bomber crew.

My refugee charges did have their upbeat moments, however. While having a few beers after potato picking, Ken altered the words to the current Glen Campbell hit "Rhinestone Cowboy" playing on the radio to "Limestone Cowboy," causing us all to sing along with Glen while loudly altering the lyrics when appropriate and laughing uproariously. This provided a special bonding moment when we all forgot their losses and found some solace. In retrospect, I would have explained that, "I am so terribly sorry it turned out like this, guys, and I wish I could make it right, but I can't. I hope you can rescue your lives and find some happiness."

After six months or so, they began to leave for different areas of the country—Ken and Hoa to the large Vietnamese community in southern California, Nguyen and Chuan to North Carolina. Nguyen would be the only one I would see again. He had married a down-home (North Carolina) girl and worked in the furniture industry near Thomasville. In the mid-eighties, I located him and visited. His wife showed off their two toddlers rampaging around the living room. Nguyen beamed proudly at his ability to display his success, and we sang "Limestone Cowboy" for his wife, who humored our silliness. I noticed an old, framed, official portrait of me on the mantle. Maybe he put it up just for my visit, maybe not.

His children reminded me of one of the great shames of our Vietnam foray, the legions of mixed-race children abandoned by their GI fathers when they went back to the world. I understand it would be impossible to bring your Vietnamese wife and child home to your American wife and children. However, the emotional carnage would prove horrific for these jettisoned children, as the Vietnamese ostracized them, taking out their anger and angst on these visible reminders of the departed American presence that had left its penniless "flotsam" in the midst of their society.

This represents another potential factor politicians must ponder before they go charging off half-cocked into a war. There can be many more casualties than the dead and wounded. Given a replay, I'd have tried to bring a few of those children out. While I'm certain I don't have any inadvertent Vietnamese offspring, I'd turn the world upside down to rescue a "half-me" from such infamy if I did. Of course, not being married at the time would make that much easier than it would for those returning to families, a terrible dilemma that must haunt these men still.

ESCAPING MAINE

My final winter in Maine, 1976-77, visited a near-record snowfall on us. It seemed it didn't stop snowing all winter. One morning I awoke to the radio telling me it had snowed twenty inches overnight. I pulled back the curtains, and the only difference I could perceive was that the snow surface was smooth, but I couldn't detect any increase in its height, so high had it already become.

Also in the late winter, I heard something scratching around in my basement. Investigating with a flashlight, I found a feral cat in an empty cardboard box with a litter of six newborn kittens. Mama kitty looked at me as if to say: "Well, we're either dead or not, now that this human has discovered us." I did the honorable thing. When the kittens were a few weeks old, I took them in another large cardboard box and set them up in front of the BX on Saturday morning with a "Free kittens!" sign. The kids loved it, the parents wanted to kill me, and I moved every one of the kittens to new homes by lunchtime.

I had been told upon assignment to Loring, and while moaning and bitching about my misfortune, that I could transfer out after four years. Well, ho, ho, ho, four years was up in the spring of 1976, so I hot-wired into the SAC assignments desk at headquarters. They had a lame alibi for me. "Gosh," they said, "we've assigned three B-52 IPs to replace you, but they all got out of the service when informed! We can't find anyone who wants to replace you!"

I reminded them that I didn't want to replace anyone when they sent me here, so I wasn't buying their excuse. I suppose it was my misfortune to have potential replacements who could escape getting tagged by getting out of the service. It would be an extra year and five days before I escaped and then only because I volunteered to take a schoolhouse instructor pilot position at Castle.

Since this would be a permanent change of station (PCS), they scheduled me to take the three-month Squadron Officer School course at Maxwell AFB, AL, en route to Castle.

In the last six months before I departed, I got my stan/eval crew and performed as an evaluator. My copilot, Tony Beat, proved a diligent paperwork manager who ran the testing program with an iron hand. As I left for Castle, he departed for aircraft commander school, after which he returned to Loring as an aircraft commander. This proved another tragic connection for me. In November 1992, Tony would die in a B-1 bomber on a low-level run when the aircraft suffered complete electrical failure. I don't know the details, but all four crew members died. They went where, but for the grace of God, my first crew and I would have gone had things transpired only slightly differently either on the underpowered takeoff or for the runaway nose-down trim on our low-level route.

SQUADRON OFFICER SCHOOL

APRIL 1977–JUNE 1977

Squadron Officer School represented the first rung of the Air Force professional education ladder, to be followed by Air Command and Staff College and then Air War College. Most of the Squadron Officer School attendees are in the five- to seven-year group as officers, finishing their first PCS assignment and en route to their second, as I was.

My 1977 class at Maxwell AFB in Montgomery, AL, formed up in the "blue bedroom" (nicknamed for the tendency of everyone to fall asleep in it for after lunch briefings), a large auditorium designed to hold the entire class. My libido radar swept the room for targets and found only one, since women were still something of a rarity in the officer corps and there were few in the class. The lock-on centered on a long-legged brunette nurse who, I later discovered, had worked with Millie of Loring/Tachikawa fame. I knew this lovely could never wind up in my section, but I watched as the large group began to be divided up. Against all hope, as the repeated halving of the group progressed, she was still with me. I refused to get my hopes up until at last we wound up in the same section. I would have eye candy for the entire course! I became repeatedly mind-numbingly distracted at Physical Training

(PT) as she stood around in her blue shorts with those legs that, as they say nonsensically, came all the way up to her ass.

The course consisted of massive numbers of professional readings and tests upon the readings and lectures delivered in the blue bedroom. I could never seem to do well on the tests, although I passed easily enough. An elite group, however, seemed to have photographic memories and could parse the difference between two nuanced answers to a question that a lecturer had explained in one sentence in the middle of a lecture weeks before. Impossible!

For PT athletic contests, the school had a novel method to parcel out athletic ability evenly. In initial interviews on the first day of class, they asked us to tell them of our athletic accomplishments. Of course, we did this with embellishment. We didn't realize we should have downplayed our accomplishments because the sections would be apportioned to equal levels of braggadocio from these interviews. There were three or four of us, all of medium height, who had run our mouths about what jocks we were and wound up being the supposed giant killers of our section, except none of us were giants. The real giants seemed to be on all the teams we faced in volleyball who had, perhaps, divined the intent of the initial interviews and soft-pedaled their athletic accomplishments. We did manage to kick some butt in flickerball and soccer, however.

The contests were designed to make a liability of previous expertise in volleyball and football. In volleyball, the rules on "carrying" the ball when hitting it were so draconian you almost had to use a fist or forearm for contact; no fingertip finesse would be allowed. That mattered little, because the giants were smashing the ball down our throats anyway.

In flickerball, the catch would be that once you had the football, you could not move forward down the field, at complete odds with our instincts and something that initially caused repeated turnovers to the bad guys. Once we got the knack of it, we managed to win two of three contests.

Our three-man jock cadre that included me managed to win two of three soccer matches since we were all fast, agile, and fearless on the pitch. We ran circles around the giants who had tormented us in volleyball; sweet revenge.

There were also several leadership exercises, one of which divided the section into two groups to brainstorm a problem and present a policy. The school configured it to see who would rise to leadership in each group to direct the investigation to meet a time deadline. We figured out what we decided was the approved school solution. Instead of allowing a half-dozen alpha males to try to convince everyone they should be the leader, I called a time out and suggested we just appoint "Allen" the leader and get over the leadership squabble so we could come up with a policy answer. It didn't really matter who led the discussion, but someone had to so we wouldn't go off on tangents and someone could cut off discussion when he felt it necessary. This worked, and we met the deadline with a thoughtful answer. In keeping with the Grim Reaper seemingly following behind me, Allen was killed in an automobile accident the next year. He survived flying F-4s in Europe only to be killed on an autobahn.

Upon graduation, I set out for California in my newly purchased Honda Accord. So popular was the 1977 Accord that I had to take whatever color would become available three months after paying $4,000 for it. I got silver and picked it up while driving from Loring to Maxwell. I awarded the Pontiac to my younger brother, Drew, who drove it another ten years.

I drove the southern route across the States because I was already on it at Maxwell. I marveled at the Accord's stupendous gas mileage after driving a gas-hog muscle car for five years. It took me four days' driving to reach Castle, including an entire day trying to get across Texas from Shreveport, LA, to El Paso. I never quite got to Los Angeles, turning north to take Highway 99 up the Central Valley to Merced.

CASTLE AFB AS INSTRUCTOR PILOT

JUNE 1977–JULY 1979

I settled into the BOQ and went looking for an apartment. I located one downtown near the mall that had the units arrayed around an arboretum-like central court containing colorful plants, bushes, and trees. The apartments were all on the second floor with parking beneath each unit.

I reported to the squadron the next week to meet my new commander, Steve, a Lt. Col. He looked the part—tall, slender, and with a trim pencil moustache. He mostly played it safe and tried to cover his bases, maybe presuming his looks would get him promoted if he didn't screw up. His appearance fit the mold that seemed to enhance promotion potential.

Then I met my chief pilot, a B-52 pilot with long experience who told me one rule that saved me from several dangerous situations. He said, "Jay, when you are in command, never assume the pilot in the other seat is on top of things. When they go flying with you as the instructor, they think they are going flying with Daddy, who will take care of them. This applies no matter what their rank or experience level. When you are in command of a training mission, you are solo and you can't forget expecting any help." He was right. The most dangerous cockpit contained three evaluators, each of whom presumed one of the others was minding the store.

I bonded with my fellow instructor pilots better than perhaps I would with any other group of pilots I flew with. We all seemed on the same wavelength. I played golf endlessly with one of the flight commanders, Bill Ivey, who proved to be my best friend for the next two years.

The larger-than-life personality of the group would be Cliff, a major who always had a joke or ribald comment to make and had the entire section in stitches most of the time.

FIGHTER PILOT'S CAMEL

Cliff's favorite joke concerned a fighter pilot who wanted to rent a camel to cross a stretch of desert. The fighter jock, personal call sign "Poodle Boy," felt it imperative he get across this thirty-mile stretch of desert to rendezvous with his grossly overweight girlfriend. I watched Cliff present this joke to the bomber instructor pilots in our training room.

The camel trader said he had only one camel left and this beast had a peculiar problem. The fighter pilot said he didn't care about any of that, he wanted the animal anyway because his lovely awaited, but to please explain the problem. The trader said on occasion the camel would sit down and refuse to move before he got a "hand job" from the rider. If he sits, the trader said, stand in front of him, make a circular fist, and stroke your hand up and down. (Cliff would elaborately demonstrate the fighter pilot's required actions, much to the audience's delight.) If he nods yes, you must perform on him to a successful conclusion. The fighter pilot grimaced but felt it worth the risk to meet his beloved since she was the only female who could tolerate endless hours of Poodle Boy's self-promotion of heroic invincibility and unfathomable fascination with reenacting aerial dogfights with his hands. "I'll take the stinking beast," he said.

All went well for five miles into the thirty-mile trek when suddenly the camel sat down. "Oh, great," thought Mr. Fighter pilot. He walked in front of the camel and performed the hand gesture as advised. The camel nodded yes. (Cliff elaborately demonstrated all the fighter pilot's and camel's actions.) The fighter pilot performed as required, and then off they went. At ten miles, the sequence repeated, although it took more effort this time with his vaunted fighter pilot "stick hand" to reach a successful conclusion for the camel. (By this point the instructor pilot audience had been reduced to covering their faces, laughing uncontrollably, and stamping their feet rapidly.) Again, with

248

visions of his rotund lovely dancing in his mind, the fighter jock took the camel to a gallop. Alas, at the fifteen-mile point, the halfway mark from water or civilization, the camel sat down again. The fighter pilot wearily stood before the now-sweaty and disgusting beast and made the standard hand motion. However, this time the camel shook his head no. (Cliff mimicked the fighter pilot's shock, setting everyone up for the punch line.) Just as Poodle Boy thought he had escaped, the camel looked him in the eye and began making loud sucking noises with its mouth.

Now, having mimicked the camel's sucking noises, Cliff had the entire instructor room howling, crying and laughing, or face down, pounding on the desk shouting for him to stop because they couldn't take it anymore! Stop! Stop! Pleeeeeease!

Later in my orientation I met the staff, the secretaries, military admin help, and the airman who ran the publications cage. The airman, a black female about nineteen, reached out and shook my hand with a smile and what I thought for a moment was a twinkle in her eye, or a flow of stardust from her eyes to mine. My libido went on full alert, scanning this slender yet fully filled-out target. She bore a strong resemblance to contemporary pop singer Leslie Uggams.

I had had little contact with black females in my nearly totally segregated education and it seemed a dirty trick to drop such a delightful, off-limits enlisted morsel before me unexpectedly like this. I feared I could get into trouble playing on the railroad tracks with her and eventually we would be walking the tracks together in violation of several norms of the time, both military and social. But that came later. For now, I would just chat with her when I reported flight planning or flight debriefing. Her eyes still seemed to sparkle when we chatted, and I must presume mine were starting to do likewise.

FIRST STUDENT CREW

After a brief checkout regimen, I got my first student crew, led by Larry, a captain, and a crew of first lieutenants, much as I had three years earlier. They would return as a crew to their home base of Grand Forks, ND. I took an immediate liking to Larry, who seemed to have a marvelously relaxed attitude, although diligent in his duties. His copilot was a wide-eyed rookie, as we all were at this stage.

The training sequence would be the same as in the field as I had learned it at Loring. Day one would be spent mission planning. The A/C would fill out the fight plan, and the copilot would run a fuel log and update his low-level chart to identify any new towers or obstructions that had been built since the last version of the manual. The copilot caught the brunt of the preparation, and Larry and I spent significant time shooting-the-shit in the lounge, drinking coffee in the morning or Tab soft drinks in the afternoon.

The day ended with the student aircraft commander briefing the mission, with each position briefing its specialty items. The sequence included takeoff, departure, cruise, and preparation for air refueling, air refueling, cruise for the two-hour navigation leg, descent for low level, the low-level route and bomb runs, and return to Castle for two hours of transition (touch-and-go) training— ten hours of fun and frolic!

USAF photo

An hour's worth of flailing for the student.

The air refueling track went straight north, track 8A to Oregon, then back south on track 7B to Ukiah, CA. We came to know well the volcano string in the Cascade Range to include Mount Hood, Mount Shasta, and Mount St. Helens. St. Helens would not blow its top for another five years or so. The student aircraft commander would be working up a sweat here because, after my initial demonstration, it was all his for an hour, flailing behind the tanker.

The navigation leg would be flown toward whatever low-level route we had been assigned. This was the only time we pilots could take off our helmets and wear headsets, a blessed relief. The helmets, aside from being heavy, would also develop hot spots where the inner pads touched the skull.

The low-level routes, initially termed Oil Burner routes, and later the more politically and environmentally correct Olive Branch routes, were spread out, in the north from Montana through Idaho (spectacular when the aspens turned brilliant yellow in the fall) with the southernmost route snaking through Monument Valley that crosses the Zuni Indian reservation in Arizona.

As the plane got ready to descend into the route, the helmets went back on. In the summer, low level is a bumpy ride, and the plane bounced, shook, and shuddered in the rising heat thermals that formed over the Western deserts. The student crew often had to be saved by the instructors because coordination was not attained until the third or fourth ride. Our instructors saved us when we were students, so we returned the favor. Flying at five hundred feet through these panoramic landscapes exhilarated and made us wonder why we were well paid to do this—when we'd pay to do it if we had to. If we could keep the students from puking on occasion, it would have been even better! When the copilot suddenly ripped off his oxygen mask, you'd best go on 100% oxygen, because if the puke smell reached your nose, you might be the next one to barf.

Flying back to Castle, it became my turn to earn my pay. I would spend the entire two hours of transition training watching closely to keep the students from crashing the airplane or turning it upside down in the pattern. Wild excursions from controlled flight were rare but had to be prepared for at any instant. For instance, I had to be ready if a student didn't heed the need to trim throughout the landing flare, as I had not with Lucky Luciano on my first B-52 flight seven years earlier. During my tour at Castle, we left the gear extended throughout the traffic pattern. As my tour ended, however, the command decided that, to save fuel expenses, we would start retracting the gear after every takeoff. This presented a dangerous new habit pattern that could bite the instructor, but I didn't hear of any gear-up landings thereafter. The C-5 would have one at Travis, and a B-1 would land gear up on Diego Garcia years later, but the B-52 escaped such disaster to the best of my knowledge.

As usual in my career, my first test at various stages seemed to be the worst I would see, as my first line check had been flying to Nha Trang in a monsoon rainstorm. This first student crew delivered two doozies.

ENGINES DANCING ON THE WING

In about the middle of the crew's three-month course, on the Friday of Thanksgiving weekend of 1977, I found the Grim Reaper seated in my jump seat. We had just started the post–air refueling navigation leg over the snow-covered Sierra Nevada mountain range. I had about an hour off since the students both rode their seats for nav leg. I slipped the *Playboy* magazine out of my helmet bag and sat on the floor behind the jump seat, the only place I could stretch out a little.

I had just opened the centerfold, a lovely naked brunette seated on a chair she had rakishly turned backwards, when the copilot came up on interphone. "Ah, IP, copilot!"

Oh, great, I thought, *what problem could this rookie have now?* I told him to go ahead.

"Ah, are there supposed to be holes in the engines?"

"Yes," I told him, "one in the front, one in the back," irritated he was dragging me away from the brunette.

"No," he said, his voice now quavering, "I mean holes in the side of the cowling."

Uh, oh, I thought. I folded up Miss Playmate and went forward, grasping his headrest and leaning around him to look at the #5 engine, the first one visible out his window.

My vision replicated a movie cinematic technique, where I initially saw the entire engine, then zoomed into the midsection in horror. The engine had two overlapping basketball-sized holes where the N2 compressor turbine resided. Looking into the holes, I could see the remnants of that turbine twirling madly and unevenly, throwing sparks wildly as its broken blades struck the side casing. Suddenly, the fire light and bell alarm on this engine's pylon mate, engine #6, came to life, the bell clanging and the light flashing ominously.

"*You, out of the seat!*" I shouted at the copilot as I grabbed my helmet and checklist and moved aside for him to clear the copilot position.

When I landed heavily in the seat, I immediately pulled the fire handle on both #5 and #6 to shut off fuel and hydraulics at the firewall at the top of the pylon. I told the student pilot to fly the plane while I handled the emergency. I also strapped tightly into my ejection seat.

Mercifully, the fire light and bell went out on #6. Engine #5 was apparently so torn up that the disintegrating compressor had probably severed the fire loop warning system, because it gave no warnings at all despite being in shambles. What I did not know until the next day was that shrapnel from the disintegrating compressor had blown into the fuselage as well as into engine #6. Fortunately, it didn't hit anything vital, to include a wing fuel tank or me and my *Playboy* magazine. Had it hit a fuel tank, the plane might have exploded and none of us would have known what happened.

Cockpit view of B-52 engines #5 and #6 on their (nearest) pylon. Engines dancing on the wing, Grim Reaper sitting in the jump seat.

Catastrophes are impossible to plan for completely. You can have an engine fire, and you know the Bold Print responses, yet you can't anticipate surrounding events, complications, or your location when the shit hits the fan. In this case I had to think quickly of where we were and where we should go to land. In these days, prior to INS and GPS navigation systems, I did what any self-respecting pilot would do—I shouted on interphone for the radar navigator to give me the nearest SAC base. A few seconds later, he reported it would be Mather AFB in Sacramento, CA, twenty minutes to the west.

I looked out at the two stricken engines on the pylon, and things had gotten worse. Engine #6, which I could not see except for the front intake, seemed largely intact, and the airstream passed through it cleanly. Engine #5, however, having torn itself apart, would not allow the airflow through unimpeded and now put heavy drag on the pylon. This uneven airflow through these pylon mates had now caused them to start wobbling, or Dutch rolling, on the pylon, a terrifying dance that threatened to tear the engines off the pylon. The Reaper had joined us in the cockpit.

Fearing what two engines departing the plane might do to my aerodynamics, to say nothing of what would happen if they hit the tail on the way by, I again shouted to the radar nav to give me the nearest runway. A moment later, he said it would be Lake Tahoe, but he didn't recommend it because it was a short runway and at the bottom of a steep valley.

"Turning for Mather!" I said.

"Heading two-seven-zero," he responded.

Now I had to start talking and coordinating. I declared the emergency on the Oakland Center frequency and told him we had two engine failures, an engine fire, and needed clearance direct to Mather with further clearance to descend and maneuver as necessary while doing so. This busy Air Traffic Control (ATC) frequency went silent except for me and the controller, pilots in a couple of dozen other cockpits, civilian and military, listening intently. As I found over the course of several emergencies, ATC can save your ass in a pinch. This controller locked into the situation immediately and professionally. He gave me the Mather weather, altimeter setting, and landing runway, which fortunately would provide a straight-in approach. He then asked for status on the engines and I reported the instability. He switched me to another frequency to free up the main frequency for everyone else. I'm sure those couple of dozen other cockpits switched a backup radio to that frequency to follow the emergency, fascinated at the drama and thankful it was me, not them.

My other UHF radio still had the Castle command post frequency in it. I switched there and gave them a brief summation of the situation, then returned to the ATC frequency to report how far out of Mather we were. He said he had notified Mather we were inbound.

255

I looked at the dancing engines again and at the sparks flying from #5. *What to do?* I thought. *Go fast and get it on the ground before the damn pylon catches fire and burns into the wing? But if I go fast, that may tear the engines off the pylon. Screw it,* I thought, *I'm going fast.* (In retrospect, this was not the best choice.) I pushed up the remaining throttles and shoved the nose into a steep descent. Mather would soon see us screaming and smoking out of the sky to them.

I have tried to imagine the scene at the Mather fire station when the call came in saying a burning B-52 would soon be on final. This was the Friday of Thanksgiving weekend and almost everyone had a four-day weekend. Castle crews had to fly, however, because the valley fog had put us behind our training timeline and we needed the extra day if it was clear, and this was a clear-and-one-million (visibility) day. Maybe the firemen were in the middle of a volleyball game, or maybe they were watching football on TV, but none of them expected to get scrambled for an emergency since Mather had stood down for the long weekend. Yet suddenly the horns and lights went off, signaling an impending crash scenario. I'm sure the predominant epithet uttered while scrambling into their silver fire suits was, "What the fuuuuuuck!"

I could now see Mather far in the distance. I could also see the engine dance getting worse. I flicked my radio control back to Castle since they would be berserk to talk to me. I also feared the DCO, the chief of stan/ eval, and an assorted multitude of other ops types would be leaning over the controller's shoulder to ask me fifty questions about my situation. I saw Mather drawing closer and decided I didn't have time for that. This was going to be over, one way or the other, in five minutes, and I didn't want to spend it talking to them.

"Castle," I said, "This is Panzer Eight-Zero. I'm on fire and I'm headed for Mather; if you want any information, ask them." Then I clicked the radio back to Mather command post. They didn't have any operations personnel on duty over the holiday and wouldn't know what to ask. Just as well. I'm sure the Castle DCO was turning back flips to know what was happening, but I hoped he would understand.

Later I got another interesting perspective on the whole scene from the instructor EW seated behind me in the cockpit. When I leapt into the copilot's seat and started shouting at everyone, the EW feared I might soon give the bailout order, so terse did the dialogue sound. He knew we were over the snow-covered Sierras and he didn't have his winter flight jacket on. He said he eyed it sitting on the floor next to him and wondered if he had time to unstrap from his parachute to put it on. He listened to the frantic discussion up front and decided he did not dare do so. He grabbed the jacket and pulled it through his chest strap, hoping it might land somewhere near him if he punched out. I had not thought I sounded that bad; I mean, I wasn't screaming or anything, but perhaps my voice went up an octave or two. I had no plans to make the ejection call unless the engines came off the pylon and resulted in a loss of control, and they had not, as yet. I didn't have my jacket on and never thought about it. It would have been a cold ride down to the snow for me if it had come to that.

Approach control switched me over to tower to get landing permission. I now had to pull the engines to idle and deploy the airbrakes to slow down so I could extend the gear and flaps. Everything came down properly, we landed, and soon we were rolling out on the runway with an armada of fire trucks chasing us. We cleared at the end of the runway and let ourselves get surrounded by the trucks. After observing us briefly, two of the silver-suited, alien-looking firemen inspected the #5 and #6 engines and decided this emergency was over.

We taxied to parking and shut down the engines. I scrambled out of the plane and raced over to the wrecked engines.

I found an engine stand already up against #5 with a crusty old guy in civilian clothes wagging an unlit cigar from his mouth. I climbed up next to him and looked into the gaping hole in the side of the engine and the tangled mess of metal within. The old guy muttered, "Five more minutes and these engines would have come off the pylon."

"Wow," I said, "are you an (enlisted) engine guy?"

"No," he growled. "I own this place!"

Oops! I don't know if he was the wing commander, the maintenance commander, or the ops commander, but I took his word for it.

The Grim Reaper had again left my aircraft empty-handed. I tell my current pilot training students that the Reaper will visit their aircraft in the future, and I wish them luck when he does.

SACRIFICIAL LAMBS

Although I felt this was easily enough excitement for Larry's crew and for me, there was more to come. We had finished the training course, and I had recommended them for their check ride when the dreaded higher headquarters (HHQ) inspection team showed up. I thought students were exempt from inspection team check rides. But, noooooo. Larry and the boys got jumped for their initial B-52 check ride. I freaked out when the flight commander informed me my lambs would be sacrificed to the CEVG wolves. "Take me," I insisted, "not them!" But there was nothing I could do.

HHQ inspection teams threw fear into the crew force. The best you could do was break even by passing or take a severe official hit if you busted. The inspections started with the two big lies: the team would say they were here to help us, and we would return their lie by telling them we were glad to see them.

I hated the teams, but I had a different philosophical view about them.

They are an imperative feature to keep the crew force safe. Curse them as I would, they were an absolute necessity. Our training program would be geared to ensuring standardization and compliance with regulations, always with the threat of HHQ evaluating us. We couldn't depend on our buddies to give us the benefit of the doubt within the wing on check rides; we had to be capable of doing it by the book and letting a neutral agency look up our skirt to make sure we had clean underwear. This is a rule for any organization; a separate, disinterested agency must check the operation. In 2008, we found out what happens when the watchdogs are asleep as Wall Street went bonkers and almost brought down the Western world's finances. Had the Securities and Exchange Commission or the bond rating agencies such as Moody's been doing their job, they might have saved us from this multitrillion dollar calamity, but they were not.

I sweated the entire ten hours Larry and the boys were in the air on the check ride. I thought of dozens of things I should have warned them about and wondered if I had given them everything they needed to succeed. They were very good, but screwy things often happen on check rides that you've never seen before, and I hoped they would escape such a test. I'd seen many highly experienced crews bust, but my guys had little experience individually or as a crew, which increased the odds against them.

Finally, they landed and headed to debriefing, to which I was not invited, so I sweated some more. They left the debriefing and headed for the base pizza parlor, but I missed their departure and searched all over for them. This was decades before I could just call them on the cell phone.

At last, I found them at the pizza joint. I walked toward them and they looked at me with neutral expressions on their faces. Bastards, they were going to play with me. I stopped next to the table and said, "Well, is this a celebration or a wake?"

Larry looked at me and put his hand up with the thumb horizontal. He tortured me for a few more seconds, then raised the thumb. Yes! My first crew survives a CEVG inspection! This ranked up with my crew's best bombs on our first ORI. I wanted to "cock-a-doodle-doo" to the pizza parlor patrons in pride for my neophyte wonders.

I've wondered in the years since if I might have received a "one" OER under the original system after the successful recovery from the engine fires and the success of my first student crew on the CEVG inspection. Even though I was a new guy, fate had given me two opportunities to shine, and these might have bagged a "one" under the original criteria. Since this system had already inflated to all "one"s, however, it didn't matter; we all got the top rating.

TRAINING INCIDENTS

I had six student crews during my two years at Castle. All successfully completed the course and there were no more hair-raising emergencies, but there were a few incidents. Two were caused by the damn fog that covers the San Joaquin Valley in the winter. I spent more than one day sitting against the wall at Base Ops with a dozen other bomber and tanker crews waiting for the fog to lift.

The first incident came in the winter of 1978, in the middle of the course for the student crew. We had exited a low-level route in Utah shortly after midnight, and I contacted Castle on phone patch with the Hill AFB command post to check the weather. They told me it was zero-zero (ceiling and visibility) and I couldn't get back that night. I requested a divert base and they came up with Minot, ND. *Oh, great,* I thought, *Minot in the middle of the winter; just my luck.*

A Minot landing would be no picnic I discovered when I called to request their weather. While Castle was fogged in, Minot had a blizzard. So we got to anticipate a landing at 0400 in the morning, after having been up for perhaps twenty hours and in the air for ten, in a blinding snowstorm. I got in the copilot's seat and let the student pilot fly the approach. The ILS precision approach started well but soon got dicey. The pilot started getting behind due to the crosswind, and I had to take it from him halfway down the approach. This is one of those freak occurrences you need experience to handle. I had it in this aircraft; he didn't.

The landing required ten degrees of crosswind gear, a peculiarity of the Buff necessary because it cannot be flown wing low to fight the crosswind. Recall my lesson from Elvis in the T-41 on crosswind; now imagine the horrendously long wing of the B-52. The wing-low method is not an option. The Boeing engineers therefore made the landing gear rotatable. The two main landing gear trucks are normally aligned with center line. For a crosswind landing, the trucks rotate left or right to compensate for the wind. This means as you approach touchdown, you might be looking down the runway centerline out the side window. Your mind must convince your brain that you must touch down looking sideways or all hell will break loose, the plane will dive toward the downwind wing, and you'll be headed off the runway toward the upwind wing.

The blowing snow proved very thick and seemed more so due to our speed. It would have been thick just standing on the ground, but flying through it at 120 knots made it a super-blizzard. I broke out near minimums and landed with the ten degrees of crosswind. I didn't curse the sky gods for this one as I had that first check ride into Nha Trang. I could handle this after years of experience, whereas the Nha Trang approach hit me before I half knew what I was doing in airplanes.

The second incident was more political than dangerous. Again, returning to Castle in the middle of the night, the fog had beat us to the runway. I saw this peculiar situation several times in thirty years of flying. The ground fog sits on the runway about fifty feet thick. If you fly over the runway at a thousand feet, you can see the runway clearly looking down, but if you approach from a low angle, such as from a visual approach, the runway disappears as you start to flare for landing. Suddenly you can't see anything, as if landing on a cloud. This condition would cause a crash landing for a C-5 in Muscogee, OK, years later on an ORI (see book two for that one) and could have done the same to me. But rather than chance blindly feeling for the runway, I again diverted to Mather, and this time I would not be on fire. As we climbed out from the missed approach, I called the Castle command post and told them I got down to fifty feet and went around due to fog.

The next day, after travelling back from Mather, I reported to the squadron commander's office after an official call to get my ass into the squadron to explain my mission from the day before. I had no idea what the problem was. The divert was warranted and nothing untoward had happened. However, it seems a tanker *toad* pilot, a Lt. Col., had been on command post frequency and railed to the ops commander that this bomber IP—me—had busted the two-hundred-foot minimums down to fifty feet before going around. This presumes I was in the clouds down to fifty feet, which was not the case. I had been totally visual down to fifty feet and *then* lost visibility in the fog. What a jerk that tanker guy had been! Anyway, that explanation got me off the hook and I never did find out who the prick was.

The final crew incident happened on a bomb run at the La Junta bomb site, when the student pilot got down to fifty feet above the ground on the radar altimeter at three hundred knots as we approached the target. We could have been throwing up dust clouds behind us, we were so low. One wrong move and we'd have been splattered over miles of cactus. Trapped in the jump seat with no access to throttles or yokes, I could do nothing but tersely order the pilot to start climbing or be in fear of his life, as I was of mine.

BEAR OF A CAMPING TRIP

Castle was not all work and no play, of course. Two treks to Yosemite National Park proved eventful. On the first, I got a late start and arrived at my campsite in the lower park just before dark. I decided I didn't have enough time to set up a camp, although the hitchhiking hippie couple I picked up on the way quickly got their tent up.

We discussed what to do with food to keep it from the bears. I said, "Hey, no problem, I'll put it in the front seat and close all the doors and windows. Besides," I continued, "I'm going to sleep in the back seat and set up my camp tomorrow." So we all turned in to sleep.

Sometime during the night, I felt cramped and opened the door by my feet to stretch out. As the sky was beginning to lighten, I awoke with a start but didn't know what had woken me. I sat up, rubbing my eyes, and realized something smelled horrible, like a wet, dirty dog but far worse. When I stopped rubbing and looked toward my feet, I froze. Two inches from my big toe, the indescribably huge head of a black bear came into focus. Mr. Bear was preparing to climb over me to get to the food in the front seat. I quickly pictured myself trapped in this compact car with five hundred pounds of hungry bear.

Fate saved me again. When I sat up, I apparently startled the bear as much as he startled me, because he stepped back a few feet. I took that opportunity to reach for the door handle and slam the door shut. This caused the still-startled bear to stand up and fall backward over a log. He then turned to other targets of opportunity and sniffed at the hippies' tent. They froze, as they should have, since there was no food in the tent and no reason for the bear to investigate. He then walked to a nearby VW van, probably also full of hippies, and stood on his hind legs to peer inside. Finding nothing to eat, he

263

left. I immediately reviewed my brilliant idea to put the food in the front seat with me in the car with a door open.

A second morning later that summer of 1979, I awoke and walked to the stream that runs out the south end of May Lake in the upper meadow. I'd brought my fishing pole and some salmon eggs as bait but didn't hold out much hope of success. However, I snagged an eight-inch trout almost immediately. I built a campfire, cleaned the catch, and ate it for breakfast. I can't remember a better tasting breakfast. This provided a potent dose of living marvelously with Mother Nature, killing my breakfast as any noble savage might and living off the land like proud pioneer stock. Then I laughed at myself for such thoughts—me, frat boy, who flew around in a metal box for a living and lived in an air-conditioned apartment? I did revel in that brief, marvelous glimpse of living in the wild, however. Thank you, May Lake.

DECISIONS

About halfway through my two-year tour at Castle, I made two decisions. First, I would get off active duty. Second, I would ask out the pubs cage airman, who I will call Tammy, despite the taboo against such officer/enlisted fraternization and against a still fragile acceptance of interracial dating. I suspect the first decision drove the second.

I discussed leaving active duty with Bill Ivey at the golf course after a round of golf followed by a few rounds of beer. As I looked ahead at a possible career, I didn't like what I was seeing. Castle would be counted as a "southern" assignment, which meant I'd be headed back north, perhaps for another half decade, to Grand Forks or Minot, ND, a possibility that did not thrill me. I also told him I looked at ops commander positions up the chain and I didn't want that job. This seems curious in retrospect, because just over a decade later, that is precisely what I would be at a C-5 reserve wing for the first Gulf War. I had ideas of entering airline management—that would not work out, I later discovered—and wanted out of the service. Ivey, who was three or four years senior to me and would soon be a DCO at Fairchild AFB, WA, said I should do what I felt I should do. So I did.

I had to report to the wing commander to tell him I would be resigning my commission. That meeting introduced me to the second superlative military leader of my career, Col H.T. Johnson.

I'm not sure what I expected of Johnson as I entered his office, but he astounded me. He told me to relax and then threw his leg over the arm of his chair as I stood stiffly at attention. He smiled and said if I wanted to get out, that was fine, but he thought I should stay.

The total insouciance of this action startled me. His display of nonchalance did not convey sloppiness or carelessness; it told me he knew to a certainty that he would be a general and could afford to be casual, that he had the program knocked, and could display his utter confidence with total informality. It seems he was entirely correct in his promotion estimation, as I discovered ten years later when we met again and he wore four stars. I'll have much more to say on Johnson in book two.

Double Taboo Dating

I also acted on my second decision and lingered at the pubs cage at the end of the afternoon one day. I think Tammy guessed what was coming because she seemed a little nervous. So was I. She was black and enlisted; I was white and an officer. Any number of taboos, political and social, militated against what we were about to do, but we both sensed it had been coming for a long time. I asked her out to dinner Friday night and she beamed and accepted. I rationalized this would be acceptable; I wasn't dating her because she was enlisted or black, I was dating her because she was Tammy.

We went to a local Italian restaurant full of ferns and talked office politics. She reported that I would be amazed at how many senior squadron pilots had hit on her in the cage. She seemed adept at fending them off, usually because she knew they were married and up to no good. (I wondered, *and what am I up to?*) Things seemed to be going well until I looked to my right at two ladies about fifty years old at another table who were looking at us in haughty disdain, as if one of us had brought a dog into the restaurant. I had expected pushback from several quarters, but I hadn't thought I'd get it out on the town and off base, but here it was. I thought momentarily about walking over and righteously setting their asses straight, or introducing ourselves and asking how their meal was, but decided that would do no good and just cause a ruckus. I smiled at them and went back to my meal.

At the end of the evening, I returned Tammy to her apartment. We paused at the door. She didn't ask me in, unsure of the situation she later told me, and I didn't ask for the same reason. My question to myself—just what are my intentions?—kept coming back to me, so I thanked her and left. We both wanted me to come in, but the apprehension was too high. I suspect I felt mild pride that I had shown I wasn't dating her just so I could rip her clothes off and throw her on the bed, except that is precisely what I wanted to do. I also feared perhaps I really was, to some degree, taking advantage of a subordinate. I didn't ask her out again for two months.

On the second attempt, she suggested making dinner for me. This, obviously, got me in the door and both of us past the "would you like to come in" question. I would already be in. What a plan! She cooked lasagna and we discussed squadron gossip and our family backgrounds.

Afterward, we walked over by the couch and she paused. The time had arrived. I stood, frozen, my good and bad angels thrashing it out again. The pause became embarrassingly long. She kept standing there and began looking distractedly at the floor, then at the couch, waiting for me to do—

266

or not do—what I would. The angels fought savagely; my jaw tightened. Suddenly, the contest ended with my good angel getting his ass kicked again. I threw my arms around her, seemingly possessed, and almost broke her in half, something she thought I might do, she said later. She asked the next morning what had taken me so long.

After several more dates, I decided to invite her to the squadron picnic, my final formation, of sorts, before I departed the Air Force. When I picked her up, I grimaced at her wardrobe, a pair of red, hot pants (loose fitting but very short, shorts). If I thought we might circulate somewhat unobtrusively through the crowd, this ensured we would not. The pilots' wives were looking daggers at their husbands, who were blundering into tables, gawking at her.

At one point, Tammy was off with the other enlisted squadron members and I was sipping a gin and tonic near the bar. A senior squadron pilot came over and stood next to me as we both looked out at the crowd. "Say, ah, Jay, I was, ah, wondering . . ."

Here it comes, I thought. I'd prepared for this. "Yes, sir, what were you wondering?" I asked.

"Ah, um, you know; how is it? I mean, you know, with a black woman?"

I rocked on my heels and said, "Well, sir, you know what they say; all cats are gray in the dark."

He sniffed, nodded, smiled, and moved on, filling in the blanks as he wished.

At no time did anyone caution me on this relationship or warn me to terminate it. The staff seemed curious spectators of the developing romance they probably suspected was in progress from my hanging around the pubs cage and getting lost in conversation with Tammy. This is the stage of the relationship where I should have been counseled to cease and desist, if they were going to, and I should have been so advised. *Wait until you are off active duty, captain,* they should have said, *then do whatever you want.*

Once again I found the bad angel forgot to ask questions, as usual. As the summer wore on, Tammy asked what our kids would look like; would they be zebras, she deadpanned? Talk of kids put me in a brace. I was not interested in marriage or kids, and our differences would make things far more difficult than most marriages, most of which seemed to have enough difficulties anyway. Then she asked me to cosign a loan for her to pay off her credit cards. Argh. Things were going downhill fast. As with Frieda five years before at this same base, the end of my tour terminated the relationship and I was free again. I packed up the Honda and headed for the East Coast, a civilian.

In closing this life chapter, I reflect that my active duty career seemed to have a disturbing feature. All my assigned bases closed behind me, and someone I knew on those bases died in an aircraft accident. The Castle casualty would be my best friend and golfing buddy, Bill Ivey, some five years later.

No matter how many family and friends might love you, we must all leave this life on that one-way, solo mission home.

DEATH SPIRAL

USAF photo

The B-52 bomber, call sign Swoon 52, swept over the dark desert landscape in a descent into the Holbrook low-level route that runs through Monument Valley, Arizona. The visibility on this October night in 1984 was acceptable but with light snow falling that made judging distances and terrain elevations more difficult on the plane's infrared radar scopes.

The plane dropped steeply down to the valley floor to simulate the primary mission to penetrate the Soviet Union and drop nuclear weapons on Russian military targets. Their newly assigned wing operations commander, Col. Bill Ivey, observed the crew and mission from the pilot jump seat. While he wore a parachute, he alone among the crew did not have a ballistic ejection seat should bailout become necessary, a factor that would doom him.

In the final part of the aircraft's descent, the infrared scopes ineffectively painted only ground returns due to the steep angle at which it approached the terrain. Undetected, the broad, flat rock formation of Hunt's Mesa lurked a short distance away.

As the plane approached the ridge, Col. Ivey could not have anticipated that he would very shortly realize he was about to die and would have about eight seconds to contemplate his fate.

269

The crew had concentrated on flying down to their prescribed route altitude five hundred feet above the ground but had done so in the valley leading to the rock formation. As the plane leveled off, Hunt's Mesa suddenly appeared above the aircraft on the crew's radar scopes that displayed the plane's position well below the mesa rim. The pilot firewalled the engines and started a steep climb to clear the ridge, but the effort proved too late. The other crew positions on the aircraft might have had an inkling of danger from the sudden application of full power, but more likely they knew nothing until the right wing tip caught the mesa rim.

I have not had access to the accident investigation report, so I must guess at the final seconds of Swoon 52.

Had an observer been standing on the Hunt's Mesa ridge line, there would have been little warning that disaster was on the way. The B-52 would have approached at three hundred mph below the level of the mesa. The sound of aircraft engines would arrive only slightly before the aircraft from the snowy darkness below. With only a faint whine as the plane neared, the roar of eight engines would have risen rapidly as the plane climbed desperately to clear the ridge.

Suddenly, the plane would have appeared, engines screaming, in a slight right bank with its right wing angling down. As it crossed the ridge, the right wing tip and outboard engine pod that held engines #7 and #8 would strike the mesa, tearing them from the wing. This would throw the plane into a right corkscrewing death spiral that would end 3,600 feet away and about eight seconds later, where it would strike the top of the rock formation, cartwheel across the mesa, explode and cascade fiery debris into a ravine on the far side of the mesa. A salvage team sent later to recover usable plane parts from the area reported no usable parts remaining, so violently had the aircraft been torn apart in the crash.

Many times in the years since, I have mentally ridden that eight-second aircraft death spiral with Bill Ivey, my fellow Castle B-52 instructor. I heard the accident report early the next morning on TV, which caused me to leap from my couch in Delaware in disbelief.

Immediately after the initial impact concussion tore off the right wing tip and two outboard engines, the aircraft would have accelerated its right turn, since the left wing would now be producing far more lift than the shortened right wing and would have four engines at power instead of the two remaining on the right wing. Because the plane had been on a fairly steep upward trajectory, it would have continued to rise briefly as the spiral began. I estimate the left wing struck the mesa on its second revolution and began the catastrophic cartwheel disintegration.

The pilot would have instinctively applied full left-turn controls with the wing spoilers in an attempt to counter the hard right rotation that had begun. The aircraft would have continued to roll toward ninety degrees of bank despite the pilot's efforts and, within about two seconds, he would have mentally acknowledged the hopelessness of his task and commenced the ejection sequence.

A reported copilot account said immediately after ridge impact, he first looked at the fireball on the right wing and then turned to see the pilot's ejection seat traveling up the rails and out of the plane in seeming slow motion. Before ejecting, the copilot reported Col. Ivey had begun a mad scramble to get out of the aircraft.

All six crewmembers with ejection seats escaped the aircraft, and five survived. The gunner bled to death on the mesa, as his leg was severed during ejection. Ivey went down with the aircraft.

The navigators should not have survived since they require four hundred feet ground clearance and level flight to have one swing in their parachute before hitting the ground. However, it appears everyone ejected as the plane neared or passed ninety degrees right bank, allowing the nav team a successful trajectory from the aircraft. The radar navigator received severe facial burns from the aircraft's initial impact fireball and explosion, so closely before the impact did he eject.

Ivey had no time to pull himself out of a pilot's overhead hatch opening, considering the instability of a spiraling aircraft, whose centrifugal force would have pressed him against the left wall of the crew compartment and the tornado-force winds beyond the hatch.

If the aircraft had been stable and at altitude, he could have clambered down the ladder to the lower compartment and leapt from a navigator's hatch more easily than transiting an upper hatch, but there was no time and no altitude.

I imagine Ivey saw vividly what was coming and finally closed his eyes to accept death in serenity.

The sweet chariot swung low to carry Bill home.

USAF photo

"Col. William L. Ivy
Deputy Commander for Operations of the 92nd Bombardment Wing
killed."

Keep a light on for us, Bill; we'll all be along soon.

AFTERWORD

As I drove out the Castle AFB gate, I felt relief as I left military restrictions behind. The primary condition I escaped would be a second northern tier assignment at Minot or Grand Forks, ND. I couldn't handle another northern assignment. The Air Force had me living in the sticks my entire career—Texas, Vietnam, Northern Maine, and the Central Valley of California. I headed for Washington, DC, the city I had grown up outside of and longed to live near again.

Soon, however, the down side of this escape would arrive. The Air Force had provided a tribe to belong to, a place where, once you showed your ID, you were automatically accepted, where I was saluted every time I came on base. Several months later I found myself flying as a BE-99 commuter copilot flying a fifteen-passenger prop for half the salary I had left. I stood at the rear entry door as the passengers embarked up the short stairway from the ramp and handed me their carry-on luggage to stow. I had gone from an elite, respected, B-52 aircraft commander to Mr. Step-n-fetch-it for airline passengers.

A second humiliation came when I wanted to buy a Daisy Wheel Printer for my computer. This top-of-the-line, end-of-the-line printer would be the last to use a metal striking surface to force ribbon ink onto the page. The slightly larger-than-a-golf-ball sphere would spin rapidly to apply the selected stroke by spinning it to the page. It moved so fast I could hardly follow it, and I just had to have one.

When I petitioned the local bank for a $1500 loan, however, they turned me down. Me, "Ace" Lacklen! I tried to explain my current low salary rate would be temporary, and the branch manager responded that when my pay went up they'd be glad to loan me the money. All my previous accomplishments meant nothing, I was a commuter copilot who made a pittance and that was the score. I will cover this travail in book two.

On the positive side, I recalled what the retired major told me, wistfully, while we were selling cameras in Hartford, CT, before my induction: that I was about to begin a great adventure. He was right. I had done things by age thirty-two I could not have dreamed of while in college. After doing these things, I couldn't imagine pursuing any other path with my life. Although, had I known how many near-death experiences I would have, I might have considered another alternative.

I thought I was leaving such things for good in 1979, but I was not. Within two years, I'd be training as a reservist in C-5s at Altus AFB, OK, to fly out of Dover AFB, DE. The entire world would open for me over the next twenty-three years to include two wars, refueling in a developing typhoon over the Pacific, two appearances on CBS's *60 Minutes* TV show opposite the Air Force, and a stupendous march-off-this-cliff episode with the mandatory anthrax shot program that put me within fifteen minutes of a court martial.

Stay tuned.

USAF photo

C-5 Galaxy.

ADDENDUM

The following movies are ones I feel best describe various aspects of the military experiences outlined in this book.

VIETNAM

PLATOON (1986)

Excellent presentation of the feel of Vietnam with the standard wartime pressures as they unfolded in this war. The author shows great insight with two quotes. First, "The beast is hungry tonight." The beast is the war itself, and more precisely, the reptilian brain core wielding human technological advancement to inflict injury on other humans as the invisible monster controlling the conflict. It suggests the soldiers on both sides are struggling against this invisible beast, not each other. Second quote: "Dying is easy, just like allowing yourself to go to sleep." This from a wounded soldier contemplating his wounds and wistfully imagining dying would not be a traumatic event, if it should occur. This movie also graphically portrays a dire event in this war, calling in an airstrike on your own position because it has been overrun.

APOCALYPSE NOW (1979)

This movie's renown comes from one of its famous quips: "I love the smell of napalm in the morning!" but also conveys the disintegrating rationale for the war replicated in the disintegrating minds of a renegade colonel hiding in Cambodia and of the soldier sent to execute him. The special effects of explosions and wild firefight exchanges capture the sense

277

of the bizarre insanity and nightmarish quality of this war. As an aside, the character of a cowgirl in a USO-style show presents the most erotically appealing female form I have encountered. I don't know why this might be, since she is fully clothed in a cowgirl outfit, but she still sends my libido into orbit at age sixty-five.

HAMBURGER HILL (1987)

Seldom do we see the North Vietnamese soldiers displayed in their full ardor contesting the American army, but this film does so by showing the NVA soldiers savagely defending their hilltop position as the Americans climb the hill. We also see an American gunship mowing down a line of Americans by mistake and the futility of abandoning a hill many lives were just sacrificed to capture.

STRATEGIC AIR COMMAND

A GATHERING OF EAGLES (1963)

The best display of the take-no-prisoners mental landscape of the command. Commanders find themselves embedded in the command matrix 24/7 under severe, relentless pressure that drives the draconian decisions it often forces them to make. One quibble—the wing vice commander, Rod Taylor, launches a B-52 on an ORI with one engine attaining only 80% power, and the decision is condoned by the ORI team chief nicknamed "Black Jack." This is precisely what happened at Loring in 1969, six years after the movie's release, that caused the plane to crash on takeoff, killing everyone on board, all for an exercise, albeit one that could end a wing commander's career.

DR. STRANGELOVE (1964)

This is a dark, often hilarious comedy of the Soviets and Americans blundering into a nuclear war. A demented wing commander launches his bombers, uncommanded, against the Soviets, and general nuclear war breaks out after American and Soviet officials attempt, unsuccessfully, to shoot down the American bombers that do not respond to the recall message.

I have several technical gripes with this otherwise superlative film. I have no idea what switches the pilot is commanding the radar navigator to throw in their struggle to open the bomb doors. The aircraft commander does not run a switch position checklist on a bomb run; the radar runs it all. If the doors do not open, I'd have no clue how to tell the radar to open them. A layman does not know this, however, so I'll attribute this to plot considerations and give the director a pass.

FAIL-SAFE (1964)

Another chilling, somewhat plausible story of America and the Soviets almost blundering their way into a nuclear war. As with *Strangelove*, a lone American B-58 bomber succeeds against all efforts of both militaries to stop it. These efforts include both the US president (played by Henry Fonda) and the aircraft commander's wife imploring him, over the command radio, to abandon his mission. Ever the faithful automaton, however, the plane's commander rejects it all as a sinister ploy and nukes his Russian target anyway. If only he had been a history major in college and noticed he did not see nuclear explosions going off from other B-58s in the fleet and realized the recall must be valid. Fonda must then order his best military pilot friend to drop a nuke on New York City, where his wife and family are visiting, to balance the equation to avert an all-out nuclear war.

TWELVE O'CLOCK HIGH (1950)

While a World War II depiction, this movie, staring Gregory Peck, displays nuances of a bomber commander's dilemma. Air Force professional education loved this movie and showed it at several of the military education schools I attended. The problem is they at least tacitly endorse Peck's actions in the film when they should not, unless qualified. This involves the complicated approach a commander must follow in dealing with his bomber crews. These commanders find themselves embedded in a horrific situation, however, where losses at one point pursuing the daylight bombing of Germany reach 71%. (More Air Force crewmembers died in the European theater than did Marines.)

The first squadron commander commits the sin of sympathy with his crews and protects them righteously, but ill-advisedly, given the situation. Yes, most of them are going to die, but they must accept that they are expendable to win the war and save the homeland; bad news, but necessary. The air group general knows this and replaces the good-guy commander with Peck.

In one of the film's crucial scenes, Peck stops outside the base before entering to assume command and shares a cigarette with his enlisted driver. He talks to the driver calmly, courteously, and man-to-man. As he finishes the cigarette, Peck throws it to the ground and adopts his new persona as hard-ass taskmaster. "All right, Sergeant," he snaps. "Let's go."

Peck assaults his new subordinates with unrelenting scorn and harshness to break them loose from the previous commander's sympathetic demeanor. We know Peck is really a softie underneath and eventually cracks under the strain, but he plays Attila the Hun to shape up his boys.

I strongly disagree with this approach, however. While the first commander suffered from the sin of unaffordable *sympathy*, Peck should have based his command on *empathy* instead. In the empathetic approach, you recognize the hardships forced on the squadron and empathize (I feel your pain) with the troops instead of sympathizing (I'll take this unreasonable pressure off you guys). That is, a *sympathizer* demands relief from the pressure; an *empathizer* will demand what is necessary while acknowledging the difficulties and hardships. Peck, instead, treats his charges as malingering slouches in need of a good ass-kicking to shape them up.

However, instead of playing the insufferable jerk, Peck should have empathized, told them, as sternly as necessary, it was a rotten deal, but the situation demanded they put up X number of airplanes every day until relief arrived, the war was won, or they were all dead. The priority must be on the mission, not the crews.

In one scene, Peck growls at the crews to assume they are already dead, then they needn't worry about dying. He could have said that with empathy instead of deprecating anger, vowed to fly with them (hard to beg sympathy when the hard-ass is going with you), and it would have worked more effectively. When Peck expressed this sentiment in his deprecating manner, he suggested that they deserved to die for being slackers and losers, something no one placed in such a position could be judged. They needed to be redirected away from sympathy to empathy, not shattered with disdain and rebuilt.

By idolizing Peck's approach, the Air Force has unleashed scores of insufferable jerks into command billets who have been taught that being a growling, screaming, unreasonable cad equates to being a good commander. What they intended, I suspect, was to produce empathetic taskmasters who could acknowledge difficulties while still demanding everything necessary for the mission. But that is not what they produced in too many instances, several of whom I encountered on active duty and in the reserves. The joke in the reserves would ask who in a given group would be promoted to colonel. The standard answer would be the guy who had proven himself a big enough jerk to handle the job. What a commentary.

Of my three superlative commanders I cite during my career, two cited in this book, I never heard one of them shout, scream, belittle, or needlessly threaten a subordinate. I realize this view may seem self-serving from an officer who did not reach full colonel (although promoted once to that rank in 1993, I turned it down because I could not find a reserve billet and would have been forcibly retired six months after pinning on. The system did not make the "mistake" of promoting me again). I recognize this and offer my viewpoints with that in mind.

I also have a marvelous episode for a sci-fi adventure. As Gregory Peck's character stands before the beleaguered bomber crews, he explains that new recruits have arrived (from verrrrry far away) who have volunteered to replace any crew that wishes to stand down that day. The doors to the back of the briefing room open and in walk me and my contemporary B-52 pilots and crews from the 1970s, now in our sixties, who have been time-warped back to 1943 and quickly trained in the B-17s and B-24s, really simple machines compared to ours.

He explains that the young bomber crews have their whole lives ahead of them, while the elderly bomber crews long for a heroic mission to perhaps finish out their lives in a great cause and have volunteered to replace the younger crewmembers on today's mission, if they wish.

I'd go in a heartbeat. Then I wonder how many of the young crews would accept?

Sound Track to Accompany the Book

Prologue

"Temptation Eyes"
The Grass Roots

OTS

"A Rainy Night in Georgia"
Brook Benton

Pilot Training

Theme from *The Good, the Bad and the Ugly*
Hugo Montenegro

"Amarillo by Morning"
George Strait

"Here Comes the Sun"
The Beatles

"Solitary Man"
Neil Diamond

"No Time" (vapid prelude, but superior long version)
The Guess Who (Canned Wheat)

VIETNAM

"Gypsies, Tramps and Thieves"
Cher

"We've Got to Get Out of This Place"
The Animals

"Susie Q" (Taiwan hooker)
Creedence Clearwater

"Yellow River"
Christie

"Fortunate Son"
Creedence Clearwater

"Run Through the Jungle"
Creedence Clearwater

Where Have All the Flowers Gone" (Vietnam Memorial)
Mary Jane Furches (Tribute to Mary Travers)

"Ohio" (Kent State Massacre)
Crosby Stills and Nash

B-52s

"Dust in the Wind" (Emergency War Order execution)
Kansas

"Living in the USA" (Low level flight anthem)
Steve Miller Band

"If You're Going to San Francisco"
Scott McKenzie

"Good Morning Starshine" (Hippie chicks)
Oliver

"California Dreaming"
The Mamas and the Papas

"Brandy" (San Francisco theme)
Looking Glass

"Philadelphia Freedom" (Dragons and silk takeoff)
Elton John

GUAM

"Riders on the Storm" (Music to accompany bomb run)
The Doors

"Have You Ever Seen the Rain?" (Rain=B-52 bombs)
Creedence Clearwater

"Bad Moon Rising"
Creedence Clearwater

"Sky Pilot"
Eric Burdon & The Animals

"Who'll Stop the Rain?"
Creedence Clearwater

"Dance to the Music" (Favorite go-go girl tune)
Sly and the Family Stone

LORING

"A Horse with No Name"
America

Ventura Highway"
America

"Pieces of April"
Three Dog Night

"Rhinestone Cowboy"
Glen Campbell

"Afternoon Delight"
Starland Vocal Band

"You Baby" (Nav-wife serenade)
The Mamas and Papas

"You Raise Me Up" (A son's salute)
Josh Groban

"Coming to America" (Vietnamese refugees)
Neil Diamond

CASTLE

"Don't Fear the Reaper" (Dancing engines)
Blue Oyster Cult

"Could It Be Magic" (Dating black enlisted woman)
Donna Summer

"Ride of the Valkyries" (B-52 death spiral)
Wagner

"Swing Low, Sweet Chariot" (Bill Ivey going home)
Kathleen Battle w/Harlem Choir

INTERNET VIDEOS ON "YOU TUBE"

B-52 MITO takeoff: "B-52 "cart-start" and Minimum Interval Take-Off (MITO)"

B-52 bomb run audio over Hanoi: "In a B-52 bomber over Hanoi, Military.com"

Fairchild Air Show, Bud Holland, crash 1994: "Mishap of B-52 at Fairchild Air Force Base Washington"

B-52 Story: "Battle Stations, B-52 Stratofortress"

"The B-52: Vietnam – 4258 Strategic Wing operations out of U Tapao Air Base, Thailand"

"Apocalypse Now: Suzie Q-Carmine Coppola"

FOOTNOTES:

1. Earthlink. Net, Vietnam as Statistics:

    http://home.earthlink.net/~aircommando1/Vietnam.htm

    "The total tonnage of bombs dropped over North Vietnam, South Vietnam, Cambodia, and Laos came to about 8 million (about four times the tonnage used in all of WWII); 2,236,000 tons of bombs were dropped on the infiltration routes in Laos alone between 1965-71."

2. Earthlink.Net, Vietnam as Statistics:

    http://home.earthlink.net/~aircommando1/Vietnam.htm.

    South Vietnam reported 185,528 of its military personnel killed in the war, with 499,026 wounded. North Vietnam and the Vietcong reportedly lost 924,048 dead in combat. Vietnam is estimated to have lost 415,000 civilians in the war, with at least 935,000 wounded.

3. Iraqi Body Count.org:

    http://www.iraqbodycount.org/analysis/numbers/2011/

    Total deaths with combatants, combining IBC and official records:

    Combining IBC civilian data with official Iraqi and US combatant death figures and data from the Iraq War Logs released by WikiLeaks, we estimate the documented death toll across all categories since March 2003 to be 162,000, of whom 79% were civilians.

4. David Johnston, U.S. Says Rendition to Continue, but with More Oversight, The New York Times, Aug 24, 2009: http://www.nytimes.com/2009/08/25/us/politics/25rendition.html?_r=0 WASHINGTON — The Obama administration will continue the Bush administration's practice of sending terrorism suspects to third countries for detention and interrogation, but pledges to closely monitor their treatment to ensure that they are not tortured, administration officials said Monday. (Author's note: Then why are you sending them to another country? Rendition is rendition that lipstick on the pig will not alter).

5. Vietnam War Casualties, Wikipedia:

   http://en.wikipedia.org/wiki/Vietnam_War_casualties

   According to the Vietnamese government, there were 1,100,000 North Vietnamese Army and Viet Cong military personnel deaths during the Vietnam War (including the missing).[34] Rummel reviewed the many casualty data sets, and this number is in keeping with his mid-level estimate of 1,011,000 North Vietnamese combatant deaths.[35] The official US Department of Defense figure was 950,765 communist forces killed in Vietnam from 1965 to 1974.

6. Bao Ninh, The Sorrow of War, A Novel of North Vietnam (New York: Riverhead Books, 1996).

7. Jim Noone, A Flight to Remember, The C-7 Caribou Association newsletter, November 2008; The Longest Flight, TAC Attack Magazine, Tactical Air Force, May 1972, reprinted in The C-7 Caribou Association newsletter, February 2003.

8. Snopes.com: "Hanoi'd with Jane";

   http://www.snopes.com/military/fonda.asp

   "It's a figment of someone's imagination says Ret Col Larry Carrigan, one of the servicemen mentioned in the "slips of paper" incident."

9. Jane Fonda, The Truth About My Trip to Hanoi

   http://janefonda.com/the-truth-about-my-trip-to-hanoi/

   "It is possible that it was a set up, that the Vietnamese had it all planned. I will never know. But if they did I can't blame them. The buck stops here. If I was used, I allowed it to happen. It was my mistake and I have paid and continue to pay a heavy price for it. Had I brought a politically more experienced traveling companion with me they would have kept me from taking that terrible seat. I would have known two minutes before sitting down what I didn't realize until two minutes afterwards; a two-minute lapse of sanity that will haunt me forever. The gun was inactive, there were no planes overhead, I simply wasn't thinking about what I was doing, only about what I was feeling, innocent of what the photo implies. But the photo exists, delivering its message regardless of what I was doing or feeling. I carry this heavy in my heart. I have apologized numerous times for any pain I may have caused servicemen and their families because of this photograph. It was never my intention to cause harm. It is certainly painful for me that I, who had spent so much time talking to soldiers, trying to help soldiers and veterans, helping the anti-war movement to not blame the soldiers, now would be seen as being against our soldiers!"

10. B-52 crash, Loring AFB, ME, 1969.

    http://www.ejection-history.org.uk/Aircraft_by_Type/b52_stratofortress.htm

11. The History Channel, This Day in History (Linebacker II).

http://www.history.com/this-day-in-history/linebacker-ii-resumes-after-christmas-pause

The North Vietnamese rejected Nixon's demand and the president ordered Operation Linebacker II, a full-scale air campaign against the Hanoi area that began on December 18. During the 11 days of Linebacker II, 700 B-52 sorties and more than 1,000 fighter-bomber sorties dropped an estimated 20,000 tons of bombs on North Vietnam--half the total tonnage of bombs dropped on England during World War II.

12. Ibid, Bao Ninh, 90.

13. Ralph Wetterhahn, Escape to U-Tapao, Air & Space Magazine, January 1997: http://www.airspacemag.com/military-aviation/escape.html?c=y&page=4

14. Mayaguez Incident, Wikipedia: http://en.wikipedia.org/wiki/Mayaguez_incident

15. Falklands War, Wikipedia: http://en.wikipedia.org/wiki/Falklands_War

16. Anthony T. Kern, Darker Shades of Blue: A Case Study in Failed Leadership, McGraw-Hill Professional Publishing, 1999.

ACKNOWLEDGMENTS:

As a self-published, first time author, I required extensive help to complete this endeavor. My first editor, Marta Tanrikulu, a freelancer with Guru.com, corrected the myriad of errors I could no longer see in the manuscript, or had been mistaken about. Most amazingly to me she corrected the spelling of the term nuoc mam, a Vietnamese fish sauce, from my incorrect estimation of how it was spelled. Once with Two Harbors Press, my second editor, Pam Nordberg, did likewise by knowing, somehow, the stars of two 1960s movies I cited had one, Kirk Douglas, out of place. Since I had messed with the manuscript extensively since Marta saw it, and had added numerous sections, Pam again saved me from myself by correcting new errors and providing a mercy killing of my many extra commas. I suppose a back-handed kudo is due the US government that furloughed me for four months in 2012 from my pilot simulator job that allowed me uninterrupted time to write most of the manuscript. I'm not sure any of this would have happened had I not been furloughed. Thanks, also, to the many military personnel who reviewed parts of the manuscript for accuracy including the Caribou Association whose members advised me on the Vietnam section and provided me with many of the photos from the time. These include Peter Bird, Stan Owens, and John Stymerski. Finally, great appreciation to my wife, Eleanor, who put up with me as I disappeared for hundreds of hours deep within my writing cave with headphones on and YouTube playing the tunes of the time, that allowed me to return mentally to my twenty-five year old self.

ABOUT THE AUTHOR

Photo by Amanda Lacklen

Jay Lacklen is a retired Air Force reserve Lt. Col. with
12,500 flying hours who teaches Air Force pilot training simulators
at Columbus AFB, Mississippi. This is his first of a three-book trilogy
on his Air Force experiences

INDEX

Page numbers in **bold** indicate photographs or illustrations.

operational readiness inspection (ORI), 181–185, 220–223

Oscar (Ox-cart or Ox-fart), 75–76, 104–106, 113

P

Pappa Tango, 86–95

parachute jumpers (PJs), 108

Pattaya Beach, 187–188

Patterson, Ken, 211–216, 220–223

pets, 73–74

Phan Thiet, 86–95

Phil, 130–131

the Philippines, 57–65

Phu Cat TDY, **96**–97

Physical Training (PT), 244–246

pilot training

    arrival, **19**–21

    graduation, 44–45

    sound track, 283

    starship troopers, 21–24, **22**

    T-37, 29–37, **30**

    T-38, **37**–44

    T-41, **24**–29

political prisoners, 91–92

prisoners, treatment of, 52–55

promised assignments, 113

R

R&R (Rest and Recreation), 104–106

refueling, 79, **80,** 122, 127, 134, 229–233

refugees, 192–193, 235–242, **237, 239**

Reno (dog), 74

rogue pilots, 233–235

rolling thunder, 117

S

Saigon, 92–95, **191**–193

Saigon tea, 95

salute to author's mother, 224–225

Scott, (OT), 8

scuba diving and snorkeling, 188

security test at Loring AFB, 126

Selvidge, Norv, 88

Shields, Roy, **41**

skiing trips, 144–147

sleep deprivation, 11

snake school, 57–65

Soldier's Code of Conduct, 52

Song Be, 86–**87**

The Sorrow of War, 98

sound track, 283–287

sponsoring refugees, 193, 236–242

Squadron Officer School, 244–246

starship troopers, 21–24, **22**

stereotypes of Vietnam vets, 117

Steve, 144, 145, 247

Strategic Air Command (SAC)

    B-52 aircraft commander school, 174–179

    Castle AFB. *See* Castle AFB, CA

    death spiral of Bill Ivey, 269–272